Procedural Justice

Oñati International Series in Law and Society

TITLES

Totalitarian and Post-Totalitarian Law
Edited by Adam Podgorecki and Vittorio Olgiati

Foreign Courts: Civil Litigation in Foreign Legal Cultures
Edited by Volkmar Gessner

Family Law and Family Policy in the New Europe
Edited by Jacek Kurczewski and Mavis Maclean

Procedural Justice
Edited by Klaus F. Röhl and Stefan Machura

Oñati International Series
in Law and Society

Procedural Justice

Edited by Klaus F. Röhl
and Stefan Machura

A Series published for
THE OÑATI INTERNATIONAL INSTITUTE
FOR THE SOCIOLOGY OF LAW

Ashgate
DARTMOUTH
Aldershot UK • Brookfield USA • Singapore • Sydney

Published by
Dartmouth Publishing Company Limited
Ashgate Publishing Limited
Gower House
Croft Road
Aldershot
Hants GU11 3HR
England

Ashgate Publishing Company
Old Post Road
Brookfield
Vermont 05036
USA

British Library Cataloguing in Publication Data
Procedural justice. – (Onati international series in law and society)
1.Justice 2.Procedure (Law)
I.Röhl, Klaus F., 1938– II.Machura, Stefan III. Onati International Institute for the Sociology of Law
340.1'1

Library of Congress Cataloging-in-Publication Data
Procedural justice / edited by Klaus F. Röhl and Stefan Machura.
p. cm. – (Oñati international series in law and society)
ISBN 1-85521-919-0 (hc). – ISBN 1-85521-921-2 (pbk.)
1. Procedure (Law)–Social aspects. 2. Procedure (Law)––Philosophy. 3. Procedure (Law)–Moral and ethical aspects.
4. Justice. I. Röhl. Klaus F. (Klaus Friedrich) II. Machura. Stefan. III. Series.
K2110.P76 1997
306.2'5–dc21 97–469
CIP

ISBN 1 85521 919 0 (Hbk)
ISBN 1 85521 921 2 (Pbk)

Printed and bound in Great Britain by
Biddles Limited, Guildford and King's Lynn

Contents

List of Figures and Tables

Preface

KLAUS F. RÖHL AND STEFAN MACHURA

If people have to make hard choices, more or less formalized procedures are preferred as means to come to decisions. To achieve acceptance of decisions, procedures have to be 'fair' or 'just'. There seems to be a shared sense about the minimal qualities of procedures. This common measure can be easily identified by such criteria as the opportunity for parties to state their case, the impartiality of decision-makers, or the ability to reach reasonable decisions. This is what everybody could imagine.

However, it was a long time before social scientists took procedures seriously enough to make them a focus of their work. In contrast to the widespread use of procedures, problems of outcome fairness ('distributive justice') occupied the social sciences. There is an exception in the realm of political philosophy. A discussion about appropriate procedures has always been central to the debate on democracy. It was nurtured by the ideological confrontation between the East and the West, as well as by the philosophical construction of underlying principles of a liberal society. The main points were free elections on the one hand and the ideal construction of a social contract on the other hand. Rawls's outstanding book *A Theory of Justice* (1971) was rooted in the liberal philosophical debate. He suggested an ideal procedure to reach the principles of a fair society. Since then, the topic of 'procedural justice' has made a remarkable scientific career. The first article in this volume sketches the history of the field in detail, so only a few words need to be said here. Procedural justice attracted people from all scientific and political camps: right-wing and left-wing thinkers, lawyers and sociologists, adherents of systems theory and those of critical theory, etc. Reading in another branch of literature, which claims a breakdown of traditional state-interventionist politics, we find ourselves in a world of 'proceduralization'. According to Teubner and Willke (1984, 7, 23), so-called reflexive law should curtail procedures which enable the self-regulation of partial systems in society. Soon after Rawls, 'positivistic' empirical research emerged. Thibaut and Walker (1975) started social-psychological research. A 'fair process effect' (Greenberg and Folger 1983) was discovered:

People tend to accept decisions if the decisions are reached by procedures seen as fair. More recently, a 'group value theory' of procedural justice was introduced by Lind and Tyler (1988). According to it, people want to be treated according to the values of the group, as a full-fledged member of the group. Procedural justice became a fascinating field of research: multidisciplinary and international.

In order to bring together scientists with different approaches, from different subjects, and from different cultures, a workshop on procedural justice was held at the Oñati International Institute for the Sociology of Law (IISIL) in June 1992. A second workshop was hosted by the IISIL in September 1993. This volume presents papers from those meetings.

In this book, all contributions have been updated to reflect the most recent level of the discussion. The volume is unique as a collection of procedural justice articles of scientists with different theoretical and methodological backgrounds, writing for an international forum. It might compare to Lind and Tyler's *The Social Psychology of Procedural Justice* (1988) in providing an overview on research, but from a more interdisciplinary and more international point of view. In German there exists a volume on procedural justice focusing on social-psychological research in Germany (Bierbrauer, Gottwald, and Birnbreier-Stahlberger 1995). Thus its scope and public are more restricted than those of this book.

There are five main questions which are discussed by the authors of this volume. The first treats the relation of procedural and distributive justice to each other. The second asks, how procedural are Rawls's and Habermas's conceptions of procedural justice? The third addresses the relevance of Luhmann's conception of procedure. The fourth analyses the place of procedural justice in autopoietic systems theory. Finally, the fifth discusses procedural justice findings to legal settings.

How are procedural justice and distributive justice related? When procedural justice research started, there was an ambitious equity theory, which stated that in allocations individuals are striving selfishly for an equitable relation between contributions (inputs) and rewards (outcomes; see Adams 1965; Berkowitz and Walster 1976). Homans (1961, 76) formulated the leading paradigm: 'Am I getting as much as other men in some respect like me would get in circumstances in some respect like mine?'. Critics argued against the anthropological assumption and highlighted the vagueness of the categories 'contribution' and 'reward'. 'Because procedural justice first came to researchers' attention at a time when disenchantment with equity theory was high, it is understandable that some may think that it was intended to be a substitute for distributive justice' (Greenberg 1996, 403). In this book, the interrelation of procedural and distributive justice is examined by Klaus F. Röhl, Volker H. Schmidt, and David Wasserman. Schmidt argues that procedures have to serve as devices to reach acceptable decisions. He concludes with a catalogue of six criteria that have to be fulfilled by procedures. Wasserman discusses conflict constellations in which procedural justice is valued more highly than outcome justice. He argues that procedural justice might well be preferred for noninstrumental reasons. Social-psychological studies reported by Röhl have shown that for the affected persons procedural justice can represent a different level of experience than outcome justice. It is time to reject a simple either/or approach to the relation between procedural and distributive justice. Both dimensions have to be considered for sociological theory. 'In the absence of a coherent overarching theory' (a formulation by Greenberg [1996, 405]), Tyler and Lind's group value theory may give us a hint of how to further develop theory on the relation of procedural and distributive justice. If people acquire during their socialization the society's (or group's) norms and values for fair treatment and fair procedures, we can argue that they also adopt norms and values for just allocations. And if people are eager to monitor their treatment by institutions and by authorities in order to estimate their social standing in the society (or the group) to which they belong, then unjust outcomes indicate discrimination, too. In situations where people cannot find a consensus about contested outcomes, parties may be able to meet in choosing a 'fair' allocation procedure. Where the 'procedural justice heuristic' (see Lind 1994) and its counterpart, which we may call the 'distributive justice heuristic', fail to come to similar results, the procedural aspect has more impact. One reason has already been mentioned; there is more controversy about just results than about fair procedures. Even people who are sentenced may often have doubts about whether their sentence is unjust in any aspect and therefore evaluate the court on the basis of procedural fairness (see Stefan Machura in this volume). Most obviously, in legal conflicts, individuals encounter a long-term social relationship (with the state) which they cannot escape. Unfair legal procedures are likely to produce unfair outcomes over and over again (see Tyler 1990). Fair legal procedures may sometimes result in questionable decisions, but can be expected to work well in the future.

When it comes to the connection of procedure and justice, many think of Rawls (1971) and of Habermas's discourse theory (see especially Habermas 1993). The connection of these two authors is not random since Habermas (1993) explicitly aims to replace Rawls's concept with his discourse theoretical of the 'reconstruction' of the *Rechtsstaat* (the state based on the rule of law). According to Habermas, decisions should be reached in 'discourses' free of domination. The 'proceduralistic paradigm of law' (Habermas 1993, 532) counts on a flow of communications channelled through democratic procedures which constitute power and law. But how procedural are the theories of Rawls and Habermas? According to Axel Tschentscher, both make a very restricted use of the procedural justice topic. They only address the 'justice-defining function' of procedures. As in traditional reasoning, procedures are seen from the justice of the results. Further, Tschentscher argues that without additional information about the qualities of procedures employed, the justice-defining function will not be convincing.

Long before the beginning of the present discussion, Luhmann evoked a debate in Germany with a publication called *Legitimation by Procedure* (1969). What is the meaning of that book when read in the context of today's procedural justice literature? Luhmann analysed procedures in the light of the early systems theory. He did not refer to justice or to legitimacy, but to obedience as achieved in formal procedures. At the end procedures socially isolate a resisting loser. Luhmann's description of trials reminds us of the dark sides of legal procedures (as does Feeley 1979), which are all too easily overlooked by authors in the streams of the discourse theory or the group value theory. On the other hand, Luhmann, who introduced social meaning as a key concept of systems theory, underestimates citizens' concerns with social values and with their confirmation by authorities in legal proceedings. Machura presents the critics' response to Luhmann's theory of procedure, especially objections against Luhmann's empirical basis. Following the group value theory of Lind and Tyler, Machura contrasts Luhmann's theory of 'procedure without justice', as Machura puts it, with an understanding of 'legitimacy by fair procedures'.

What is the place of 'procedural justice' in the light of Luhmann's subsequent work? In this volume, Kai-D. Bussmann and Alfons Bora represent recent systems theory. Later in his theoretical development, Luhmann analysed law as a symbolic generalized medium of communication. Bussmann's work shows strong elements of that theory: In relation to law, people have to act using legal meanings which are produced exclusively in the legal system. Here is the root of their concern with the fairness of the judgement process, according to Bussmann. At the second workshop in Oñati, Lind recalled social-psychological studies which detected procedural justice concerns in numerous social settings in answering Bussmann (see Machura 1993a). It appears that procedural justice is important wherever people are confronted with procedures, not only in legal disputes (see Lind 1994). Bora also criticizes Lind and Tyler's group value theory from a sociological viewpoint. The group value theory certainly faces a problem in situations in which different groups with different values meet (Bora), or in which individuals find themselves between conflicting demands of groups to which they belong (Machura 1993b). Bora's and Bussmann's analysis of procedural justice is deeply influenced by the autopoietic systems theory, which was developed mainly by Luhmann (especially: Luhmann 1984) for the social sciences. Both contributors conceive procedural justice as 'adequate complexity'. Bussmann argues that procedural justice means adequate complexity of the transformation of everyday descriptions of a conflict into the code of law. Bora depicts procedural justice as serving the balance between demands for complexity of a procedure as a social system and demands for consistency. He develops a typology of patterns of structural complexity. 'In the absence of a coherent overarching theory', to quote Greenberg again, it remains important to develop different theoretical concepts, as Bussmann and Bora do for the systems theory.

This volume also contains texts which advance knowledge on procedural justice by focusing on its clinical and political dimensions.

In the United States, in Germany, in Great Britain, there are debates about inefficiencies in the court system. Critical legal scolars have long detected political efforts to cut costs by cutting back access to legal procedures. Qualities of procedures are the starting point of Christoph Rennig's review of recent developments in German law. He discusses political strategies to cope with the problems of case-load and of delay. What might be the impact of these strategies on citizens' feelings of fairness? Rennig's contribution is especially valuable because he addresses the topic for the first time using findings of social-psychological research. The questions Rennig raises are relevant for other countries as well, since all face the same main alternatives in shaping the justice system of the future. Alternative dispute resolution (ADR) procedures are sometimes suspected of serving mainly administrative interests. As Fischer, Vidmar, and

Ellis (1993, 2156) argued for so-called 'domestic issues', 'mediation . . . helps clear court dockets of troublesome cases'. In this volume, Neil Vidmar criticizes a stream of literature and empirical studies which recommend ADR procedures. Differences are too often constructed between ADR procedures and litigation which do not withstand proof. Vidmar doubts whether ADR in general is better to provide a fair process. There is no easy rule of thumb available which favours ADR or litigation.

The study of communications in legal proceedings has become a major focus of process analysis. Diversion and victim-offender mediation with juvenile offenders are the topics of Heinz Messmer's contribution to this volume. He employs methods of communication analysis to sketch conversations between social workers, offenders, and victims. In his conclusion Messmer points out that 'justice and the sense of justice can only be achieved and extended in cooperative relations in which the fostering of social and personal development will be the dominant goal'. However, court trials (Luhmann 1969) and ADR procedures similar to court procedures are not the places for such an education. Here, it seems that the application of values of procedural and distributive justice are decisive, not for bettering the personality, but for more modest aims: the acceptance of decisions and at least a minimum of trust in legal authorities.

Since law is always applied in procedures, knowledge about procedural justice theories, including knowledge of psychological research on procedural justice, is required for legal scholars. May this volume serve to spread the most current thinking on procedural justice. And may these ideas reach to the practicioners of law. In modern society, legitimacy, as Bourricaud 1961 said (7, our translation) is attributed to 'un pouvoir qui accepte ou même qui institue son propre procès de légitimation' [a power which accepts or institutionalizes its due process of legitimation].

References

Adams, J. Stacy. 1965. Inequity in Social Exchange. In *Advances in Experimental Social Psychology*. Vol. 2, edited by L. Berkowitz. New York: Academic.

Berkowitz, Leonard, and Elaine Walster, eds. 1976. *Equity Theory: Toward a General Theory of Social Interaction*. New York: Academic.

Bierbrauer, Günter, Walther Gottwald, and Beatrix Birnbreier-Stahlberger, eds. 1995. *Verfahrensgerechtigkeit: Rechtspsychologische Forschungsbeiträge für die Justizpraxis*. Köln: Verlag Otto Schmidt.

Bourricaud, François. 1961. *Esquisse d'une théorie de l'autorité.* Paris: Plon.

Feeley, Malcolm M. 1979. *The Process Is the Punishment.* New York: Russell Sage.

Fischer, Karla, Neil Vidmar, and Rene Ellis. 1993. The Culture of Battering and the Role of Mediation in Domestic Violence Cases. *Southern Methodist University Law Review* 46: 2117–74.

Greenberg, Jerald. 1996. *The Quest for Justice at the Job.* Thousand Oaks: Sage.

Greenberg, Jerald, and Robert Folger. 1983. Procedural Justice, Participation and the Fair Process Effect in Groups and Organizations. In *Basic Group Processes,* edited by P. B. Paulus. New York: Springer.

Habermas, Jürgen. 1993. *Faktizität und Geltung.* 3rd ed. Frankfurt am Main: Suhrkamp.

Homans, George C. 1961. *Social Behavior: Its Elementary Forms.* London: Routledge and Kegan Paul.

Lind, E. Allan. 1994. Procedural Justice and Culture: Evidence for Ubiquitous Process Concerns. *Zeitschrift für Rechtssoziologie* 15: 24–36.

Lind, E. Allan, and Tom R. Tyler. 1988. *The Social Psychology of Procedural Justice.* New York: Plenum.

Luhmann, Niklas. 1969. *Legitimation durch Verfahren.* Darmstadt: Luchterhand.

———. 1984. *Soziale Systeme.* Frankfurt am Main: Suhrkamp.

Machura, Stefan. 1993a. Vom Eigenwert des Verfahrens. Zweiter Internationaler Workshop on Procedural Justice in Oñati. *Zeitschrift für Rechtssoziologie* 14: 303–5.

———. 1993b. Zur Erklärungskraft von Eigennutzaxiom und Group Value Theory am Beispiel des Managements öffentlicher Unternehmen. In *Soziale Disparitäten als Folge ungleicher Wirtschaftsentwicklung,* edited by K.-H. Hillmann and E. Lange. Bielefeld. Duplicated.

Rawls, John. 1971. *A Theory of Justice.* Cambridge: Harvard University Press.

Teubner, Gunther, and Helmut Willke. 1984. Kontext und Autonomie: Gesellschaftliche Selbststeuerung durch reflexives Recht. *Zeitschrift für Rechtssoziologie* 6: 4–35.

Thibaut, John, and Laurens Walker. 1975. *Procedural Justice: A Psychological Analysis.* Hillsdale/N.J: Laurence Erlbaum.

Tyler, Tom R. 1990. *Why People Obey the Law.* New Haven: Yale University Press.

1 Procedural Justice: Introduction and Overview

KLAUS F. RÖHL

From Substantive to Procedural Justice

At first glance, procedures seem only a means to bring about the just allocation of rewards and punishments, of benefits and burdens. Thus, in a discussion of procedural justice, we might first expect an analysis of how procedures should be be shaped in order to achieve the most just distribution possible. In this sense, a distribution is just if it is made as accurately as possible according to a measure outside of the procedure. We usually call this kind of justice distributive justice, substantive justice, or outcome justice.

The question, however, of the objective suitability of procedures for the establishment of distributive justice is only the starting point. For, on the one hand, it has proven to be the case that participants and observers evaluate procedures as more or less just or fair independent of their outcome, and that this estimation is quite relevant to whether the distribution resulting from a procedure is accepted as just. On the other hand, modern societies lack objective or generally agreed-upon standards for the just distribution of life's chances and risks. In many cases, it seems easier to agree on a procedure than on the distribution itself. As a result, material distribution standards are replaced by procedures.

What Is a Procedure?

The answer to the question, What is a procedure? is not at all obvious. If we try to identify the essence of the concept of procedure, we could get lost within an endless philosophical discussion of form and substance. But we cannot totally refuse to draw a line. There exists a danger that the notion of procedure could lose its contours, for in a broad sense all social institutions are 'procedures' (Peters 1991).

As we work within a legal context, different kinds of resolution and decision procedures come to mind. The most prominent are court and administrative procedures. Arbitration is a procedure, too. Mediation and negotiation, however, may be considered procedures only if they develop in a preordered framework, not spontaneously.

Thibaut and Walker (1975) used to argue that procedures are necessary only when allocation is in dispute, because only then does the question of procedure arise. Sociologists no longer accept this limitation. The field of research has been considerably extended by including procedures which are not aimed at dispute resolution but oriented toward shaping the future; procedures, in other words, which are not reactive but proactive. In this manner, administrative procedures and the procedure of parliamentary legislation also come under scrutiny. The same is true for many allocation proceedings both inside and outside organizations. These need not even entail allocation by a third party or a higher authority. Rule-governed negotiations, such as collective bargaining, also constitute procedures in this sense.

On the other hand, I would exclude from our field technical procedures, symbolic operations, and discourses (discussions). I am not so sure about investigations and inquiries (see Peters 1991). A scholarly investigation is probably not a procedure. A legally regulated investigation, however (as done, for instance, by a parliamentary commission), would certainly draw our attention.

I doubt, however, that processes which do not aim at a decision should be considered procedures. Lind and Tyler (1988) contend that excluding such processes places artificial restrictions on procedural justice phenomena. They argue that recent studies have shown 'that judgements of procedural justice arise in contexts in which no real decision is made and that procedural judgements are stimulated by factors such as respect or politeness, which have nothing really to do with decision making'.

It seems to me that sociologists tend to use a much narrower concept of procedure than do psychologists. Also holding a narrower concept is Luhmann (1969), who limits his concept of procedure to a social system which has the specific function to work out a single binding decision and is therefore only a short-term phenomenon. He points to the prestructured framework and to differentiation from a social environment as preconditions for a procedure. Only by these features does a procedure become to some extent independent from its environment and autonomous.

The distinction between distributive justice and procedural justice always makes good sense in those cases where more or less rule-governed procedures have developed which precede any allocation. To me it seems important, as it does to Luhmann, to stress the difference between an actual procedure which is conducted over time and the general framework within which procedures of the same kind can be repeated. Even the encounters between citizens and police which have been studied by Tyler and Folger (1980) can be procedurally structured. Encounters of this kind may lead to a decision by a police officer to issue a ticket or to file a formal charge. I doubt, however, whether informal processes within an organization which do not aim at a decision belong to our topic, although there may be concerns about 'fairness'. After all, Greenberg and Tyler (1987) concede that within an organizational context, fairness may mean something different from what it means in dispute processing or in allocation. I would also exclude from our field a study by Tyler and Caine (Tyler and Caine 1981; Tyler, Rasinski, and Spodick 1985) on the evaluation of group leaders and political authorities, or research on voting behaviour as dependent upon the perceived fairness of politicians, or the interviews (mentioned by Wasserman 1992) with venture capitalists and entrepreneurs who referred to procedural justice criteria to explain their level of satisfaction. I am afraid that an unrestricted notion of procedure leads to the conclusion that every interaction is a procedure, so there would be no difference between procedural justice research and general communication analysis.

Dimensions of Procedural Justice

In the context of research in the fields of sociology and social psychology, the notions of 'justice' or 'fairness' with regard to procedures do not refer to a normatively binding judgement of the sort that moral philosophers have in mind. Instead, they focus on a factual phenomenon that can be empirically observed.

According to Thibaut and Walker, we have to distinguish between objective and subjective procedural justice. Lind and Tyler (1988, 3) define objective procedural justice as 'the capacity of a procedure to conform to normative standards of justice, to make either the decisions themselves or the decision-making process more fair, by, for example, reducing some clearly unacceptable bias or prejudice'. I only want to add that the 'normative standards of justice' need not be objective themselves. Sometimes they may be 'clearly unacceptable', but often they are highly disputable.

Lawyers are mainly interested in questions of objective procedural justice. They want to know what kind of evidence is appropriate to find the truth, and how procedure should be structured in order to lead judge and jury to an unbiased and substantively justified decision. However, it is not common to count studies on the quality of evidence or jury studies as procedural justice research. The field is dominated by social psychologists who are mainly interested in subjective procedural justice, i.e., with the response of participants and observers to particular procedures (Lind and Tyler 1988).

There exists, however, one exception. I think of the numerous studies appearing during the last decade, which spoke of 'quality of justice' and dealt with alternative dispute resolution as compared to court proceedings. Studies of this kind offer a strange mixture of objective and subjective aspects. Vidmar gives a comprehensive overview in this volume.

Distributive and Procedural Justice

The goal of a procedure is to distribute benefits and burdens. At the end of the procedure, one party is the winner, another the loser. If we assumed that people are primarily motivated by self-interest, we would conclude that the winner is always content and the loser always dissatisfied. For the winner a positive outcome would always be just, and for the loser a negative outcome would always be unjust (the principle of absolute outcome). However, things are not so simple. Usually the people involved do not look only at the last event in time; they take a longer chain of events into account, and eventually they strike a balance. Research on distributive justice deals with how the relevant situation is defined and what principles are used in evaluation.

Such research has long been a tradition among social psychologists. A very prominent line of thought which developed during the 1960s was so-called equity research (Adams 1963; Berkowitz and Walster 1976). Equity theory assumes that people continually strive to maximize the difference between the rewards they receive and the costs they incur. This leads to the assumption that every individual who is involved in, or merely observes, an exchange, draws a balance more or less consciously by judging this exchange as just or unjust. Accordingly, the individual strives to repeat or continue an exchange judged to be just, to discontinue an exchange judged to be unjust, or to take actions aimed at re-establishing justice.

The systematization of the justice judgements observed in numerous studies has led to distinctions between three principles of orientation for the evaluations. These are

the principle of proportional equity,
the equality principle, and
the needs principle.

These principles of substantive justice are old acquaintances. However, unlike philosophers, social psychologists don't ask for the normative justification of these principles. Social psychologists' studies deal with determining which variables affecting an individual or a situation are responsible for the choice of a particular principle of justice. In addition, social psychologists have investigated what impact a particular principle of justice may have upon relations within a social group. Numerous studies have provided many interesting details, but, of course, they have not been able to answer all questions. Two prominent points of debate remain open: whether the three material principles of distribution can be reduced to the one principle of proportional equity, and what the respective effects of the proportional equity principle and the equality principle are upon the performance and solidarity of a social group.

We need not go into the details of distributive justice here. I only want to mention that, with regard to our topic, the equality principle has an interesting feature; namely, it is very close to procedural justice. Once this principle has been chosen, its application is not difficult: If one wants to distribute the cake, one just counts the number of people who sit around the table and cut the cake into that many pieces.

The application of the proportional equity and needs principles is much more difficult. Both principles confront us with the problem of measurement. What price is adequate? How should the damage be assessed? Does the crime call for prison or is a fine sufficient? Who is needy? What kinds of needs shall be compensated? Questions of this sort very often lead to discussions.

The people who are involved in an exchange do not encounter a measurement problem at the beginning. The parties agree on a voluntary exchange only because they measure differently, with each valuing the other's contribution more highly than his own. The interest of both parties in making an exchange is motivated by this very difference. It makes the interaction a bargaining game. If the parties agree on an exchange, this means that they have come to view their respective contributions as equivalent. They take the outcome of their negotiation as just unless the bargaining process has been distorted by a striking difference in bargaining competence or by the greater power of one party to threaten the other.

Evaluation of the respective contributions by the parties themselves depends primarily on their needs and on their capabilities to offer a good in exchange. Whether the buyer sees the price as just depends above all upon the urgency of his needs and upon his means. In addition, however, the buyer also compares how much others must pay for a similar item. Where a going rate is known, it may become the primary measurement. In this case, the equivalence of input and output is, at least to some extent, replaced by the principle of equal treatment.

In a more highly organized group, a second supporting principle applies; namely, the principle of entitlement and obligation. Lawyers tend to consider this principle not as supplementary but as the basic principle of justice. From a psychological point of view, however, the principle's supporting character becomes apparent: every entitlement can be evaluated against the basic principles of distributive justice. Equality, entitlement, and obligation can usually be assessed more easily than proportional equity. Nevertheless, the judgement is not obvious. At this point, one understands procedural justice as a principle of the second order, as a supporting principle.

Procedural justice scholars consider different variables to be of potential relevance for the acceptance of a decision (Tyler 1984):

— the outcome as such, i.e., the quality of the outcome as reward or punishment (absolute outcome)
— the outcome expected or hoped for by the participants (relative outcome)
— the outcome which is expected from the observation of similar cases (equal treatment)
— the outcome which the participants deem just according to their own standards (distributive justice)
— the evaluation of the authority which is conducting the procedure (legitimacy)
— the fairness of the procedure leading to the outcome.

These variables are not independent but interconnected. For example, the expected outcome depends, among other things, on what is considered just. In general, legal and equal treatment should coincide. The evaluation of a procedure may be influenced by the legitimacy of the institution which is responsible. Many studies, however, claim to have demonstrated that both participants and observers evaluate distributive and procedural justice more or less independently, so that the acceptance of a decision depends not only on the outcome but also on whether the procedure as such is considered fair. The more the adversaries involved—according to the basic hypothesis—evaluate a procedure as fair or just, the sooner they will accept the distribution resulting from the procedure as 'just', even in those cases where the outcome of the procedure represents an objective disadvantage for them. That is the so-called *procedural justice effect*. The most comprehensive explanation for this phenomenon is offered by Lind and Tyler: They argue that an adequate judgement of outcome fairness is a much too difficult task even for professionals. Therefore procedural justice judgements work as a kind of shortcut, as a heuristic for the overall justice evaluation (Lind 1994a). Schmidt in this volume gives a more detailed explanation of how procedural and distributive justice are interrelated. Also in this volume, Wasserman discusses the relationship between procedural and outcome justice from a psychological point of view.

On the Development of Procedural Justice Research

Procedural Justice by Thibaut and Walker, which was published in the United States in 1975, was the pioneering work in this field. Although the idea of procedural justice was not completely new at the time, Thibaut and Walker, together with a group of affiliated scientists, started to apply it in a programme of empirical experiments. With their conception and execution of a whole series of experiments, they set the standards for later research and immediately achieved remarkable results.

In their 1975 study, Thibaut and Walker assumed that the different procedures of conflict resolution with the help of a third party can be conceived as a continuum ranging from bilateral negotiations with the third party's assistance to dictatorial decisions by the third party. At the one end, the disputing participants have complete control of the procedure (*process control*) as well as the decision (*decision control*). At the other end, both types of control are placed in the hands of a third party. In traditional court procedures, the judge makes the decision. Control of procedure, however, is more or less left up to the participants. In lawsuits following the American or adversarial model, control of procedure remains to a large extent in the hands of the parties themselves. They determine the spectrum of facts which are discussed as well as the manner and extent of the hearing of evidence. In lawsuits following the continental European and especially the German inquisitorial model, the judge assumes to a large extent the control of the procedure as well.

Thibaut and Walker assume that three factors in particular determine one's preference among these possible procedures. The need to reach a quick decision is the first factor. Delays mean costs, whether in the form of loss of money or time or fewer options. The authors suspect that such cost pressure is the basis for the preference for increased intervention by a third party. The other side of the coin, however, is loss of control over the outcome of the procedure, control which increases with the degree to which the adversaries, rather than the third party, control the process. The second factor is the existence or absence of a decision-making standard that binds the third party. The more such a standard is lacking, the more important it is for the adversaries to run the procedure themselves, in order to negotiate ad hoc a distribution rule. The authors' third variable is the type of distribution problem. According to their hypothesis, stronger procedure control by the third party is required in zero sum conflicts than in situations more like a negotiation game.

In their empirical experiments, Thibaut and Walker focused on a comparison of the adversarial and the inquisitorial model. They came to the conclusion that the American-style process is superior to the inquisition process both objectively, as an instrument for reaching just decisions, and subjectively, in the evaluation of the participants. The various experiments are supposed to have shown that the adversarial process

— offers better protection against wrong judgements based on insufficient evidence, since, in the adversarial process, lawyers confronted with evidence which is to their clients' disadvantage search for favourable evidence more carefully and persistently,
— offers more protection against prejudiced opinions on the part of the judge, and
— is better able to prevent distortions which can occur as a result of the temporal sequence in the presentation of evidence.

Subjectively the adversarial process leads to greater acceptance of the decision, regardless of the outcome and regardless of whether the person concerned feels guilty or innocent. Even behind the veil of ignorance (Rawls) with regard to their role in a court case in which they would be involved, the experimental subjects preferred the adversarial model unequivocally.

The early critics (Damaska 1975; Diamond and Zeisel 1977; Hayden and Anderson 1979) claimed that the results from laboratory experiments with students on the basis of mere fictional conflicts or in disputes over small sums of money could hardly be applied to real procedures with important matters in dispute. But in the first half of the 1980s, Tyler and Folger (1980) were able to observe the procedural justice effect, first in confrontations between citizens and police, and then in court decisions on traffic violations and in minor criminal cases (Tyler 1984). In the second half of the 1980s, the procedural justice hypothesis also passed the critical test in major criminal cases: There can be no question about how much is at stake for someone on trial for a serious crime. Furthermore, convicted criminals usually have pronounced ideas about the relative appropriateness of their sentences. Nevertheless, three studies were able to show that here, too, the criminals' evaluations of their convictions were to a large extent positively correlated to their acceptance of the procedure as fair (Heinz 1985; Landis and Goodstein 1987; Casper, Tyler, and Fisher 1988). Lind and Tyler (1988) claim that Thibaut and Walker actually underestimated the procedural justice effect which they had discovered. They contend that the procedural justice effect plays at least as large a role as distributive justice in determining overall justice judgements in the dispute settlement arena.

Components of a Fair Procedure

Procedural justice is a complex variable. Many studies try to assess procedural justice by asking direct questions like: 'How fairly were you treated by the police'? or 'How just and impartial were the procedures used by the judge in trying your case'? (Lind and Tyler 1988). Sometimes there is an additional question asking about the fairness of the judge or the legitimacy of the court or other institution responsible for the procedure in question. These general evaluations of procedural beliefs cannot reveal the particular features of a procedure that make it appear fair to the participants. Thibaut and Walker used as their key variable process control. However, this, too, is a relatively complex property of a procedure which can be operationalized in different ways. Other studies replace process control with voice. Lind and Tyler (1988) occasionally combine 'process control or voice' in such a way that the difference between them seems to disappear.

From different studies one can extract at least a few special circumstances which seem to promote procedural justice. For example, it is remarkable that the evaluation of criminal proceedings is influenced by the way the defendant has been treated during his first contact with the police (Casper, Tyler, and Fisher 1988). Also of some importance is whether the lawyer spends time with his client, listens carefully, and does not make unrealistic promises. It comes almost as a surprise that defendants sentenced after plea bargaining do not evaluate their sentences as more appropriate than do defendants who stand trial. A reasoned opinion by the decision-maker seems to enhance procedural justice (Lind and Tyler 1988). It likewise enhances procedural justice when the decision-maker explains the special features of the procedure (Lind and Tyler 1988). On the other hand, people do not like 'naked statistical evidence' (Wasserman 1992, referring to a study done by Wells).

Particularly the research done by Tyler has been inspired by the Leventhal scheme (1980), which offers an elaborate analysis of the special features of procedural justice. It contains several important criteria for the degree of subjectively perceived fairness of a procedure (similarly, Bierbrauer 1982; Lerner and Whitehead 1980): correctness of the information, consistency, avoidance of prejudice, equal representation of the parties, reviewability of the decision by an appellate tribunal, and ethical appropriateness (for a discussion, see Lind and Tyler 1988; Tyler 1988). Tyler in his Chicago study (1990) found that judgements of procedural justice were highly related to the subjects' perception that the authorities cared for fairness. In formal courtroom settings, process control as defined by Thibaut and Walker turned out to be an important procedural justice criterion, too. However, the subjects placed unexpectedly little weight on consistency. From German research we know that people put much weight in the correctability rule (Barrett and Lamm 1989).

During the initial phase of empirical research, most studies focused on analysing these internal variables of procedure. Later and more sophisticated studies included the external variables which form a procedure's social context.

One of these external variables—namely, the kind of dispute—had already been considered by Thibaut and Walker. In 1978 they extended their approach, which takes as its starting point different types of disputes, into a prescriptive theory of procedure. On this subject I want only to mention that Aubert in 1963 had developed a very similar approach, which apparently did not come to the attention of Thibaut and Walker. Vidmar (1990) complains that the more recent research on procedural justice has neglected how type of dispute operates as a variable.

The involvement of the parties in social networks and settings which exist independently of procedure are also considered relevant. Studies by Fry and Leventhal (1979) and by Fry and Cheney (1981) varied not only the gender of subjects but the social setting by comparing family and business relations and by distinguishing among harmonious, disharmonious, and unspecified social settings. To summarize roughly, I would say that the procedural justice effect turned out to be little affected by variations in the social context of the procedure.

From the beginning, the general cultural context of procedure drew the most attention. Thibaut and Walker found a strong preference for the American-type adversarial process. Of course, they soon considered whether this preference could be due to a cultural bias, because most people seem to like best what they know best. Therefore, members of the research team conducted similar experiments in France and Germany. Some authors conclude from these replications that the preference for adversarial procedure is quite universal (Lind et al. 1978; Vidmar 1990). Thibaut and Walker themselves were more cautious. They took the results from Germany as inconclusive. I think they were right. Now Vidmar also has expressed his doubts (this volume). He claims that the experiments by Lind et al. (1978) used a model of the inquisitorial process that was far from accurate. In fact, the German-type inquisitorial process offers the parties some process control, as Rennig will explain later in this volume. Bierbrauer, together with Lind, Leung, and Tyler, tried to overcome this kind of critique by experimenting with a more adequate hybrid procedure (Bierbrauer et al. 1994). All this, however, is not really a rebuttal of the study done by Lind et al. 1978 because these experiments were not designed to test whether the subjects preferred the real American-type or the real European procedure, but were intended only to experiment with the variable 'process control'. Nevertheless, their results are not really convincing. First, the sample of 30 students was simply too small. More importantly, the popular image of court procedure is probably much more influenced by TV and movies than by experience in the courtroom. The media, however, have transferred the image of the American adversarial procedure to Europe, too. A state attorney told me that during a break in a trial, the defendant approached him, asking: 'Sir, when does the jury come in'? More recent studies by Leung and Lind (1986) have indeed presented some evidence that the preference for a procedure may depend upon the general cultural context.

Theoretical Explanations of Procedural Justice

Different explanations are offered for the legitimation effect of procedure. I will try to sort and label them even though they do not have the status of established theories yet.

According to the *instrumental theory*, the legitimating power of procedures derives from the fact that, in principle, they are especially well-suited to reaching materially just decisions. They help in ascertaining the facts and in searching for appropriate decision-making standards. The instrumental rationality of the procedure has an objective and a subjective aspect. The subjective aspect involves evaluations on the part of the participants in the procedure, who may consider eyewitness testimony to be suitable evidence, whereas many 'objective' observers consider it very unreliable.

The counterpart to the instrumental theory is provided by an explanatory suggestion whose idea at least has been familiar in the literature of legal philosophy for a long time, and which I shall call the *substitution theory*. In many situations it remains unclear what a materially just distribution would look like. The truth cannot be ascertained at all, or only at great cost. The decision-making standards are either vague, in dispute, or completely lacking. In such cases, procedure replaces material distribution standards. The most striking example is the 'pure procedural justice' achieved by a lottery (Rawls 1971).

Between the poles of these two 'extreme' theories can be found what I characterize as the *expressive theory*. Purely expressive means something different from value-expressive, as Lind and Tyler (1988) label their theory. Expressive behaviour is the opposite of instrumental behaviour; in other words, it is not a means to an end but an end in itself. Someone who sings in the shower is doing it just for fun. That is expressive behaviour. In the morning, we eat breakfast [illegible] order to stay healthy and efficient, but the smell of fresh coffee [illegible] hot biscuits transforms the meal from a means to an end by [illegible]roviding some immediate satisfaction. Quite similarly, proce[illegible]re not only about profits and losses but also about participa[illegible] self-presentation. Participation as such may assume the [illegible]f a reward, whereas its denial can be experienced as punishment. Thus, it is possible that a defendant leave the courtroom aquitted and yet dissatisfied, because he has not 'had his day in court'. The expressive theory also promises to demonstrate its value in the search for fair procedures when decisions must be made within organizations (Lind 1994b), and above all at the workplace. It seems to be the basis for the idea of worker participation, regardless of whether one's perspective is that of the employees, for whom codetermination is a means for pursuing their interests and achieving some self-realization, or that of management, whose goal is to foster employees' acceptance of decisions. However, the participation effect does not work so well in hierarchical institutions as it does in the courtroom. In the workplace, participation can even lead to a reverse effect. Psychologists talk about a frustration effect (Cohen 1985, Folger 1977). The participation effect is apparently not strong enough to make workers reduce their pay demands in exchange for participation.

Lind and Tyler (1988) do not like the explanation that people can enjoy participation in a procedure to such an extent that voice itself becomes a reward. They claim that this explanation stretches the self-interest model to the point where it could account for virtually any finding and would therefore be of little value. They prefer a position which is called *value-expressive*. They claim that people look at procedure not as a means to an end or as an end in itself but take a normative perspective. Normative aspects of experience include neutrality, lack of bias, honesty, efforts to be fair, politeness, and respect for citizens' rights. I do not want to attack the theory of a value-expressive function of procedure. I only claim that the rewarding effect of procedure itself can also be real. To support my position, I refer to the opposite effect. A procedure can function not only as a reward but also as a sanction.

A book by Malcolm Feeley was published in the United States in 1979 with the title *The Process Is the Punishment*. In that work the author uses the example of a criminal court in New Haven to describe how, throughout the entire court case but especially during the proceedings, sanctions are levelled against the accused. Arrest and detention while awaiting trial or bail are only the most obvious examples. Lind and Tyler themselves mention a Chicago judge who, on the day of trial, dismissed some cases because he thought that the defendants had suffered enough by spending a day in the courthouse.

In the last few years of the Federal Republic of Germany, when numerous doctors were investigated because of fraudulent billing practices, the investigators were able to exert nearly unlimited pressure by threatening to confiscate a doctor's patient index, or by describing to the accused in detail how he would not be able to continue his practice during a trial several weeks long, and how his office staff and patients would have to appear as witnesses if he didn't confess. A random glance at police and court statistics shows the large difference between the number of charges filed and the number of convictions, and gives rise to the suspicion that many sanctions have been imposed here on people who have not been convicted of anything.

Of course, according to the rhetoric of the participants, procedures—and especially legal procedures—are not intended as sanctions but rather as preparation for sanctions. But procedures are de facto always burdensome, and they often represent restrictions which are hardly less severe for the people concerned than a conviction itself would be. This situation has not escaped the attention of legal experts. Thus, with regard to the restrictive effects for the defendant, the German Federal Constitutional Court (BVerfGE 7, 109) has granted a complaint against the opening resolution, which as an intermediate reply was previously incontestable. In response to this, legislators have introduced the closing address (section 169 a StPO). The extended duration of a criminal proceeding is a recognized reason for reducing a defendant's sentence. With regard to civil rights, the question of damage suits on grounds of unjustified legal action must be taken into account. Procedure is often so burdensome in a practical sense that the stress it produces cannot be ignored. The effect of procedures resembles that of sanctions, but is different to the extent that, normatively at least, it is not intended.

Lind and Tyler in particular (1988) emphasize another possible explanation of the specific effects of procedures, which they call the *group value theory*. A decision resulting in an unjust outcome is an isolated case, whereas an unfair procedure is a long-term establishment, which reflects the value system of a group or society. Consequently, unfair procedures are perceived as a greater threat than erroneous individual decisions. But even more importance must be given to the fact that a group's or a society's allocation procedures ve its members a sense of their social status. The procedure gives individuals concerned a feeling for whether and how they are ted by their group, and thus determines in a crucial way their about their own worth and standing. This effect causes the react very sensitively to different procedural arrangesely because the individual confronts societal authorities in procedures, how he or she is treated in the procedure, whether he or she is recognized as a person and treated with respect and dignity is important for the individual's self-esteem. Lind et al. (1990; see also Vidmar in this volume) have supported this theory with astonishing observations. For a long time, it was assumed as beyond question in the sociology of law that traditional court procedure, as a type of 'distorted communication', had to lead to frustrations, and that informal conflict resolution procedures were preferable in every case. Now the exact opposite is claimed: the participants prefer the court case and procedures in courts of arbitration to informal alternatives, because they have a sense that they are being taken seriously as individuals and so are their concerns. There seems, however, to exist a difference between pre-experience procedural preferences and post-experience evaluations of procedure (Tyler, Huo, and Lind 1993).

Criticizing theories which maintain and explain the positive effects of procedure, Wasserman (1989) has suggested a 'displacement' theory. It assumes that most of the participants in a procedure could accept a negative outcome as something inevitable. In this case critique of procedure serves as a vent, an opportunity for them to make known and explain their disappointment. This 'theory' is interesting because its refutation, which would implicitly confirm the other theories, requires the answer to a chicken-and-egg question: Does acceptance of a procedure lead to acceptance of the outcome; or, on the contrary, does the acceptance of an outcome make the procedure seem fair? This question can hardly be answered on the basis of the experimental research thus far discussed. To me it seems remarkable that we also find in Luhmann's essay a displacement argument. Luhmann (1969) analyses how the losers may explain their disappointment. They look for a culprit and find one in the person of a biased judge, an incompetent lawyer, or a lying witness. Luhmann explains the stereotyped negative image that lawyers have among the public as serving to change unavoidable disappointment into diffuse and private resentment.

Procedures and the Legitimation of Institutions

In their approach, studies in social psychology aim at individuals and individual experience with procedures. A generalization, however, is implicit in this approach, namely a transition from questions about the acceptance of concrete procedures and their outcomes to questions about the evaluation of a procedure as an institution and the legitimacy of the authorities responsible for a decision. Here connections can be made to studies about the prestige of political institutions. Lind and Tyler hold that procedural justice 'plays a much larger role than distributive fairness in determining reactions to legal authorities and institutions' (1988).

Tyler and Rasinski (1991) claim, using the example of the United States Supreme Court, that nonparticipants are even more apt to draw conclusions about the legitimacy of an institution on the basis of the fairness of its procedures than are those individuals immediately affected by the procedures. Gibson (1991) emphasizes, in contrast, that general support for institutions, which results from political socialization in childhood, political values, and accumulated satisfaction or dissatisfaction with the results of institutional decision-making, fosters acceptance for individual decisions. According to Gibson, since citizens know little about distant institutions, they tend to assume that an institution they consider legitimate also incorporates a fair procedure. The perception of procedural justice plays no part in the legitimation of an institution or in the acceptance of decisions, as long as firsthand experience is not involved. Gibson thus claims, contrary to Tyler and Rasinski, that the generalized legitimacy of political and legal institutions has a countereffect on the individual acceptance of concrete procedures and outcomes. In effect he comes quite close to Luhmann's functional systems approach of 'legitimation through procedure'.

German Research

So far I have referred largely to American studies. In Germany, empirical research on procedural justice was until recently almost nonexistent. One reason for this lack is that in continental Europe, and particularly in Germany, procedure in general is valued less highly than in common-law countries. For a long time, procedure was seen in Germany only in its instrumental function (Gilles 1981, 1992). In addition, German and American research traditions differ. I want to mention two details which in my country have been obstacles for several empirical projects. First, it is difficult, or impossible, to ask a court for details about litigants, because the court would refuse on grounds of confidentiality. Second, the relatively inexpensive method of telephone interviews which has been used in several American studies is still not widely accepted. Therefore, one finds more research plans than results in Germany. Occasionally, studies appear that centre on other topics but also include some aspects of procedural justice (e.g., Rottleuthner 1983).

There are, however, very few empirical studies which focus on procedural justice.

In Germany, Bierbrauer (1982) was one of the first to come out with relevant publications. Barrett and Lamm (1989) took American studies as the point of departure for their study on how West German students evaluate the relationship between procedural and distributive justice, and they arrived at the conclusion that Germans place comparatively great importance on the possibility of appellate review. An experiment by Klein and Bierhoff (1991) tested the reactions of employees toward their superiors' evaluations of their work performances under a variety of degrees of participation in the process and of channels of appeal. The section on 'norm development and environment' at the Wissenschaftszentrum (Scientific Centre) in Berlin, has been studying a procedure for the mediation of conflicts in the planning of large-scale technical waste-treatment facilities and a procedure for the estimation and evaluation of the consequences of technology (Bora 1993, 1995; van den Daele 1991). The Centre for Social Policy at the University of Bremen is engaged in a research project on 'local justice'. This is the national subproject of an internationally coordinated research project with further subprojects in Chicago, Paris and Oslo. The topic is 'local', i.e., allocation decisions immediately relevant to the citizen in the areas of health, work, and education (Elster 1990; Schmidt 1992, 1993). The study covers the allocation of life-saving medical resources, especially of organs for transplantation; the hiring, promotion, and firing policies of private and public employers; and admission procedures at universities. It is obvious that, apart from the relevant allocation criteria, distribution procedures are of decisive importance.

There are two German studies on procedural justice at courts using Tyler's research approach. They show that procedural justice matters for German defendants. Haller (1987; Haller and Machura 1995) surveyed juvenile prisoners and their opinions on their process and on legal authorities. The juveniles' evaluations of procedural justice and of distributive justice contributed to their satisfaction with their verdicts, which was the strongest correlated with the outcome compared to expectations. Moreover, procedural justice was the only factor of all measured which was moderately related to the evaluation of the judge. The juveniles experienced a trial type with lay assessors. The influence of the lay assessors correlated moderately with procedural and distributive justice evaluations. Even the judges were not seen throughout negatively but rather as differentiated in their behaviour. Judges were evaluated by the same criteria American defendants use for their judges' behaviour (see Tyler 1984). All in all, Haller's study provides some support for the group value theory (Haller and Machura 1995.)

Defendants at German lower criminal courts were examined by Machura (1994a, 1994b). Again, the same criteria for fair behaviour of judges were used as in American studies (see Tyler 1984, 1990). Regardless of the favourability of the outcome, the defendants tended to evaluate the judge, the public prosecutor, and their lawyer positively. Distributive fairness and procedural fairness were related, but conceptually different. Whereas distributive justice evaluations were mainly driven by outcome favourability, procedural justice evaluations were driven by the fair behaviour of the judge. Satisfaction with the outcome, procedural fairness, and distributive fairness shaped evaluations of courts and judges as well as perceptions of possible future court trials. The findings largely confirm the group value theory (Machura 1994a, 1994b). Messmer in this volume gives an account of a study of the communication processes which develop in victim-offender mediation.

A recent publication (Bierbrauer, Gottwald, and Birnbreier-Stahlberger 1995) contains a study by Bierbrauer on gender and procedural justice which found only very faint differences in the attitudes of men and women toward different kinds of procedures. A contribution by Richli extends the focus of research on legislation, and a contribution by Schünemann shows a strong effect of the cooperation of the attorney general and the judge on the judge's neutrality.

Systems Theory Approaches

Legitimation Through Procedure

In 1969, Luhmann developed the thesis of 'legitimation through procedure'; i.e., that the political administrative system procures legitimacy for its decisions through procedures as such. Luhmann treats as procedures those social systems which are limited in their duration from the outset due to their specific function of reaching a single binding decision. The examples which he refers to and describes are legislative procedure which begins with a political election; administrative procedure; and, most impressively and in the most detail, court procedure. Here I will focus only on the last of these.

If I had to label Luhmann's theory I would call it the 'isolation theory'. Luhmann's starting point is the thesis that every conflict has a tendency toward generalization; i.e., toward inclusion of more and more topics, toward involvement of more and more people, and toward an escalation of weaponry. Procedure counteracts this tendency by restricting the parties to certain fighting tools, by specifying the topic, and by isolating the parties from their social environment.

Luhmann considers the instrumental character of procedures completely beside the point. He also gives little importance to procedural fairness. The recognition of a decision as legitimate is not supposed to depend on whether the parties involved are convinced of the necessity, correctness, or justice of the decision. Instead, the procedure exposes the individuals concerned to a learning process, resulting in their acceptance of the outcome of the procedure as the basis for their future behaviour. The only thing that matters is success in an external sense. Even if defendants who have been found guilty are dissatisfied with the verdict, they will still act in accordance with it, because they are forced to realize that they can mobilize neither their friends nor the general public against the verdict. This kind of success is only to be achieved in a social climate in which the recognition of decisions which are meant to be binding is institutionalized. That is the contribution of procedure, which does not require that individuals be convinced that they were treated fairly but instead changes the structure of the expectations of the parties involved and their environment, and integrates them in the procedure in such a manner that in the end they have no alternative but to accept the decision (the way we all accept the weather even if we don't like it).

Luhmann has drafted a sociological, not psychological, theory of procedure. However, he has built in several psychological hypotheses. The most important could be characterized as a *commitment hypothesis*. Luhmann interprets procedure as a learning process by first describing how consensus is developed in a transitory social system. He considers decisive the expectations of continuity which every self-presentation awakens among other participants. They form the 'funnel of the procedure'. Luhmann then describes the preconditions on which the success of the procedure depends, especially its openness and its relevance to decision. These in turn are not possible until procedure differentiates itself from other social contexts. In a further analytical step, with the supposition that consensus with regard to nonparticipating third parties can be assumed, the procedure is recoupled with its surrounding social systems: the public nature of the procedure, which may be only a fiction, and the habits of reasoning of the judge, which in Germany takes the 'if A, then B' form, are supposed to remove the chance of public criticism of the result and to reinforce the public belief that everything is going the way it should. Everywhere in social life people are expected to behave consistently. He who takes part in a procedure without being brutally forced to do so has already signalled to his environment that he will accept the outcome. If the outcome is disappointing, he can't protest. He has renounced this possibility by participation.

Initially, Luhmann's book evoked a great deal of criticism and even furious protest, which was based mainly on the misunderstanding that the critics thought Luhmann was addressing the question of whether the legal system could legitimately command recognition, whereas in fact he was merely giving a description of how it functions. Machura in this volume gives an account of Luhmann's critics. Bussmann's contribution places the procedural justice approach into the context of systems theory, building on Luhmann's concept of law as a symbolic generalized medium of communication.

Proceduralization Through Reflexive Law

Even those not able to accept Luhmann's analysis of 'legitimation through procedure' do accept the hypothesis, advanced as an empirical claim, that the basis of legitimacy of modern law has changed, that a consensus on values has been lost and either has been or will have to be replaced to an increasing extent by a consensus on the rationality of procedures. The theory of reflexive law goes a step further. It reacts to the widespread assumption that the direct regulation of society by state law, especially regulation by injunctions and prohibitions, taxes and material incentives, is doomed to failure in light of the internal complexity of the subsystems of society, which have grown enormously (e.g. Teubner 1982; Teubner and Willke 1984; Teubner 1986, 1989). The modern welfare state is, according to this hypothesis, a victim of its own success, for the subsystems—political parties and associations, churches and unions, commercial concerns and media, and so on—which have grown under its protection and influence have achieved such size and autonomy that they are in increasing measure able to escape the influence of the state. They have become serious competitors for power and control in society, having already forced the state into a defensive position (Teubner and Willke 1984). For the authors, this results in the development of reflexive law, which will in the future replace the interventionist law of the welfare state and constitute the definitive medium of the regulation of society through law. It is supposed that law will supply only procedures by means of which decisions are to be worked out. This refers not so much to court procedures as to the creation of organizations and the distribution of competences, thus constituting the framework within which the immediately involved individuals are to resolve their conflicts and regulate their affairs themselves. The most common examples are the collective industrial agreement act and the various codetermination regulations in companies and government departments. But also in all important administrative procedures, the participation of different bureaucracies as well as of the concerned parties is foreseen. In technical areas, the state legislators refer to rules below the level of laws in the strict sense, to technical norms or ethical standards which are to be developed by those immediately involved. With regard to environmental protection legislation, it has been noted that the courts have increasingly shifted the focus of their attention from difficult judgements of controversial technical and scientific issues to review of the behaviour and procedures of the actual decision-makers (minority vote of the judges Simon and Heusner on the *Muelheim-Kaerlich resolution*, BVerfGE 53, 30-96). Even more generally, Germany's highest court tends to protect constitutional rights by procedural means. If I am informed correctly, there is a similar development in American constitutional law, known as the 'due process revolution'.

The concept of reflexive law gains its particular attractiveness and its specific problem contours from the fact that Teubner and Willke (1984) have anchored it in a theory of self-referential or autopoietic systems. In the context of the subject matter of procedural justice that is quite important, because this theory was initially introduced into the sociology of law by Luhmann. Consequently, Luhmann also participated later in the discussion on reflexive law. Thus there is hope that 'legitimacy through procedure' and 'reflexive law', too, can eventually be placed in relation to one another in a comprehensive framework of systems theory.

Those who advocate the theory of reflexive law are not satisfied with the mere description and explanation of the current state of law, but rather make the explicit claim to be able to describe a new stage in the evolutionary development of law (Teubner 1982). In this respect the reflexive law theorists find themselves in agreement with the ideas that Habermas and Eder have developed with regard to evolution theory, i.e., that the legitimacy problems of modern times can be solved only by new forms of law which meet the requirements of communicative or procedural rationality.

The concept of 'reflexive law' is by no means generally accepted, it is also the object of strong attack (Hartmann 1987; Nahamowitz 1987, 1988); this has to be mentioned here for the sake of completing the picture. For a complete grasp of the topic at hand, it is more important to point out that the empirical-analytical concept of reflexive law is often connected with the normative demand for a further-reaching proceduralization of law (see, for example Eder 1990; Peters 1991). The connection is forged by explicit reliance on the discourse theory of the Frankfurt School (e.g., Habermas 1987).

The concept of procedural justice not only forms a bridge between types of procedure and social development as a whole but also offers a model for the solution of conflicts within anticipated future structures of postindustrial society and, furthermore, is not completely impervious to empirical testing. The major problems of 'postregulatory law' arise according to this thesis, not in the realm of regulation as such but rather in the evaluation and selection of alternatives (Eder 1990). In essence, these are questions of the rational, but morally justified, creation of opportunities for appropriate participation in formal as well as informal procedures. Eder (1990, 157), for example, states: 'The specific functions of procedural legal norms for this problem are the distribution and allocation of discourse chances, duties with regard to the public sphere and with regard to justification. Procedures in the traditional sense just process things. Procedures in the normative sense now mobilize actors and present them intervention chances in ongoing discussion and decision making processes'. Peters (1991) confronts the traditional execution model of procedure with the notion of procedure as a device for problem- and conflict-solving.

The theories of proceduralization and reflexive law may be characterized as substitution theories because they eventually aim at distributive justice. The distribution principle, however, must first be invented through procedure. To me it came as a surprise to find an even more radical proceduralization hypothesis in the writings of American empiricists. Lind and Tyler (1988, 151) refer, though only in a footnote, to Thibaut's 'insight . . . that procedural justice might provide an ever more important source of satisfaction as society's resources become more and more limited'. Here it seems that procedural justice will someday replace material distribution. I have not been able to verify the source in Thibaut's writings. Probably I am stretching a mere footnote too far if I take it as the final theory of procedural justice.

Normative Philosophical Concepts

The normative philosophical concepts, derived from the idea of law as rational, which aim at a morally and ethically grounded 'procedural theory of justice' (see Habermas 1987), can be considered the counterpart to the perspective of systems theory in the philosophy of law. Rawls (1971) and Habermas (1983, 1987, 1992) are well-known representatives of such a position. The philosophic origins of their concepts are as diverse as imaginable, and yet both lead to a theory of procedural justice. In both men's views the legitimacy of procedures in a state under the rule of law is traced back to a necessarily developing procedural rationality, to empathetic understanding, or to both. In Rawls, the rational egoism of free and equal individuals directs the choice or acceptance of right principles; the justice of an outcome is guaranteed by the procedure from which it stems. The procedure in question, however, is not a real one: rather, 'procedure' remains a regulative idea. In Habermas the validity—in the sense of being morally justified and rationally grounded—of procedurally achieved outcomes springs, on the contrary, from the common, cooperative search for truth within a rational communicative discourse (discourse theory). This procedure, too, is initially just a regulative idea but becomes, in a juridical context, a real procedure (Alexy 1978, 1981; Kaufmann 1989). 'Moral consciousness and communicative action'—as the programmatic title of the book published by Habermas in 1983 reads—'is thus rendered the foundation of rationality and, accordingly, the foundation of the legitimacy of procedure in the modern state under the rule of law. Legal procedures are unique therein, because they approach the requirements of absolute procedural rationality since they are connected to institutional (i.e., independent) criteria on the basis of which, from the perspective of a nonparticipant, a decision can be evaluated with regard to whether it has been reached in accordance with the rules or not' (Habermas 1987, 13, my translation). Tschentscher in this volume gives a detailed comparison of how Rawls and Habermas make use of the concept of procedural justice.

Research Perspectives

On the basis of the widely diversified research spectrum, which includes empirical as well as normative and micro- as well as macro-theoretical approaches, it is hardly an exaggeration to call the viewpoint of procedural justice one of the most important starting points for interdisciplinary theory construction in the field of law. In light of these circumstances, the fact that the possibilities and opportunities for comprehensive theory construction have not yet been exhausted is all the more relevant. There are various reasons for this.

Studies by social psychologists draw a sharp dividing line between procedural justice and distributive justice. When one looks back at the research tradition in which the studies by Thibaut and Walker (1975) were developed in the 1970s, it seems obvious to ask whether procedural justice cannot be, in the final analysis, traced back to distributive justice after all. This refers to the research tradition of those sociologists and social psychologists who tried to account for all social relations, with the help of the idea of reciprocity, in an exchange theory. The works of Blau (1964), Gouldner and Sprehe (1965) and Homans (1960, 1972) from the 1960s and early 1970s pointed out the direction and were soon succeeded by numerous empirical studies on social justice and equity. The enormous theoretical and practical potential of newer studies on procedural justice cannot perhaps be fully exploited until these studies are integrated into a more comprehensive exchange theory.

The most important element missing from the literature is the lack of empirical studies in Germany, and perhaps also in other European countries. However, empirical research on the social psychology of procedure is not to be the focal point of the procedural justice workshops at Oñati. Rather, this research approach is to be combined with the more macro-theoretically oriented approaches. Unlike the social psychologists' research on procedural justice, the macro-theoretical studies until now have been almost exclusively oriented towards theory construction. In general, one could say that social psychology lacks an encompassing theoretical perspective, whereas the systems theory approach fails to offer empirically testable hypotheses.

Luhmann's more recent works are receiving attention and recognition outside of Europe, not least in the United States. An exception to this recognition is *Legitimacy Through Procedure*, which seems to be completely unknown in that country since it is not included in the comprehensive bibliographies even of the most recent works. This is noteworthy since the book has become better known in Germany than most of Luhmann's other works and can almost boast of a certain popularity, and because it seems in comparison to Luhmann's other works particularly accurate on an empirical level. Luhmann's fundamental premises are of a psychological nature. Until now no attempt has been made to pursue what seems, in light of the situation sketched above, the obvious course: to bring Luhmann's systems theoretical analyses of legitimacy through procedure together with the empirical studies of procedural justice which have been pursued in such great numbers by social psychologists in the United States.

The effort to combine the systems functional approach with the empirical results of social psychology promises a reciprocal enhancement of the different studies of procedural justice. Such a combination would furthermore be of considerable general interest since the transition from the micro to the macro level of theory construction, which is demanded again and again in sociology, could succeed here. The possibility of connections to ideas in the theory of evolution about proceduralization through reflexive law also seems desirable and should not be ruled out from the start.

The policy implications of procedural justice research are obvious. Here are only two examples: in the United States the courts had to decide whether an appointed defense attorney is required to file all petitions which the defendant demands in a criminal case, so long as these petitions are not frivolous. The Supreme Court answered this question in the negative in 1981 (*Barnes v. Jones*). Wasserman (1989) comments that the decision certainly would have been different if the court had been familiar with and taken seriously those studies showing that participants in court cases by no means evaluate the fairness of the procedure purely instrumentally. In Germany new laws have restricted remedies in minor cases. The fact that, generally, the evaluation of the fairness of a procedure also depends on whether it is possible to correct mistakes (Leventhal 1980) is certainly relevant in this context, as are the findings by Barrett and Lamm (1989) that the subjects in German experiments place comparatively more importance on the possibility of appeal.

The philosophers who have discussed procedural justice, on the other hand, have so far failed to recognize the extensive empirical results available. Until now, however, a systematic critical evaluation of theories of legal procedure on the basis of the empirical studies has also been lacking (Lind 1994a). The procedural justice workshop is thus presented extensive and rewarding tasks. The first conference in 1992 concentrated on a summary and critique of the available results, theories, and suggestions. The second conference, held in 1993, tried to integrate theories with empirical results and to search for a satisfactory theory of procedural rationality. This volume presents some of the work done. A third conference in 1996 continued these efforts and applied the procedural justice approach to such new fields as public acceptance of exceptional procedures (e.g., the Nuremberg trials), procedures as a means for allocating research funding, law-making procedures in the European Union, procedural justice and conflict resolution in the workplace, doing 'local justice' by procedure, and 'due process' in private organizations.

References

Adams, J. Stacy. 1963. Toward an Understanding of Inequity. *Journal of Abnormal and Social Psychology* 67: 422–36.

Alexander, L. 1987. The Relationship Between Procedural Due Process and Substantive Constitutional Rights. *University of Florida Law Review* 39: 323–43.

Alexander, Sheldon, and Marian Ruderman. 1987. The Role of Procedural and Distributive Justice in Organizational Behavior. *Social Justice Research* 1: 177–98.

Alexy, Robert. 1978. *Theorie der juristischen Argumentation.* Frankfurt am Main: Suhrkamp.

———. 1981. Die Idee einer prozeduralen Theorie der juristischen Argumentation. *Rechtstheorie Beiheft* 2: 177–88.

Aubert, Vilhelm. 1963. Competition and Conflict Discussions: Two Types of Conflict and Conflict Resolution. *Journal of Conflict Resolution* 7: 26–42.

Austin, William, and Neil C. McGinn. 1977. Sex Differences in Choice of Distribution Rules. *Journal of Personality* 45: 379–94.

Barrett, Edith J., and Helmut Lamm. 1989. The Role of Procedural Justice in the Allocation of Limited Resources: A West German Perspective. *Social Justice Research* 3: 21–30.

Barrett-Howard, Edith, and Tom R. Tyler. 1986. Procedural Justice As a Criterion in Allocation Decisions. *Journal of Personality and Social Psychology* 50: 296–304.

Bayles, Michael D. 1990. *Procedural Justice: Allocation to Individuals.* Dordrecht: Kluwer.

Berkemann, Jörg. 1989. Fairneß als Rechtsprinzip. *Juristische Rundschau*: 221–28.

Berkowitz, Leonard, and Elaine Walster, eds. 1976. *Equity Theory: Toward a General Theory of Social Interaction.* New York: Academic Press.

Bierbrauer, Günter. 1982. Gerechtigkeit und Fairness im Verfahren. In *Alternativen in der Ziviljustiz*, edited by E. Blankenburg et al. Köln. Bundesanzeiger.

Bierbrauer, Günter, Walther Gottwald, and Beatrix Birnbreier-Stahlberger, eds. 1995. *Verfahrensgerechtigkeit. Rechtspsychologische Forschungsbeiträge für die Justizpraxis*: Köln. Verlag Otto Schmidt.

Bierbrauer, Günter, Kwok Leung, E. Allan Lind, et al. 1994. Cultural and Situational Determinants of Disputing Preferences and Disputing Behavior. Working paper, American Bar Foundation, Chicago.

Bierhoff, Hans Werner. 1986. Sozialer Kontext als Determinante der wahrgenommenen Gerechtigkeit. *Zeitschrift für Sozialpsychologie* 13: 66–78.

———. 1992. Prozedurale Gerechtigkeit: Das Wie und Warum der Fairneß. *Zeitschrift für Sozialpsychologie* 23: 163–78.

Bierhoff, Hans Werner, Ernst Buck, and Renate Klein. 1989. Attractiveness and Respectability of the Offender As Factor in the Evaluation of Criminal Cases. In *Criminal Behavior and the Justice System*, edited by H. Wegener, F. Lösel, and J. Haisch. New York: Springer Verlag.

Bies, R. J., and J. S. Moag. 1986. Interactional Justice—Communication Criteria of Fairness: In *Research on Negotiation in Organizations*, edited by R. J. Lewicki, B. M. Sheppard, and H. M. Bazermann. Greenwich, Conn.: JAI Press.

Blau, Peter M. 1964. *Exchange and Power in Social Life.* New York: Wiley.

———. 1968. Interaction—Social Exchange. In *International Encyclopedia of the Social Sciences*, Vol. 7, edited by D. L. Sills. New York: Macmillan.

Bora, Alfons. 1993. Gesellschaftliche Integration durch Verfahren—Zur Funktion von Verfahrensgerechtigkeit in der Technikfolgenabschätzung und bewertung. *Zeitschrift für Rechtssoziologie* 14: 55–79.

———. 1995. Procedural Justice As a Contested Concept: Sociological Remarks on the Group Value Model. *Social Justice Research* 8: 175–95.

Brett, Jeanne. 1986. Commentary on Procedural Justice Papers. In *Research on Negotiation in Organizations*, edited by R. Lewicki, B. M. Sheppard, and H. M. Bazermann. Greenwich, Conn.: JAI Press.

Capelletti, Mauro. 1988. Trends of 'Procedural Justice' in Contemporary Europe. In *Festschrift für Werner Maihofer zum 70. Geburtstag*, edited by Arthur Kaufmann, E.-M. Mestmäcker, and H. Zacher. Frankfurt am Main: Vittorio Klostermann Verlag.

Casper, Jonathan D. 1978. Having Their Day in Court: Defendant Evaluations of the Fairness of Their Treatment. *Law and Society Review* 12: 237–51.

Casper, Jonathan D., Tom R. Tyler and Bonnie B. Fisher. 1988. Procedural Justice in Felony Cases. *Law and Society Review* 22: 483–507.

Cohen, Ronald L. 1985. Procedural Justice and Participation. *Human Relations* 38: 643–63.

———. 1987. Distributive Justice: Theory and Research. *Social Justice Research* 1: 19–40.

Connolly, Paul R. J., and Saundra Smith. 1983. The Litigant's Perspective on Delay: Waiting for the Dough. *Justice System Journal* 8: 271–86.

Cook, Karen S., ed. 1987. *Social Exchange Theory*. Newbury Park: Sage.

Damaska, M. 1975. Presentation of Evidence and Fact-Finding Precision. *University of Pennsylvania Law Review* 123, 1083–1106.

van den Daele, Wolfgang. 1991. Zum Forschungsprogramm der Abteilung 'Normbildung und Umwelt'. Veröffentlichungsreihe der Abteilung Normbildung und Umwelt des Forschungsschwerpunkts Technik, Arbeit, Umwelt des Wissenschaftszentrums Berlin für Sozialforschung Nr. FS II: 91–301.

Diamond, Stanley, and H. Zeisel. 1977. Book Review. *Duke Law Journal*: 1289–96.

Eder, Klaus. 1990. Prozedurales Recht und Prozeduralisierung des Rechts. Einige begriffliche Klärungen. In *Wachsende Staatsaufgaben, sinkende Steuerungsfähigkeit des Rechts*, edited by Dieter Grimm. Baden-Baden: Nomos Verlagsgesellschaft.

Elster, John. 1990. Local Justice, *Archives Européennes de Sociologie* 31: 117–40.

Emerson, Richard M. 1972. Exchange Theory. In *Sociological Theories in Progress*, Vol. 2, edited by J. Berger, M. Zelditch, and B. Anderson. Boston: Houghton-Mifflin.

Feeley, Malcolm. 1979. *The Process is the Punishment*. New York: Sage.

Fischer, Karla, Neil Vidmar, and René Ellis. 1993. The Culture of Battering and the Role of Mediation in Domestic Violence Cases. *Southern Methodist University Law Review* 46: 2117–74.

Folger, Robert. 1977. Distributive and Procedural Justice: Combined Impact of 'Voice' and Improvement on Experienced Inequity. *Journal of Personality and Social Psychology* 35: 108–19.

———. 1987. Distributive and Procedural Justice in the Workplace. *Social Justice Research* 1: 143–59.

Folger, Robert, and Jerald Greenberg. 1985. Procedural Justice: An Interpretive Analysis of Personal Systems. In *Research in Personnel and*

Human Resources Management, Vol. 3, edited by K. M. Rowland and G. R. Ferris. Greenwich, Conn.: JAI Press.

Fry, W. R. and Cheney, G. 1981. Perceptions of Procedural Fairness As a Function of Distributive Preferences. Paper presented at the annual meeting of the Midwestern Psychological Association, Detroit.

Fry, W. R., and G. S. Leventhal. 1979. Cross-Situational Procedural Preferences: A Comparison of Allocation Preferences and Equity Across Different Social Settings. Paper presented at the annual meeting of the Southeastern Psychological Association, Washington, D. C.

Gibson, James L. 1989. Understanding of Justice: Institutional Legitimacy, Procedural Justice, and Political Tolerance. *Law and Society Review* 23: 469–96.

———. 1991. Institutional Legitimacy, Procedural Justice, and Compliance with Supreme Court Decisions: A Question of Causality. *Law and Society Review* 25: 631–5.

Gilles, Peter. 1981. Zum Bedeutungszuwachs und Funktionswandel des Prozeßrechts. *Juristische Schulung*: 402–09.

———. 1992. Material vs. Formal View of Procedure and Legitimation of Judicial Decisionmaking Through Procedural Norms. Paper prepared for an Oñati workshop on procedural justice, 8–11 June, Oñati, Spain.

Gouldner, Alvin W., and J. Timothy Sprehe. 1965. *The Study of Man.*

Greenberg, Jerald, and Robert Folger. 1983. Procedural Justice, Participation, and the Fair Process Effects in Groups and Organizations. In *Basic Group Processes,* edited by P. B. Paulus. New York: Springer Verlag.

Greenberg, Jerald, and Tom R. Tyler. 1987. Why Procedural Justice in Organizations? *Social Justice Research* 1: 127–42.

Habermas, Jürgen. 1983. *Moralbewußtsein und kommunikatives Handeln.* Frankfurt am Main: Suhrkamp.

———. 1987. Wie ist Legitimität durch Legalität möglich? *Kritische Justiz* 20: 1–16.

———. 1992. *Faktizität und Geltung*. Frankfurt am Main: Suhrkamp.

Haller, Volkmar. 1987. Zum Einfluß von Urteilshöhe und empfundender distributiver und prozeduraler Gerechtigkeit auf die Urteilszufriedenheit sowie auf die Beurteilung von Richter und Gerichtsbarkeit bei jugendlichen Strafgefangenen. Diss., Faculty of Psychology, Philips-Universität Marburg.

Haller, Volkmar, and Stefan Machura. 1995. Procedural Justice at German Courts As Seen by Defendants and Juvenile Prisoners. *Social Justice Research* 8: 197–215.

Hartmann, Michael. 1987. Reflexives Recht am Ende? Zum Eindringen materiellen Rechts in die Tarifautonomie. *Zeitschrift für Soziologie* 16: 16–32.

Hayden, Robert M., and Jill K. Anderson. 1979. On the Evaluation of Procedural Systems in Laboratory Experiments: A Critique of Thibaut and Walker. *Law and Human Behavior* 3: 21–38.

Heinz, A. M. 1985. Procedure Versus Consequence: Experimental Evidence of Preferences for Procedural and Distributive Justice. In *Courts and Criminal Justice: Emerging Issues*, edited by S. Talarico. Beverly Hills, Calif.: Sage.

Hoffmann-Riem, Wolfgang. 1989. *Konfliktmittler in Verhandlungen*. Baden-Baden: Nomos-Verlag.

Hofmann, Roland. 1992. *Verfahrensgerechtigkeit*. Paderborn: Ferdinand Schöningh.

Homans, George C. 1960. *Theorie der sozialen Gruppe*. Opladen: Westdeutscher Verlag.

———. 1972. *Elementarformen sozialen Verhaltens*. 2nd ed., Opladen: Westdeutscher Verlag.

Houlden, Pauline. 1981. Impact of Procedural Modification on Evaluations of Plea Bargaining. *Law and Society Review* 15: 267–316.

Kahn, Arnold, Robin E. Nelson, and William P. Gaeddert. 1980. Sex of Subject and Sex Compositon of the Group as Determinants of Reward Allocations. *Journal of Personality and Social Psychology* 38: 737–50.

Kahn, Arnold, V. E. O'Leary, J. E. Krulewitz, and Helmut Lamm. 1980. Equity and Equality: Male and Female Means to a Just End. *Basic and Applied Social Psychology* 2: 173–97.

Kaufmann, Arthur. 1989. *Prozedurale Theorie der Gerechtigkeit*. München: Verlag der Bayerischen Akademie der Wissenschaften.

Klein, Renate, and Hans Werner Bierhoff. 1991. Responses to Achievement Situations. The Mediation Function of Perceived Fairness.

Ladeur, Karl Heinz. 1990. Selbstorganisation sozialer Systeme und Prozeduralisierung des Rechts. In *Wachsende Staatsaufgaben—sinkende Steuerungsfähigkeit des Rechts*, edited by Dieter Grimm. Baden-Baden: Nomos Verlagsgesellschaft.

Landis, Jean M., and Lynne Goodstein. 1987. When is Justice Fair? An Integrated Approach to the Outcome Versus Procedure Debate. *American Bar Foundation Research Journal* 7: 675–707.

Landy, Frank J., Janet Barnes-Farell, and Jeanette N. Cleveland. 1980. Perceived Fairness and Accuracy of Performance Evaluation: A Follow-Up. *Journal of Applied Psychology* 65: 355–56.

Lane, Robert E. 1988. Procedural Goods in a Democracy: How One Is Treated Versus What One Gets. *Social Justice Research* 2: 177–92.

Lerner, Melvin J., and Linad A. Whitehead. 1980. Verfahrensgerechtigkeit aus der Sicht der Gerechtigkeitsmotiv-Theorie. In *Gerechtigkeit und soziale Interaktion*, edited by G. Mikula. Bern: Huber.

Lerner, Melvin J., and Sally C. Lerner, eds. 1981. *The Justice Motive in Social Behavior*. New York: Plenum.

Leung, Kwok, and E. Allan Lind. 1986. Procedural Justice and Culture: Effects of Culture, Gender, and Investigator Status on Procedural Preferences. *Journal of Personality and Social Psychology* 50: 1134–40.

Leventhal, Gerald S. 1980. What Should Be Done With Equity Theory? In *Social Exchange: Advances in Theory and Research*, edited by K. J. Gergen, M. S. Greenberg, and R. H. Willis. New York: Plenum.

Lind, E. Allan. 1994a. Procedural Justice, Disputing, and Reactions to Legal Authorities. Working paper, American Bar Foundation, Chicago.

———. 1994b. Justice and Authority in Organisations. Working paper, American Bar Foundation, Chicago.

Lind, E. Allan, Bonnie E. Erickson, Nehemia Friedland, and Michael Dickenberger. 1978. Reactions to Procedural Models for Adjudicative Conflict Resolution: A Cross-National Study. *Journal of Conflict Resolution* 22: 318–41.

Lind, E. Allan, Robert J. MacCoun, Patricia A. Ebener, William L. F. Felstiner, Deborah R. Hensler, Judith Resnik, and Tom R. Tyler. 1990. In the Eye of the Beholder: Tort Litigants' Evaluations of their Experiences in the Civil Justice System. *Law and Society Review* 24: 953–96.

Lind, E. Allan, and Tom R. Tyler. 1988. *The Social Psychology of Procedural Justice*. New York: Plenum.

Luhmann, Niklas. 1969. *Legitimation durch Verfahren*. Darmstadt: Luchterhand.

Macdonald, R. A. 1981. A Theory of Procedural Fairness. *Windsor Yearbook of Access to Justice*, Vol. 1: 3–34.

Machura, Stefan. 1994a. Procedural and Distributive Justice as Seen by German Defendants. Paper presented at Law and Society annual meeting, 17 June, Phoenix, Arizona.

———. 1994b. Trust and Procedural Fairness: How Are Lawyers, Judges, and Public Prosecutors Seen by German Defendants? Paper presented at the thirteenth World Congress of Sociology, 18 July, Bielefeld, Germany.

Martin, Guido, Heidemarie Renk, and Margaretha Sudhof. 1989. Maßstäbe, Foren, Verfahren: Das Prozeduralisierungskonzept Rudolf Wiethölters. *Kritische Justiz* 22: 244–57.

Matsamura, Yoshiyuki. 1991. Procedural Justice in Dispute Resolution—Japan and the West. Paper presented at the Law and Society annual meeting, 26–29 June, Amsterdam.

McEwen, Craig A., and Richard J. Maiman. 1986. The Relative Significance of Disputing Forum and Dispute Characteristics for Outcome and Compliance. *Law and Society Review* 20: 439–47.

Nahamowitz, Peter. 1987. Effektivität wirtschaftlicher Steuerung—ein Beitrag zur Autopoiesis-Debatte. *Kritische Justiz* 20: 411–33.

Nahamowitz, Peter. 1988. Autopoiesis oder ökonomischer Staatsinterventionismus? *Zeitschrift für Rechtssoziologie* 9: 36–73.

Nelson, William. 1980. The Very Idea of Procedural Justice. *Ethics* 90: 502–11.

Neumann, Ulfrid. 1989. Materiale und prozedurale Gerechtigkeit im Strafverfahren. *Zeitschrift für die gesamte Strafrechtswissenschaft* 101: 52–74.

Nothdurft, Werner. 1987. Die Ordnung des Konflikts. Gesprächsanalyse der Konfliktbehandlung in einer Güteverhandlung vor dem Schiedsmann. In *Das Güteverfahren vor dem Schiedsmann*, edited by Klaus F. Röhl. Köln: Carl Heymanns Verlag.

O'Barr, William M., and John M. Conley. 1985. Litigant Satisfaction Versus Legal Adequacy in Small Claims Court Narratives. *Law and Society Review* 19: 661–701.

———. 1988. Lay Expectations of the Civil Justice System. *Law and Society Review* 22: 137–61.

Peters, Bernhard. 1991. *Rationalität, Recht, und Gesellschaft*. Frankfurt am Main: Suhrkamp.

Rawls, John. 1971. *A Theory of Justice*. Cambridge: Harvard University Press.

Rie, Michael A. 1990. Ökonomische Grenzen der Lebensrettung? Zur Mikroallokation in der Gesundheitspolitik. In *Sicherheit und Freiheit*, edited by C. Sachsse and E. H. Tristam. Frankfurt am Main: Suhrkamp.

Röhl, Klaus F. 1987. *Rechtssoziologie*. Köln: Heymanns.

Rottleuthner, Hubert. 1983. Befriedigungswirkung und Befolgung bei Vergleichen. In *Der Prozeßvergleich*, edited by W. Gottwald, W. Hutmacher, K. F. Röhl, and D. Strempel. Bonn: Bundesanzeiger.

Schmidt, Volker H. 1992. Lokale Gerechtigkeit. Perspektiven soziologischer Gerechtigkeitsanalyse. *Zeitschrift für Soziologie* 21: 3-15.

———. 1993. Zum Verhältnis prozeduraler und distributiver Gerechtigkeit. *Zeitschrift für Rechtssoziologie* 13: 80–96.

Sheppard, Blair H., and Neil Vidmar. 1980. Adversary Pretrial Procedures and Testimonial Evidence: Effects of Lawyer's Role and Machiavellianism. *Journal of Personality and Social Psychology* 39: 320–32.

Spittler, Gerd. 1967. *Norm und Sanktion—Untersuchungen zum Sanktionsmechanismus*. Olten: Walter.

Teubner, Gunther. 1982. Reflexives Recht. *Archiv für Rechts- und Sozialphilosophie*: 14–59.

———. 1989. Recht als autopoietisches System. Frankfurt am Main: Suhrkamp.

———., ed. 1986. *Autopoiesis in Law and Society*. Berlin: de Gruyter.

Teubner, Gunther, and Helmut Willke. 1984. Kontext und Autonomie: Gesellschaftliche Selbststeuerung durch reflexives Recht. *Zeitschrift für Rechtssoziologie* 6: 4–35.

Thibaut, John, and Laurens Walker. 1975. *Procedural Justice: A Psychological Analysis*. Hillsdale, N.J.: Laurence Erlbaum.

———. 1978. A Theory of Procedure. *California Law Review* 66: 541–66.

Treiber, Hubert. 1975. Verfahren als Herrschaftsmechanismus: Zu Niklas Luhmanns 'Legitimation durch Verfahren'. *Kriminalsoziologische Bibliographie* 8: 19–24.

Tyler, Tom R. 1984. The Role of Perceived Injustice in Defendants' Evaluations of Their Courtroom Experience. *Law and Society Review* 18: 51–74.

———. 1987a. Conditions Leading to Value Expressive Effects in Judgements of Procedural Justice: A Test of Four Models. *Journal of Personality and Social Psychology* 52: 333–44.

———. 1987b. Procedural Justice Research. *Social Justice Research* 1: 41–65.

———. 1988. What Is Procedural Justice? Criteria Used by Citizens to Assess the Fairness of Legal Procedures. *Law and Society Review* 22: 103–35.

———. 1990. *Why People Obey the Law*. New Haven: Yale University Press.

Tyler, Tom R., and Andrew Caine. 1981. The Influence of Outcomes and Procedures on Satisfaction with Formal Leaders. *Journal of Personality and Social Psychology* 41: 642–55.

Tyler, Tom R., Jonathan D. Casper, and Bonnie Fisher. 1990. Maintaining Allegiance to Political Authorities: The Role of Prior Attitudes and the Use of Fair Procedures. *American Journal of Political Science* 33: 612–28.

Tyler, Tom R., and Robert Folger. 1980. Distributional and Procedural Aspects of Satisfaction with Citizen-Police Encounters. *Basic and Applied Social Psychology* 1: 282–92.

Tyler, Tom R., Yuen J. Huo, and E. Allan Lind. 1993. Preferring, Choosing, and Evaluating Dispute Resolution Procedures: The Psychological Antecedents of Feelings and Choices. Working paper, American Bar Foundation, Chicago.

Tyler, Tom R., and E. Allan Lind. 1990a. Intrinsic Versus Community-Based Justice Models: When Does Group Membership Matter? *Journal of Society Issues* 46: 83-94.

———. 1990b. A Relational Model of Authority in Groups. American Bar Foundation Working Paper Series. Chicago: American Bar Foundation.

Tyler, Tom R., and Kathleen McGraw. 1986. Ideology and the Interpretation of Personal Experience: Procedural Justice and Political Quiescence. *Journal of Social Issues* 42: 115–28.

Tyler, Tom R., and Kenneth A. Rasinski. 1991. Procedural Justice, Institutional Legitimacy, and the Acceptance of Unpopular U.S. Supreme Court Decisions: A Reply to Gibson. *Law and Society Review* 25: 621–30.

Tyler, Tom R., Kenneth A. Rasinski, and Eugene Griffin. 1986. Alternative Images of the Citizen: Implications for Public Policy. *American Psychologist* 41: 970–8.

———. 1988. Fairness and Vote Choice in the 1984 Presidential Election. *American Politics Quarterly* 16: 5–24.

Tyler, Tom R., Kenneth A. Rasinski, and Nancy Spodick. 1985. The Influence of Voice on Satisfaction With Leaders: Exploring the Meaning of Process Control. *Journal of Personality and Social Psychology* 48: 72–81.

Vidmar, Neil. 1987. Assessing the Effects of Case Characteristics and Settlement Forum on Dispute Outcomes and Compliance. *Law and Society Review* 21: 155–64.

———. 1990. The Origins and Consequences of Procedural Fairness. *Law and Social Inquiry* 15: 877–92.

Vidmar, Neil, and Nancy Laird. 1983. Adversary Social Roles: Their Effects on Witnesses' Communication of Evidence and the Assessments of Adjudicators. *Journal of Personality and Social Psychology* 44: 888–98.

Vidmar, Neil, and Jeffrey Rice. 1991. Jury-Determined Settlements and Summary Jury Trials: Observations About Alternative Dispute Resolution in an Adversary Culture. *Florida State University Law Review* 19: 89–104.

Wasserman, David. 1987. Pure Procedural Justice in Law, Sports, and Organ Transplants. Paper presented at a meeting of the New York Society for Philosophy and Public Affairs, 18 November, New York.

———. 1989. Procedural Justice and the Convicted Criminal Defendant. Paper presented at Law and Society annual meeting, June, Madison, Wisconsin.

———. 1992. The Procedural Turn: Social Heuristics and Neutral Values. Paper prepared for an Oñati workshop on procedural justice.

Wells, Gary L. 1992. Naked Statistical Evidence of Liability: Is Subjective Probability Enough? *Journal of Personality and Social Psychology* 62: 739–52.

Wiethölter, Rudolf. 1986. Materialization and Proceduralization in Modern Law. In *Dilemmas of Law in the Welfare State*, edited by G. Teubner. Berlin: de Gruyter.

———. 1989. Proceduralization of the Category of Law. In *Critical Legal Thought: An American-German Debate*, edited by C. Joerges and D. M. Trubek. Baden-Baden: Nomos Verlag.

The Author

Klaus F. Röhl. Born 1938. Professor of Law, Chair for Philosophy and Sociology of Law at the Law Faculty of the Ruhr-Universität Bochum. Since 1993, editor of *Zeitschrift für Rechtssoziologie.* Major publications are: *Über die lebenslange Freiheitsstrafe* (Berlin: Dunker and Humblot, 1969), *Das Dilemma der Rechtstatsachenforschung* (Tübingen: Mohr, 1974), *Rechtssoziologie* (Köln: Heymanns, 1987), and *Allgemeine Rechtslehre* (Köln: Heymanns, 1995).

Address: Ruhr-Universität Bochum, Gebäude GC 8/135, Universitätsstraße 150, D-44780 Bochum, Germany.

Abstract

Procedures are not only a means to bring about the just allocation of rewards and punishments, benefits and burdens. Participants and observers evaluate procedures as more or less just or fair independent of their outcome, and this estimation is relevant to whether the distribution resulting from a procedure is accepted as just. On the other hand, modern societies lack objective or generally agreed-upon standards for the just distribution of life's chances and risks. In many cases it seems easier to agree on a procedure than on the distribution itself. As a result, material distribution standards are replaced by procedures.

Two consecutive workshops at the Oñati International Institute for the Sociology of Law (in 1992 and 1993) tried to explore the progress that has been achieved in research since the pioneering work on procedural justice by Thibaut and Walker was published in 1975. A third workshop in 1996 continued these efforts. This volume contains nine contributions prepared for the Oñati workshops on procedural justice in 1992 and 1993. The first contribution is a general introduction to the field of procedural justice.

2 The Procedural Turn: Social Heuristics and Neutral Values

DAVID WASSERMAN

Introduction

This paper discusses a variety of reasons for rejecting a strictly instrumental evaluation of procedures in terms of their success in achieving just outcomes. It outlines several ways in which ambiguity and conflict about outcome justice may increase the importance of procedural features such as neutrality and respect in evaluating outcome justice, and it considers several ways that procedures can display neutrality and respect in the face of ambiguity and conflict about outcome justice. It considers the suggestion that judgements of procedural fairness serve as a heuristic for judging outcome fairness.

Procedural Evaluations As Social Heuristics

In several recent papers (e.g., 1992), Tyler and Lind make an interesting suggestion about the value of procedures in complex modern societies: that because the criteria for correct outcomes are complex, obscure or debatable, and the success of procedures in achieving them correspondingly hard to assess, disputants seek something more and less in a procedure: indications of the neutrality and trustworthiness of the authorities administering the procedures, and of their own standing in the social order which employs the procedures. Thus, Tyler (1988, 8) observes that although it may seem simple to evaluate the quality of one's outcomes, it is actually very difficult. He suggests that this difficulty is eased by focusing on the procedures by which decisions are made.

One way of understanding the simplifying role of procedural evaluation is as a shortcut or expedient for making more complex outcome judgements. In a recent paper, Lind (1992) suggests that judgements of politeness, respect, and neutrality function as a 'social heuristic'; as a rule of thumb for more complicated and demanding judgements of procedural and outcome fairness. Lind finds this heuristic a reasonable response to cognitive complexity, but recognizes that its use carries a risk of error and deception. He sees social heuristics in much the same way that Kahneman, Slovic, and Tversky (1982) view cognitive heuristics: as features of 'bounded rationality' (Herbert Simon's term [Newell and Simon 1972]), necessary to compensate for our cognitive limitations but susceptible to over-reliance and abuse.

Lind suggests two ways in which politeness, neutrality, and respect may function as heuristics: they may be taken as indicators that the authorities are using reliable procedures to resolve the present dispute or encounter, so that the outcome is likely to be fair or correct. But they may also be taken as indicators that the authorities are benignly disposed to the disputant generally, whatever the merits of the procedures employed in this case. In either instance, the disputant's inference may be mistaken and her reliance on the procedure's neutrality, politeness, and respect misplaced.

Although Lind favours the second interpretation, the first is closer to Kahneman, Slovic, and Tversky's treatment of cognitive heuristics. In this interpretation, social heuristics serve as shortcuts for making outcome judgements that really require a more demanding calculus. For Kahneman, Slovic, and Tversky, the proper calculus is given by an expected utility model, which requires rational decision-makers to assign a utility to every possible outcome, discount it by the probability of its occurring (a probability calculated by the Bayesian formulae for subjective probability), then pick the option with the greatest expected utility. The analogous presupposition in the case of social heuristics is that disputants should judge procedures by their success at producing the most valuable outcomes, with the most valuable outcomes understood as those yielding the greatest utility or good. On this instrumental assumption, procedures are valuable solely as means for achieving or maximizing independently specifiable goods. If the disputants prefer outcomes that yield suboptimal results, it can only be because they rely too much on such features as politeness, neutrality, and respect, which are imperfect indicators of instrumental success.

This instrumental assumption invites a response analogous to that made by Kahneman, Slovic, and Tversky's critics (Cohen 1980): that departures from the models of subjective probability and expected utility are not evidence of cognitive error, but evidence against those models; that probability estimation and rational decision-making must be modelled in ways that capture the inferential processes that lay decision-makers actually engage in. Similarly, it can be argued that the tenuous connection of procedural evaluations to the instrumental success of the procedure does not reflect the difficulty disputants have in assessing success, but the limited importance it has for them. To assess this response, it is necessary to spell out the instrumental model of procedural value and the alternatives to that model.

Valuing Procedures Instrumentally and Noninstrumentally

The instrumental model provides one answer to the question of why procedures matter: they are valuable as means of achieving ends that, however complex, can be described independently of the methods that yield them. What makes any action or policy right is that it maximizes, or at least increases, the good. This approach takes an expansive view of what counts as a good, but it insists that a procedure can only be valued for the good it produces, and that whatever is valuable about a procedure can be treated as a good subject to a maximizing calculus.

While this approach might be thought to place a premium on accuracy—the minimization of expected error—it can readily accommodate competing values, and tradeoffs among values.[1] Features such as consistency and impartiality may also be defined as tendencies to produce certain kinds or patterns of outcomes;[2] to value those procedures, because of that tendency is to value them instrumentally. Rather than assigning all errors the same weight, the model can assign different weights to different kinds of error, such as repeated errors favouring the same disputant. The weighting techniques may be complicated, but the principle is simple: we favour the procedure that minimizes expected weighted error.

Even the qualities of a procedure that cannot be defined in terms of outcome characteristics, like dignity and restraint, can be treated as side-effects of the procedure, like modest cost or quick results, effects which merely constitute part of the good to be maximized. To reject this elastic model of instrumental value, it is necessary to deny that whatever is valuable in a procedure can be reduced to its consequences.

I will consider several alternative accounts of procedural value. Each denies that disputants' judgements about the politeness, respect, and neutrality of the procedure merely serve as evaluative shortcuts, relied on in the face of cognitive complexity. Although the noninstrumental accounts of procedural value are quite diverse, I will attempt to map the territory by describing two general, complementary approaches. One defends the intrinsic value of procedures, either as expressing values independent of the outcomes or as providing necessary validation for those outcomes; the other challenges the instrumental role by stressing the uncertainty, indeterminacy, and conflict in applying outcome criteria. The two approaches reinforce each other: the more difficult or controversial it is to apply independent criteria for correct outcomes, the easier it is to make out a non-instrumental role for procedures. The approaches converge in the notion of pure procedural justice: the idea that any outcome yielded by a fair procedure is *ipso facto* fair or correct.[3]

Forms of Intrinsic Value

Expressive Value

One prominent alternative is an expressive theory of procedure: we value procedures that are polite, respectful, or neutral not as means to valuable outcomes but as expressions of important values: we affirm the dignity of individuals not, or not merely, by giving them appropriate outcomes, but by adopting procedures that treat them with dignity and respect. A proponent of expressive value would agree that procedures could promote dignity instrumentally, but would insist on a contrast between promoting and expressing a moral good.

That contrast is suggested by the controversy over the exclusionary rule. We would like the authorities to treat criminal suspects with dignity and restraint, but the only effective way of deterring them from treating suspects in undignified ways may be to suppress any evidence yielded by their misconduct. While the purpose of the rule is to protect dignity, there may be a great deal of indignity in its administration, which requires the courts to void arrests and reverse convictions for reasons that have little or nothing to do with the defendants' innocence or the weakness of the evidence against them. Critics of the exclusionary rule complain that it treats the case, and the defendant, as a means to ulterior social goals. If we value the procedures associated with the exclusionary rule at all, we must therefore value them instrumentally for their long-term effect in promoting police respect for the Fourth Amendment.

In contrast, we may admire procedures that treat disputants with dignity and restraint even if we do not regard those procedures as effective means of promoting dignity and restraint. Conversely, we would not countenance brutal and degrading criminal procedures even if they were certain to produce a kinder, gentler, society; we must sometimes sacrifice the *achievement* of dignity and restraint to *express* them.

More broadly, critics of utilitarianism often insist that we express certain values through constraints on our conduct that may hamper our achievement of those same values. Thus, we express the great value we place on human life by prohibitions on murder and by extravagant rescue efforts, even though we might be able to save more lives by permitting an occasional murder, or by diverting resources from rescue to prevention.

One does not have to be a utilitarian, however, to question the coherence of the idea that we can honour a value by imposing constraints that limit its achievement. The devotion to a procedure at the expense of the values it is intended to express strikes some people as a kind of fetishism. Thus, Simon (1978, 100) argues that a ritualist approach to adversary procedure

> simply ignores that at the end of the trial one of the parties may imprison or coerce the other or deprive him of property. To ignore such facts is to commit the reverse of the mistake which ritualists attribute to instrumentalists . . . to collapse result into process. The problem is not that procedures cannot be seen as expressive phenomena, but that the results which are produced by the procedures must also be seen as part of what is expressed. The Ritualist cannot acknowledge that because, more often than not, the results of the judicial proceeding contradict the values the procedures are supposed to express.

The claim that we value procedures for what they express, rather than what they achieve, is certainly easier to defend when we do not have clear, applicable outcome criteria against which to assess their performance. Thus, an expressive theory of procedure seems more at home in settings where the application of outcome criteria is less certain.

Outcome Validation

There are also a number of ways in which the procedure may be valued for its role in producing the outcome without being valued instrumentally. Unlike an expressive account, these ways of valuing the procedure take account of the outcome; unlike an instrumental account, they do not view the outcome as justifying or subsuming the procedure. In each case, the procedure is seen as validating the outcome by generating it in the right way. The procedure may validate the outcome epistemically, not (only) by making it more likely that the outcome is correct, but by giving participants and observers reason to believe that it is correct.[4] Or it may justify the outcome in a more elusive moral sense, by providing fair and equal consideration of opposed points of view, participation by the disputants, or attention to the individual details of the case. While an outcome can be justified in any of these senses and still be mistaken, it cannot be correct or valid unless it is so justified.

Justification in an epistemic sense is distinct from accuracy, since the most accurate procedure or decision rule may not provide the requisite justification. The 'gatecrasher' case provides the most notorious example: most people would think it wrong to allow the owner of a rodeo to recover against a spectator solely on the grounds that the turnstile showed that fewer than half of the spectators had paid, though in the (justifiable) absence of other evidence, it would be more probable than not that the spectator was liable, and a rule favouring the owner against any spectator would yield the least expected error. In one interpretation, the resistance to imposing liability arises from the fact that naked statistics cannot sustain a belief in the liability of any particular spectator. In another interpretation, the rejection of naked statistics expresses a moral, not an epistemic, conviction: that justice requires a dispute to be settled by facts that are specific to the disputants rather than by statistical generalizations.[5] In either interpretation, we would demand evidence more specific to the spectator, such as eyewitness testimony, even if it was no more likely to yield a correct result.

Similarly, the burden of proof beyond a reasonable doubt may be seen as characterizing the process of validation we require to impose criminal sanctions. This suggests that we cannot understand reasonable doubt in terms of weighted accuracy, as a standard of proof that we arrive at by giving greater negative value to a mistaken conviction than a mistaken acquittal. Rather, the purpose of the standard is to honour the presumption of innocence by requiring that every reasonable attempt be made to falsify the hypothesis of guilt, a testing process which only incidentally yields different rates of false conviction and acquittal.[6]

How can we characterize the relationship of validation more generally? The procedure is not a necessary means to an independently specifiable end: e.g., if we regard the end of a trial as the factually correct result, then the constraints of particularized evidence or proof beyond a reasonable doubt are not necessary for achieving it, and may sometimes hamper its achievement. And if the end is characterized in terms of the confidence the result inspires by virtue of its pedigree, then it is not independently specifiable. Kateb (1979, 229) argues that in many settings, procedural means and the ends they achieve cannot be evaluated independently:

> [T]hough the need to attain some end is (conceptually) at the origin of a means (method, procedure), a means, once established, may come to be seen as the only right and permissible means; and . . . the valuable ends thought to be attained by some other means are not really the ends they are supposed to be but rather a shadowy or elusive form of those ends.

This, however, is more of a psychological explanation than a moral defence of the unity of procedure and outcome. If the expression of values at the expense of their achievement seems fetishistic, an insistence on the organic unity of means and ends, requiring the rejection of any alternative means, seems blindly conservative. As with expressive value, the organic unity of procedures and outcomes may be easier to defend in settings where the assessment of outcomes is uncertain, indeterminate, or disputed. I now turn to considering the roles of procedures and procedural evaluations in those settings.

Uncertainty, Indeterminacy, and Conflict

There are several distinct kinds of difficulty involved in judging outcomes that encourage a reliance on procedures: (1) we may recognize independent criteria for correct outcomes but find it impossible to assess their satisfaction in most or all cases; (2) we may not believe that there is a uniquely correct outcome, because we accept a criterion that makes any outcome within a range equally acceptable; (3) we may disagree about the criteria for fair or correct outcomes. While these sources of uncertainty may be hard to distinguish—it may not be clear if the right outcome is hard to ascertain, indeterminate, or controversial—they may have different implications for the coherence and stability of procedural evaluations. In (1), the procedure is valued for yielding presumptively correct outcomes, but the presumption may be overridden in specific cases, and the validity of the procedure is always subject to reappraisal. In

(2) and (3), the procedure plays a more significant role: it effectively replaces outcome criteria. Any outcome that results from the procedure (within a given range) will be *ipso facto* fair; the outcome can be challenged only by a claim that the proper procedure was not followed.

The default role of the procedure in (1) is unstable, since the outcomes are in theory subject to review by an independent standard of outcome fairness. The role of the procedures in (2) and (3) is more robust but more elusive: the idea that an outcome is fair just because it is yielded by a specific procedure, or a procedure with certain attributes, is ambiguous and perplexing: how can we regard a procedure as fair or neutral if we are not sure about or cannot agree on what constitutes a fair outcome?[7]

Uncertainty

The instrumental model assumes that we can evaluate the success of the procedure at achieving correct results, even if we are uncertain about occasional cases. It is possible to reject this assumption without denying that there may be, in theory, a uniquely correct outcome. In making allocative decisions, we may, for example, accept the formal principle that outputs should be proportional to inputs, but find it difficult or impossible to compare different kinds of inputs or outputs. In making factual findings, we may aim to make our findings correspond as closely as possible to the true state of affairs, but we may also believe that in many or most cases, the truth is simply unknowable. In these settings, procedural judgements will not serve as heuristics, as shortcuts for a full evaluation of the outcome, but as the only basis we have for assessing its correctness.

The problem of commensurability is illustrated by Tyler (1988, 8): 'A faculty member seeking to evaluate the quality of his outcomes relative to others, for example, would have to consider salary, office size, teaching load, and a wide variety of other issues'.

Similarly, Dees (1992) notes that venture capitalists and entrepreneurs are reluctant to assess the equity of their arrangements, because they find comparisons of inputs and outputs too difficult. They rely instead on norms of minimal procedural fairness, such as honesty.

Thus, we may rely on the procedure when the criterion for a correct outcome requires a proper balance between goods that are difficult to compare. If we regarded those goods as truly incommensurable, we would be drawn to the purely procedural view described in the next section, which regards any balance struck in the right way that falls within a 'latitude of acceptance' as *ipso facto* correct. But we may be more agnostic, believing that there is an independently correct balance while doubting our capacity to recognize it. Obviously, it may be hard to tell atheism from agnosticism in practice.

In factual disputes, the uncertainty will be felt by observers more than disputants, at least where the latter have 'privileged' access to the disputed events. Nesson (1979, 1195) argues that the complexity of ordinary litigation lies behind the deference accorded to jury verdicts: 'The trial system presents jurors with an array of facts, assertions, contradictions and ambiguities, and then obtains a verdict difficult to disagree with because the secrecy of the jurors' deliberations and the general nature of the verdict make it hard to know precisely on what it was based'. Since it is difficult to second-guess the jury, a procedurally proper verdict will be presumed correct.

In order to give a procedure this significant default role in validating outcomes, we must have some reason to believe that it generally yields correct results. It is not necessary, however, to have confirmed the accuracy of the procedure in this kind of dispute. Our confidence may rather reflect our more general beliefs; e.g., about the wisdom of ordinary people engaged in structured deliberation.

While we may rely on procedural indices of fair treatment, our deference is not boundless. It is only within a limited range of outcomes that procedural fairness will be dispositive. There may be disparities in allocation too great to be justified by a belief in the general fairness of the allocative process, and there may be factual findings about which reasonable people could not differ.

In cases where the evidence (and lack of evidence) leaves the decision-maker with clear, undisputed probabilities (cases of 'naked statistical evidence'), the decision-making process will lack the ambiguity it needs to command respect: the observer will know the precise odds that the jury faced and the decision rule it applied to those odds. The transparency of the process highlights the independent standard for a fair outcome and the probability that it has not been satisfied. But even where the evidence is complex, special circumstances may increase its transparency and thereby reduce deference to the fact-finder. The usual respect accorded jury verdicts was conspicuously absent in the acquittal of four white Los Angeles policemen in the beating of a black motorist; a videotape of the incident appeared to many observers to remove any factual doubts about the case. Thus, even if we do not believe that it is possible in most cases to second-guess the procedure, we will recognize exceptions where the outcome is 'beyond the pale' or the application of the outcome criterion unusually transparent.

We face a form of cognitive dissonance when a procedure that confers presumptive correctness on any outcome it reaches yields an outcome that appears mistaken by an independent standard of outcome fairness. In resolving this conflict, we may display our commitment to a strongly procedural view of justice by insisting that any outcome yielded by the procedure is *ipso facto* correct, or by changing our belief about the correct outcome. But rather than deny the possibility of a mistaken outcome, we may display our procedural commitments by attempting to attribute the error to the procedure; by seeking a procedural explanation. We can see the strength of this commitment in the public response to the acquittal of the Los Angeles police in the Rodney King assault trial in 1992. While some observers simply dismissed the verdict as mistaken, others searched heroically for violations of fair procedure, from the change of venue to a suburban white community to judicial instructions that appeared to require the jury to identify too fully with the policeman's lot.

In an earlier paper (1989), I treated such outcome-driven reassessment of the procedure as a form of displacement. I now think it can often be seen less reductively, as a strong but limited cognitive commitment. An observer's readiness to find flaws in the procedure before condemning the outcome as unfair may be as principled as a scientist's attempt to find flaws in his measurements or equipment before he rejects an otherwise powerful theory. Within limits, both are reasonable displays of intellectual allegiance.

But there is a striking lack of analogy with the accommodation of discrepant results in science: the 'theory' of presumptive correctness predicts errors even if the procedure is flawless. Try as she may, the disputant may not be able to attribute a mistaken outcome to a flawed procedure.

When no procedural flaw can be found, the disputant faces a conflict between two sources of authority. The procedure commands allegiance because it is the fairest or most accurate overall, because she agreed to abide by its results, or just because it is a reasonable and accepted way of resolving disputes among equals. But she also accepts an independent standard of fairness which rejects the outcome of the procedure. Her dilemma belongs to a family of conflicts arising between different forms of justification or authority: between short- and long-term accuracy, accuracy and consistency, accuracy and fair play. The dilemma is a familiar and general one.

Indeterminacy

We may accept a criterion of outcome correctness that does not yield a uniquely correct outcome. There will be a range of outcomes acceptable under that criterion, and any outcome within the range will be acceptable if it is reached by an appropriate procedure. In practice, it may be hard to distinguish epistemic from substantive latitude, to determine whether we find different outcomes equally acceptable because we have a robust presumption of correctness or broad indeterminacy in our outcome criteria.

We can find indeterminacy in a number of decision settings: where the issue is conformity to a legal standard like reasonable care (in which reasonable judges can disagree about some cases but not others); where the issue is the fairness of an outcome reached by bargaining, negotiation, or another consent-eliciting process (in which the range of acceptable outcomes is limited, if at all, only by a doctrine of unconscionableness); where the issue is the range of claimants eligible for scarce resources (e.g., potential organ recipients must have something seriously wrong with their present organs).

These decisions are all instances of what I called in an earlier paper (1987) 'bounded procedural justice': if certain background conditions are satisfied, like equal information for bargainers or equal resources for adversaries, then any outcome within a range that is reached by an appropriate procedure, like bargaining or adversary adjudication, will be *ipso facto* fair. This conception of procedural justice may be suggested by Dees's (1992) interviews with venture capitalists and entrepreneurs. Both groups may invoke procedural criteria not because they think independent outcome criteria are too difficult or controversial to apply, but because they regard them as inherently indeterminate. As long as certain background conditions and procedural rules are satisfied, they will regard as fair any arrangement that gave the parties outcomes as good or better than their default options: fair bargaining is not just a necessary but a sufficient condition of outcome fairness.

The question remains of why we should prefer some procedures over others in the face of indeterminacy. If any outcome within the range is acceptable, why should we care how it is selected? Our strongest concern may be negative: there are many bad reasons for selecting an outcome, and the minimal virtue a procedure can have is in insulating us from those reasons. Thus, we would object to an allocator giving a scarce organ to his mistress, even if she was as needy and deserving as any other potential recipient; an organ lottery would safeguard the selection from such objectionable preferences.

But the range of indifference also gives greater scope to consent: consent to an outcome, as in bargaining, or consent to a procedure for selecting the outcome, like a contest or competition. The less concern we have about ending up with a mistaken result, the greater the importance of agreement and participation in evaluating the procedure.

If we believe that there is at least in theory a correct outcome, we will reject such a strongly procedural conception of justice. In a notorious 1982 case, Judge Friess of the New York City Criminal Court tossed a coin to decide whether a pickpocket would get twenty or thirty days in jail. A fellow jurist argued that this unorthodox procedure was justified in the face of recalcitrant indeterminacy—there was no principled basis for choosing between twenty and thirty days (Shipp 1983b). The Commission on Judicial Conduct, however, held that 'abdicating such solemn responsibilities, particularly in so whimsical a manner . . . is inexcusable and indefensible' (Shipp 1983a). One reason the Commission may have been offended was that the coin toss mocked the belief that there was in theory a uniquely appropriate sentence.[8]

Similarly, someone who believed that agreements for dividing the profits and losses of entrepreneurial ventures were a matter of substantive justice would reject a purely procedural approach to bargaining. Someone who believed that resources should generally be allocated on the basis of effort or need would reject a purely procedural criterion of fair competition, and would deny that any allocation yielded by a properly functioning market was fair. Someone who believed that scarce organs should go to the most deserving or productive, and who believed there were substantial differences in desert and productivity, would find an organ lottery as unacceptable as the coin toss by Judge Friess. When there are disputes over the proper standards for resolving conflicts or distributing goods, the use of facially neutral procedures may be seen as part of the problem, not part of the solution. I now turn to the question of how, or whether, procedures can play a mediating role in moral conflict.

Conflict

Procedures may play their most important role where we cannot agree on criteria of outcome fairness. Thus, Tyler (1990, 109) writes,

> Because there is no single, commonly accepted set of moral values against which to judge the fairness of outcomes or policies, such evaluations are difficult to make. *People can, however, agree on procedures for decision making.* Evaluations of authorities, institutions, and policies therefore focuses on the procedures by which they function rather than on evaluations of their decisions or policies.

Difficulties in balancing inputs and outputs, for example, may result from conflict rather than uncertainty or indeterminacy. Even if the disputants all accept the formal rule that inputs and outputs should be proportionate, they may disagree about what inputs or outputs should be counted or how much weight they should be given.

The procedural turn in micro-disputes has its counterpart in liberal proposals for resolving fundamental moral conflicts in a pluralistic society. Citizens who have basic moral disagreements on issues from religion to abortion must fall back on neutral or impartial principles that are 'intended to transcend disagreement on specific policies' (Gutmann and Thompson 1990, 64). This conviction underlies much recent United States constitutional jurisprudence. Ely (1980), for example, claims that the lack of an adequate substantive theory of justice compels a procedural interpretation of the Constitution, in which its amendments are understood as remedying defects in the democratic process.

Like indeterminacy, conflict promotes the recognition of noninstrumental procedural values: we value trustworthiness, respect, and dignity in the decision-maker and in the decision procedure because they are the only universally recognized virtues a procedure can have in settings where the disputants cannot agree on criteria for correct outcomes. In resolving conflicts among disputants who lack shared criteria of outcome fairness, the 'transcendent' virtue is procedural neutrality: impartiality, consistency in application, and fair and equal consideration for the parties (Rawls 1988), qualities which appeal to disputants even, or especially, when they do not agree on an outcome criterion.

The problem lies in explaining how we judge procedures as fair or neutral when we cannot agree on what constitutes a fair outcome.

The difficulty in invoking 'neutral' principles is that they often presuppose some criterion of outcome fairness or they merely displace rather than resolve conflict over the correct criteria.

The first difficulty is illustrated by the use of a lottery to allocate scarce resources. For someone who thought that organs should go to the most deserving or productive, the use of a lottery that included all needy patients would hardly be neutral: its use would presuppose the equal entitlement of those patients. Moreover, it would favour one interpretation of equal entitlement over others. As Broome has pointed out (1984), an equiprobable procedure for assigning organs treats claimants of different ages unequally, in the sense that it does not treat a year saved by the younger claimant as having the same value as a year saved by the older claimant.

Similarly, the decision to resolve a conflict by a democratic vote accords a formal equality to the voters but involves strong substantive assumptions about the nature of the underlying entitlements. Those who believe in strong property rights will hardly be appeased by the use of democratic procedures to determine the distribution of property; to subject property disputes to such procedures is already to reject their claims. Perhaps the single most important political development leading to the American Civil War was the decision to resolve the question of slavery in the territories by 'popular sovereignty' rather than by geographical latitude, a recourse rejected by those opposed to the spread of slavery. The idea that a majority of voters could decide to permit slavery was repugnant to the abolitionists; the idea that a majority could introduce that institution into a community of small farmers and wage-labourers was unacceptable to Free Soilers.

If the choice of procedure has substantive implications, the substance of the dispute may also impose procedural constraints. This may be illustrated by another major event leading up to the Civil War, the *Dred Scott* decision. The Supreme Court did not reject the substantive claim of Dred Scott that he had been freed by the peregrinations of his master; it refused to even hear his claim, on the ground that as a slave he lacked the standing to raise it. The legal system that treated Dred Scott as property could not even permit him a forum to challenge his status. There was no procedural recourse in the controversy over slavery.

As Gutmann and Thompson (1990) point out, the recourse to neutral principles is also problematic in resolving the great moral issue of our time: abortion. The principle that we should let individuals decide for themselves what we cannot collectively resolve is hardly neutral; it begs the question of who the relevant individuals are.[9] The way to consensus, if there is one, is more likely to lie in substantive compromise, e.g., in restrictions on when and how abortions can be performed, than in an overarching principle.

The second difficulty, that neutral procedures may displace rather than resolve conflict, is suggested by the use of 'aresponsible decision-makers' like juries to make hard choices (Calabresi and Bobbitt 1978). It seems disingenuous to tell a decision-maker that she must give fair and equal consideration to the opposing claims when those claims concern the criteria by which a decision should be made. Reliance on the unrecorded deliberations of an unaccountable group to resolve intractable conflict seems a form of mystification.[10]

Perhaps the most influential recent account of conflict-transcending agreement, Rawls's (1987) idea of an overlapping consensus, is hedged with contingency. Consensus on neutral principles is a historical fortuity, not a triumph of abstraction. It is only when divergent views or ideologies happen to converge on such principles that we can avoid divisive social conflict. When they fail to converge, as they failed over slavery, and as they may fail again over abortion, there is no recourse to disagreement-transcending principles. As Rawls reportedly said when asked about the case of slavery in the antebellum United States, 'Sometimes, you've just got to fight'.

Social Heuristics and Group Values

As I noted at the beginning of the paper, Tyler and Lind (1992) understand fairness judgements as a heuristic, not for outcome correctness but for overall justice. Certain characteristics of the procedure serve as indicators of broader societal attitudes and arrangements; the dispute or encounter serves as an occasion for the individual to assess his social standing and the attitude of the authorities toward him. The importance of procedural fairness lies not in the favourable outcomes it promises the disputant, even in the long term, but in the group values it affirms.

Procedures may serve as heuristics not only for judging the attitude of the authorities toward the disputants, but for judging the fairness of the social order. A procedure may convey society's commitment to accurate and impartial dispute resolution, even if it works to the disputant's disadvantage or involves a rejection of her specific claims.

Outcomes may also have heuristic value, revealing broader social attitudes whose significance goes far beyond the case or the disputants. The acquittal of the Los Angeles police defendants in the first Rodney King case did not merely deny redress to a particular victim of police violence, or frustrate efforts to deter police misconduct. It also reinforced the sense that the American legal system devalues black victims, in much the same way as it is alleged to do by imposing the death penalty less frequently on those who kill blacks than on those who kill whites.

It is not necessary to see the shift from the specific dispute to the social order merely as a heuristic for avoiding cognitive complexity or evaluative stress. It may not be appropriate to judge fairness on the basis of a single outcome or procedure. A procedure or outcome that might seem unfair if viewed in isolation may assume a different character if viewed in a broader context. For example, several controversial features of adversary litigation, such as contingency fees and punitive damages, are defensible in part because they serve as rough equalizers in a society that has vast disparities in income between potential adversaries; they might be far less acceptable in a more egalitarian society with a more extensive social welfare system. Many of our dispute-resolution procedures acquire their strongest justification by being seen in such a broader social context: in their direct and indirect impact over time, across disputes, and in conjunction with other social practices.

Conclusion

Procedures matter to people as much or more than outcomes in a wide range of disputes and other transactions, in a way that cannot be easily accounted for by any nonvacuous theory of self-interest. And procedures *should* matter to people as much or more than outcomes in a wide variety of settings, in a way that cannot be easily accounted for by any nonvacuous theory of instrumental value: they express important values, validate outcomes in ways that preclude their separate evaluation, and give definitive results in the face of uncertainty, indeterminacy, and conflict.

We need to develop both the psychological and normative accounts of procedural justice more fully. Equally important, we need to understand their relevance to each other. The moral judgements that people make are shaped and distorted by self-interest, social conditioning, and malleable expectations; perhaps less obviously, the psychological reactions people have to their treatment by authorities and adversaries are shaped and constrained by transcultural moral judgements.

The difficulty in understanding the mutual relevance of moral and psychological accounts of procedural justice is compounded by internal disagreements about what morality and psychology are about. Philosophers regard morality as everything from a mental faculty to an algorithm for social action; psychologists understand their own subject matter in equally diverse ways. But the attempt at understanding has to be made, because procedural justice is a truly important, and truly interdisciplinary, concern.

Notes

1 We could also value accuracy in a noninstrumental way. A doctor might prefer an expensive, intrusive diagnostic procedure to a trivially less accurate one that was far less expensive and intrusive, just because he had a 'fetish' for accuracy.

One complexity in instrumental valuation is that the procedures that maximize good consequences in the present case may not be the procedures that maximize good consequences overall. This conflict may arise with respect to accuracy or other goods. Thus, we may value a rule or procedure that promotes overall accuracy even though it is less likely to yield the correct result in the case at hand. To take a notorious hypothetical, we would not allow the owner of a rodeo to recover the admission fee from a spectator based solely on proof that a majority of spectators had crashed the gate, even though, in the absence of other evidence, we would be more likely than not to achieve the correct result by doing so. One reason for our refusal might be that even if no other evidence could have been discovered in this case, a rule requiring other evidence to impose liability would improve the quality of evidence in other cases and enhance overall accuracy.

This example may be taken to contrast what Michelman (1973) calls 'effectuation' and 'deterrence': a reliance on naked statistics would effectuate accuracy, while their rejection would deter inaccurate evidentiary practices and promote the discovery of more reliable evidence. There will also be conflicts between the short- and long-term effectuation of accuracy: a procedure less likely to yield error in some cases may be more likely to yield error in most cases, and there may be no reliable way to distinguish the cases where it is more accurate. For example, adversarial procedures might be more accurate in most disputes, while inquisitorial procedures might be more accurate in disputes with no credibility issues. If there are no reliable means of screening disputes for credibility issues, it might be best to utilize adversarial procedures for all disputes.

2 Thus, the lack of bias in a coin is defined in terms of its tendency to produce equal numbers of heads and tails. No matter how 'fair' a coin appeared, we would regard it as biased if it continued to turn up only one face.

3 In analysing the possible relationships between procedural and outcome justice, I begin with Rawls's (1971, 84–5) analysis, which recognizes three kinds of procedural justice: perfect, imperfect, and pure, defined by two factors:

1. Whether 'there is an independent criterion for a fair [outcome], a criterion defined separately from or prior to the procedure adopted'
2. Whether 'it is possible to devise a procedure that is sure to give such an outcome'

Perfect procedural justice is found where there is an independent criterion for a fair outcome and a procedure able to satisfy it with reasonable certainty; Rawls's example is a pie-slicing among equally entitled claimants, in which the slicer takes the last piece—a procedure that is virtually certain to yield an equal distribution. Imperfect procedural justice is found in the more common situation where there is an independent criterion but no procedure sure to satisfy it; Rawls's example is a criminal trial, in which the fairest procedure may still permit a guilty defendant to be acquitted.

Finally, pure procedural justice is found where there is no independent criterion for an outcome, and where an outcome is fair just because it results from the operation of the procedure; Rawls's example is a series of fair gambles in which any outcome will be fair. The procedure must actually be followed, however, since almost any distribution *could* be produced by a fair procedure.

4 Resnick (1977) has analogized the role of a fair procedure in justice to the role of justification in knowledge, analysed as justified true belief.

5 Wells (1992) has done a series of experiments on the resistance of lay fact-finders to naked statistical evidence. His findings suggest that we demand not only specific evidence, but evidence whose reliability is affected by the truth of the verdict: we may be reluctant to find someone liable unless we can blame a mistake on an infirmity in the evidence.

6 It is formally possible to accommodate such concerns in an instrumental model by giving a sufficiently high negative value to the absence of an appropriate justificatory relationship between the procedure and outcome. But this accommodation reflects the elasticity of that model more than its plausibility.

7 Some of the most interesting issues in procedural justice arise from shifts in, or disputes about, the role of the procedure: e.g., a procedure seen as defining correct outcomes may be subsumed by an independent standard of outcome correctness; the advent of a more reliable procedure for achieving correct outcomes may force us to choose between devaluing the old procedure or redefining its role.

8 Lewis Kornhauser (personal communication, October 1987) suggests that what is objectionable about the coin toss is that it creates gratuitous inconsistency among like cases—the next pickpocket might get thirty days. The inconsistency is gratuitous, since the judge could have chosen a compromise that would have avoided it: he could have 'split the difference' and imposed a twenty five day sentence in all such cases. Kornhauser suggests that when such a compromise solution isn't possible, a coin toss might be acceptable, e.g., when 'the best interests of the child' preclude joint custody but do not favour one parent over the other.

9 An important difference between the controversies over slavery and abortion concerns the inferences drawn by the adversaries about those holding the opposite position. A fair number of participants in the abortion debate are converts from one position to the other, and the accounts of their conversion make it possible for those on both sides of the debate to see how reasonable people might take the opposing position. Even if that position is seen as evil, it is not seen as irrational. Opponents in the slavery debate seem to have been less willing to concede that reasonable people could reach different conclusions. By the time of the Civil War, both opponents and proponents of slavery considered their positions so self-evident that only a corruption or abandonment of reason could lead people to reject it.

10 It is less problematic to operationalize the criterion of outcome fairness to the decision of a deliberative body when there is uncertainty or indeterminacy rather than conflict, e.g., reasonable care is whatever a jury of twelve average people think it is. To avoid circularity, it is necessary that the legal standard mean something different for the decision-maker than it does for the claimants; for

the jury, reasonable care is defined by the vague, obscure, and elastic instructions read by the judge. The meanings of reasonable care for the participants and the jury are thus related but not identical. Glaring inconsistency in the treatment of like cases is avoided by judicial review: there are limits to the verdicts that can be reached on a given set of facts and limits to the range of facts that will support a given verdict.

References

Broome, John. 1984. Selecting People Randomly. *Ethics* 95: 38–55.

Calabresi, Guido, and Philip Bobbitt. 1978. *Tragic Choices*. New York: Norton.

Cohen, L. Jonathan. 1980. Whose Is the Fallacy?: A Rejoinder to Daniel Kahneman and Amos Tversky. *Cognition* 8: 89–92.

Dees, Gregory. 1992. Deciding What's Fair: Building Durable Relationships Between Entrepreneurs and Venture Capitalists. Paper prepared for the 18th annual Venture Capital Institute, St. Charles, Illinois.

Ely, John Hart. 1980. *Democracy and Distrust: A Theory of Judicial Review*. Cambridge: Harvard University Press.

Gutmann, Amy, and Dennis Thompson. 1990. Moral Conflict and Political Consensus. *Ethics* 101: 64–88.

———. 1995. Moral Disagreement in a Democracy. *Social Philosophy and Policy* 12: 87–110.

Kahneman, Daniel, Paul Slovic, and Amos Tversky, eds. 1982. *Judgment Under Uncertainty: Heuristics and Biases*. New York: Cambridge University Press.

Kateb, George. 1979. Remarks on the Procedures of Constitutional Democracy. In *Nomos 20 (Constitutionalism)*, edited by J. R. Pennock and J. W. Chapman. New York: New York University Press.

Lind, E. Allan. 1992. The Fairness Heuristic: Rationality and 'Relationality' in Procedural Evaluations. Paper presented at the fourth international conference of the Society for the Advancement of Socio-Economics, 28 March, Irvine, California.

Lind, E. Allan, and P. Christopher Early. 1992. Procedural Justice and Culture. *International Journal of Psychology* 27: 227–42.

Lind, E. Allan, Robert J. MacCoun, Patricia A. Ebener, William L. F. Felstiner, Deborah R. Hensler, Judith Resnick, and Tom R. Tyler. 1990. In the Eye of the Beholder: Tort Litigants' Evaluations of Their Experiences in the Civil Justice System. *Law and Society Review* 24: 953–96.

Lind, E. Allan, and Tom R. Tyler. 1988. *The Social Psychology of Procedural Justice*. New York: Plenum.

Michelman, Frank I. 1973. The Supreme Court and Litigation Access Fees: The Right to Protect One's Rights. *Duke Law Journal*: 1153–1215.

Nelson, William. 1980. The Very Idea of Pure Procedural Justice. *Ethics* 90: 502–511.

Nesson, Charles. 1979. Reasonable Doubt and Permissive Inferences: The Value of Complexity. *Harvard Law Review* 92: 1187-1225.

Newell, Allen, and Herbert A. Simon. 1972. *Human Problem-Solving*. Englewood Cliffs, N.J.: Prentice-Hall.

Rawls, John. 1971. *A Theory of Justice*. Cambridge: Harvard University Press.

———. 1987. The Idea of an Overlapping Consensus. *Oxford Journal for Legal Studies* 7: 1–25.

———. 1988. The Priority of the Right and Ideals of the Good. *Philosophy and Public Affairs* 17: 251–76.

Resnick, David. 1977. Due Process and Procedural Justice. In *Nomos* 18 (*Due Process*), edited by J. R. Pennock and J. W. Chapman. New York: New York University Press.

Shipp, E. R. 1983a. Friess Is Barred From Ever Being New York Judge. *New York Times*, 7 April.

———. 1983b. Two Justices Defend Friess at Hearing on Misconduct. *New York Times*, 6 February.

Simon, William. 1978. The Ideology of Advocacy: Procedural Justice and Professional Ethics. *Wisconsin Law Review* 1978: 29–144.

Tyler, Tom R. 1988. The Psychology of Procedural Justice: A Test of the Group Value Model. Working paper 28, Northwestern University, Kellogg Graduate School of Management, Evanston, Ill.

———. 1990. *Why People Obey The Law*. New Haven: Yale University Press.

Tyler, Tom R., and E. Allan Lind. 1992. A Relational Model of Authority in Groups. In *Advances in Experimental Social Psychology*. Vol. 25, edited by M. Zanna. New York: Academic.

Wasserman, David. 1987. Pure Procedural Justice in Law, Sports, and Organ Transplants. Paper presented at a meeting of the New York Society for Philosophy and Public Affairs, 18 November, New York.

———. 1989. Procedural Justice and the Convicted Criminal Defendant. Paper presented at Law and Society annual meeting, June, Madison, Wisconsin.

———. 1991. The Morality of Statistical Proof and the Risk of Mistaken Liability. *Cardozo Law Review* 13: 935–76.

Wells, Gary L. 1992. Naked Statistical Evidence of Liability: Is Subjective Probability Enough? *Journal of Personality and Social Psychology* 62: 739–52.

The Author

David Wasserman. Research scholar at the Institute for Philosophy and Public Policy at the University of Maryland, College Park, Maryland. Research and writing focus on ethical issues in criminal justice, social welfare, biotechnology, and environmental policy. Author of *A Sword for the Convicted: Representing Indigent Defendants on Appeal* (Westport, Conn.: Greenwood Press, 1990) and of numerous articles on law, philosophy, and public policy.

Address: Institute for Philosophy and Public Policy, 3111 Van Munching Hall, University of Maryland, College Park, MD 20742, USA.

Abstract

This paper explores several dimensions of the relationship between procedural and outcome justice. It examines how procedural justice may be evaluated independently of outcome justice, and how procedural justice plays a default role when criteria for outcome justice are controversial or difficult to apply. It argues that psychological research on procedural justice requires a clearer understanding of the possible relationships between procedural and outcome justice.

3 The Procedural Justice Approach in the Context of Systems Theory: The Theoretical Impact of Law As a Symbolic Generalized Medium of Communication

KAI-D. BUSSMANN

The Problem

Previously, despite Luhmann's 'legitimation through procedure' (1975), it was accepted as undisputed that the outcome of a procedure is decisive for the acceptance of its decisions. From the perspective of the judiciary or other authorities and their addressees, it is therefore, above all, material justice or distributive justice that is important. The procedure itself is a mere means to an end. Recently, doubts have been raised, not only theoretically but also empirically, about this relation between material justice and either procedural justice or the legitimacy of authorities.

Although from a systems theory perspective the outcomes of this research on procedural justice are rather unsurprising, they, just like the systems theory approach, almost turn the relation between legitimacy, procedure, and distributive justice upside down. In the following, these individual findings and previously proposed theoretical explanations will be discussed from the perspective of systems theory. In order to address within a short paper the complexity of these relationships, attention is restricted to the major field to which procedural justice research is applied: the legal system and its court proceedings. Nonetheless, these analyses can be also generalized to processes in other social subsystems, as discussed briefly at the end of the paper. The issue that has to be addressed theoretically concerns why procedural justice and the legitimacy of authorities are important variables in any explanation of the acceptance of the outcome of proceedings.[1] Closely linked to this is another unanswered question: whether this relationship is to be expected in all cases of conflict, or whether there are borders beyond which it no longer applies.

From all the approaches to a theoretical explanation that have been offered (for an overview, see Röhl 1993), two come relatively close to a systems theory concept of the problem. Lind and Tyler (1988, 230) proceed from a group value theory. They assume that a procedure reflects the value system of a group or society, so that unfair decisions are accepted more easily in the single case than is an unfair procedure that applies to all cases. Gibson's (1989, 1991) version is even closer to a systems theory explanation, which is also pointed out by Röhl (1993, 16). In his criticism of Tyler and Rasinski (1991), Gibson assumes that addressees of the law generally know very little about court proceedings, so that judgements on whether proceedings have been carried out fairly must come from other sources. Gibson suspects that this source can be found in a general judgement of institutional legitimacy that is acquired during the early socialization of the addressees of law. General attitudes toward the legitimacy of authorities are therefore responsible for the perception of procedural justice (Gibson 1991, 633).

However, both perspectives still explain their observations only from the micro-perspective of the actors. In contrast, Luhmann's systems theory analysis of the 'legitimacy of procedure is based on a macro-level, and is therefore theoretically unable to extend to the work on the phenomenon of procedural justice with its social-psychological orientation. However, systems theory has developed further. Since the first publication of *Legitimation durch Verfahren* in 1969, the entire theoretical structure has become considerably more flexible and differentiated. Significant in this context is the introduction of symbolic generalized media of communication, which I wish to address in this paper.

I believe that this theoretical building block makes it possible to improve our theoretical understanding of procedures on the micro-level of the actors without having to depart completely from the macro-structural dimension of the law. Such a systems theory reformulation of the (missing) connection between material and procedural justice then permits a more promising interconnection and extension of the two theoretical approaches. It will become possible to better apply social-psychological theories to this reformulated interface between micro- and macro-levels.

Theoretical Sketch: The Impact of Law as a Medium of Communication

For both Durkheim and Parsons, shared values are a necessary condition of social stability. For this reason, the normative orientation of the actors becomes an indispensable component of any activity, with culture, in the sense of a 'shared symbolic system' (Parsons), serving all actors as a sort of 'connecting theme'. Hence, they solve the problem of order in their theoretical approach by defining it *a priori*. The above-mentioned social-psychological studies of procedural justice proceed on this basis also, while implicitly assuming the existence of a generally accepted notion about justice for any conflicts and for any groups within society. In contrast, systems theory takes a radical constructivist perspective.

The systems theory approach is geared decisively to the concept of contingence (Luhmann 1991, 1993; see also Rorty 1993, 21–51); that is, the possibility that activities can also be possible in another way, and it therefore disassociates itself from other consensus-oriented initial positions. The twofold contingence[2] of communicative interaction between alter and ego or between differentiated systems becomes the pivot and central issue of the problem of social order and the development of modern society (Luhmann 1984, 148–163). In this way, the problem of order in an increasingly segmented society and its subsystems can be reformulated as a problem of contingent options. It can then be assumed that society could not exist if the outcome of basically contingent communication was left to chance (Luhmann 1991, 176). In addition, the more complex social systems become, the more oppressive the burden of deciding between contingent options will become for their actors. How does a modern society solve this problem, and how must it solve it, in order to ensure its further development?

For Luhmann, two structural achievements are involved in increasing the chances of communicative success, and these function as auto-catalysts: first, symbolic generalizations; and, second, the formation of codes (Luhmann 1991, 177). Although, in principle, the symbols used have no intrinsic value, with the help of symbolic generalizations it becomes possible for every communication partner to coordinate his or her own selections with an interpretable reality and intentionality in other partners without any necessity for actual communication.

Using these codes increases the probability that the meaning proposed in the communication will be accepted despite the enormous range of potential meanings in the world. The codes increase the probability of reaching agreement, and they do this on three dimensions: material, temporal, and social. On the material dimension, they make it possible to interpret extremely heterogeneous situations in the same way and to generalize the criteria for this to other situations. On the temporal dimension, these codes facilitate the connection to further social operations. Finally, on the social dimension, the formation of codes permits the construction of binary schemes that then make it possible to discriminate only between right and wrong or between permitted and prohibited. Hence, the coding permits only a restricted distinction; for example, only between right or wrong or between payment or non-payment (in the economic system), or between true or false (in the scientific system). This is precisely where their advantage lies: The codes simplify by reducing enormous social complexity, and thus a variety of options, to a level that is easy to deal with. Through their generalizations, the symbols can be applied to a variety of situations and contexts.

The idea of introducing communication media into a theory of society can be traced back to Parsons (1980). For Parsons, classical communication media are money, power, influence, and commitments. In recent media theories,[3] law is also viewed as a communication medium that is more or less independent from power. Media are generally regarded as special languages or supplements to language that help to reduce communication problems in societies. One example, which provided Parsons with his model for the development of media theory, is money. Media convey highly compressed information that is used further because of its symbolic form and that can develop into long chains of communication within a society without any need to renegotiate the contents of communication (see Willke 1991, 161).[4]

It was particularly the introduction and expansion of symbolically generalized media that were decisive for the development of individual functional systems in society. This was the only way in which functional systems achieved closure and began a process of autonomous internal differentiation (that is, to grow by developing specific forms). The enormous importance of the economic system, but also of, for example, the educational system and the legal system, can be traced back to the introduction of symbolically generated codes. Thus, alongside their facilitation and specialization functions, media must also encourage 'understanding'[5] between the various languages of the individual subsystems.

For example, even the unavoidable social conflicts of everyday family life, which are frequently dealt with through the media of power and money, are transformed into this specific code of law and interpreted. In this way, these media (power and money) and the rationalities of the respective systems that are available to interpret them (Künzler 1987, 324) possess a limited role in the processing of conflicts. It is not power and money but law as an at least ideally independent medium that is contrasted with these media, and it is in this way that the rationality of social justice, equality, or punishment can gain a meaning. By subjecting unequal power relationships to the law, a stronger interaction partner, for example, can be bound to the legal principle of equality.

According to media theory, one further important operative condition is necessary for the success of media: The law must not just circulate through the subsystems but must also be institutionalized. In the case of law, these are the justice or criminal justice institutions. The judiciary represents a central authority that translates between the medium of law[6] and the other media circulating within society. One can view the judiciary as a bank that administers, protects, and provides an equivalent to the medium of 'law'. As for the medium of money, there must also exist a degree of trust in the law if it is not to lose its status as a medium. Thus, a certain equivalent must also exist for the medium of law. Hence, when a social event is interpreted as a judicial case or as a criminal offence with the help of the medium of law, actors must be able to see that there is a basic possibility of also being able to put in a claim for this norm violation. It must also be possible to cash in the value that this code symbolizes. Even this implementation of law in principle suffices.

Perception and Construction of Reality Through Law

This is the point at which research on procedural justice comes in and determines that the perceived legitimacy of (legal) authorities and the fairness of procedures has a direct, or at least indirect, effect on the acceptance of procedural outcomes. The group value theory of Lind and Tyler overlooks the fact that the legal system does more than just provide procedures for making and applying law. This deficit also cannot be resolved completely by applying socialization theory, as, for example, in Gibson's approaches (1991). Law as a communication medium is not restricted to social learning processes, but is already involved in guiding the perception of the actors. The current theoretical explanations of procedural justice effects reduce the legal system too much to its instrumental performances, and this overlooks its contribution to the construction of reality. Law is exclusively effective in that, as a symbolic code, it provides a verbal space and the semantic instruments that determine the interpretations and constructions of reality of its addressees. Therefore, criminal law works exclusively by providing a linguistic environment; that is, those semantic instruments that determine the legal addressee's interpretations and constructions of reality.

Similar speech-oriented, constructivist approaches or ideas can also be found in various studies in legal sociology (e.g., Hunt 1993, 301; McIntyre 1994, 109; Rottleuthner 1989; 1992, 136; and Teubner 1989b) and criminology (e.g., Garland 1990). But they can also be found in sociological classics such as Mead's symbolic interactionism or the phenomenological approaches of Husserl, Schütz, and, taken further, of Berger and Luckmann (1980, 42). The role of framing for Goffman (1974) should also be mentioned. Both the (radical) constructivism of von Foerster, Maturana, Varela, or Paul Watzlawick and others (see also Rorty 1993) and the so-called postmodernism of Foucault (e.g., 1977), Lyotard (1987) or Derrida (1991; see also Schwartz and Friedrichs 1994) work with such ideas, as do linguistic or semiotic approaches which partly criticize precisely the law's role constructive impact (e.g., Henry and Milovanovic 1994; Milovanovic 1986, see also Habermas 1985, 1993).

All these theoretical approaches, just like the systemic media theory proposed here, emphasize to a greater or lesser extent the role of language, language horizons, and reference systems in the perception of reality. This list is no way exclusive and could be expanded much further. However, this constructivist aspect has not yet been taken up in procedural justice research.

From the perspective of systems theory, law as an operative closed system (see below) cannot guide behaviour. However, through its medium of communication, it can, at best, guide the communication of, and in particular the construction of reality of its addressees. Therefore law has an impact only in this sense. It achieves this in a highly remarkable way, as the following findings from our sociolegal survey on family violence against children suggest.[7] Violence cannot just be observed; it initially also has to be defined as violence (Honig 1992, 371; Neidhardt 1986). Thus, because violence is dependent on which measure of evaluation is applied, we asked respondents about their concept or definition of violence, and we did this in various social situations. We anticipated that parents would view a slap in the face of a child as being least associated with violence, bearing in mind that this is a legally permissible form of corporal punishment available to them (see Fig. 3.1).

Figure 3.1: Definitions of Violence in Various Social Contexts

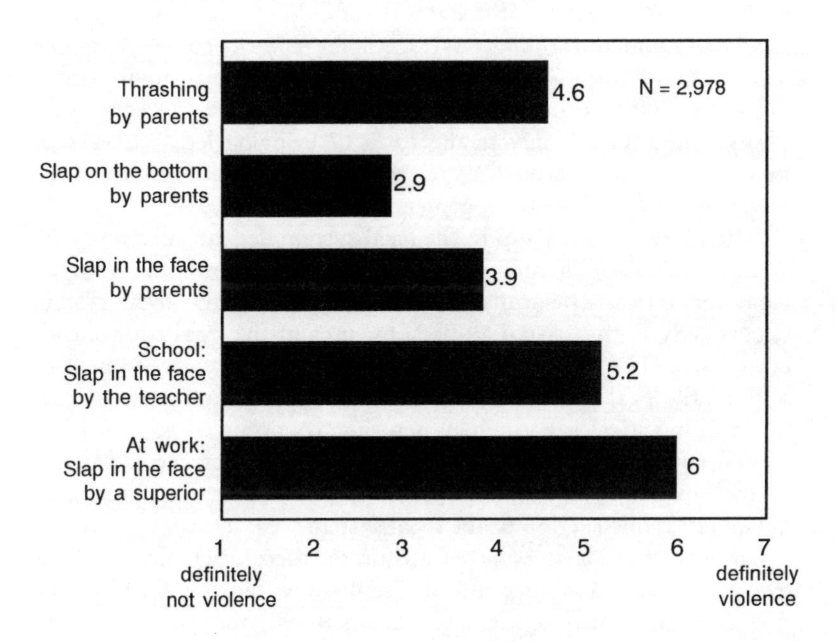

We found that all actions that are prohibited by law tended to be labelled as violence. Law justifies a mother slapping her child, so respondents did not view this action as being particularly violent; neither social norms nor the law evaluate this as violence or physical injury.[8] Our qualitative interviews with adolescents showed that they tended to label as violence those actions that had no justification. The law provides an important justification basis because it introduces discriminations between right or wrong. Thus, a slap from a teacher is already held to be violence because it is no longer permitted in Germany.

Law As a System of Reference

Unlike the explanatory approaches of procedural justice research, systems theory does not conceive the actors as outsiders or strangers to the law who approach the legal authorities equipped with their own criteria of justice. According to the consequences of distinctions mentioned above, it is not only the professionals in their institutions (administration, police, courts, etc.) who belong to the legal system but also all other 'nonprofessional' actors insofar as they refer to the law in their everyday communication (Luhmann 1986, 20). As a result, for systems theory, there is no law outside of the law (Luhmann 1986, 20–1; Teubner 1989a, 105–6), and the legal system, for its part, fabricates its own social environment (Teubner 1989a, 97). When the law is mobilized (see this concept in Blankenburg 1980) only in the form of bringing legal charges or private lawsuits, it is possible to explain why the addressees of the law also tend to view its judgements as just.

Therefore, membership in the legal system depends decisively on whether the actors in any way interpret a social conflict in terms of legal semantics. The transfer of a conflict into the legal system occurs only in this case. Lay persons' uses of the legal code suffice completely. The mere communication in conflicts with the help of apparently legal positions (that is, the discrimination between justice and injustice) is enough. When this has occurred and, in addition, even legal authorities have been mobilized, then the addressees of the law are compelled to operate within the semantic and programmatic construction of the legal system.

As the legal addressees have transformed their (originally) nonlegal everyday-world discourse into a discourse within the world of the law (which means to use legal distinctions), they must tend to perceive the decisions of the legal authorities as just, because no decision-making authority capable of reaching a decision can exist outside of the legal system. The addressees can only provide the judiciary with the facts and then receive their ruling (decision). They may experience disappointments, but they finally lack 'justice-free' categories to evaluate the outcomes of procedures (distributive justice) given.[9]

In this way, legal concepts occupy our everyday language and guide our perceptions, our interpretations of reality, and our judgements (see also Henry and Milovanovic 1994). They do this by introducing specific distinctions through the use of these codes. When actors recur to the law, they are obliged to make distinctions as assumed by systems theory with reference to the work on the theory of decision-making of Spencer Brown (1969, 1–3) or the information concept of Bateson (1972). The essential impact of these theories is that one cannot communicate without distinguishing. One does not have to select the distinctions of the legal system; but when one does, one commits oneself to the specific legal construction of reality and the judgement of law. One is obliged to differentiate in the same way as the law does. Who apart from the institution that generalizes and stabilizes this code should say what is law?

This understanding of the impact of law has many consequences; for example, it implies a different concept of acceptance. According to media theory, this does not depend on acceptance in the usual sense, but only on the communication of the code. The simple communication of observations with reference to this new code means that this code and its distinctions have been 'accepted', and this means accepted in the sense of a semantic anticipation of the adoption or rejection of a communicated proposal of meaning. For example, one can have a very critical or even totally rejecting attitude toward money, but in this sense, one has to accept it in one's interaction with other actors (that is, in daily life). In this way, the legal code circulates in the communication within society by guiding the perceptions and interpretations of the actors, whether in schools, in families, or elsewhere. Once symbolic generalized codes of communication have been introduced into the world, they guide our communication and perceptions at a very early stage, as the various definitions of violence have shown.

Therefore, from a systems theory perspective, the results of procedural justice research are at risk of producing empirical artifacts.[10] The scientific system also enters into the world of the law through its observations; for example, through surveys of the law's addressees. With its methods for ascertaining the truth, social science necessarily links itself to the constructions of reality of the legal system and its code when it interviews the actors, and the actors, at least in their perceptions, are thinking within the framework of this legal code or categories when surveyed. Hence, the legal code not only organizes the legal system but, in this context, also mediates other codings such as that of the scientific system (true/not true, Luhmann 1986, 40). Lind and Tyler (1988, 3) define procedural justice from the perspective of the respondent and correctly treat it as a purely subjective construct, but without drawing radical theoretical and methodological consequences. It is not so much the group or the individual person who is considered here as the evaluating subject, but far more the law as a central reference system for all distinctions that are shaped by law.[11]

The following example provides an illustration of the proposed theory of media: Just as when one exchanges currencies, one has no external criteria for ascertaining the true value of, for example, the American dollar, German mark, or Hungarian florin when one goes to the bank, one cannot state without referring to legal norms which legal case has been decided correctly and which incorrectly. One can only say whether the authority that hands out the currency performs appropriate computations in relation to the other currencies, and one has an idea of whether this institution is authorized to do this and whether it is worthy of trust, that is, legitimized.[12] Law is created only by legal authorities. The legitimacy of the decision is thus of necessity a performance of the procedure (see Luhmann 1975). Procedures are a necessary component in the circulation of the code of law, because through them, other everyday-life semantics or codes in the procedure are finally transformed into the legal code in order to then return to social circulation as law. In this way, the procedure simultaneously authorizes the permanent production of the code of law. At the same time, this means that the social reference of perceptions of justice has to be abandoned completely (Luhmann 1986, 39). Evaluating legal decisions as unjust and hence as unfair can then be derived only from the law itself. Within the framework of the legal system, material justice can be discussed only with reference to other legal decisions or conflicting legal norms. In this way, justice becomes a concept in communications, using the law that determines the consistence of a decision with the normative complexity of the entire legal system. The concept of 'justice' therefore becomes a consistence formula of individual legal decisions in their relationship to other legal norms and decisions; for this reason, Luhmann defines 'justice' as the 'adequate complexity of the legal system' (1981, 388, my translation).

If these ideas are generalized to other domains of society, one can understand why this procedural justice effect can also be found in nonlegal procedures. Educational examinations are a good example (Luhmann 1987b): Here as well, a code is established that always discriminates only between better and worse without taking into account alternative evaluations such as mental or social disadvantage or political opportunity. Every decision has to be based on this selection code if the evaluation of (for example), examination performance is not to be viewed as arbitrary or unfair. The only institution that can rule on this is the one that operates within this code. All who communicate with this code are dependent on it and its specific reduction of reality.

Although one can reject the choice of options that this code offers, the result is that one finds oneself outside the educational system. One can criticize the judgement criteria, suspect unacceptable unofficial reasons, but one cannot suspend the code itself. Otherwise, one becomes an outsider with all the attendant positive and negative social consequences. The law, however, always remains aloof from such judgements of performance because it does not possess any legal criteria for deciding on bad or good examination performance. The courts correct examination results only when reasons for decisions are clearly arbitrary and the intended examination procedures have been violated. The legal consequence is always that the examination has to be repeated. The legal system does not replace the decision of the educational system, it only suspends it.

Law and Other Social Norms

Just pointing to a specific legal understanding of justice shows clearly that the law has greater difficulties than other domains of society because legal norms frequently compete with other social norms. Other 'authorities' or 'institutions' such as the family, the church, the economy, social milieus, or subcultures also use, to some extent, the same distinction between right and wrong. Therefore, one would be unable to say that opinions about material justice are completely dependent on the legal system.[13] The question is whether extralegal ideas about a just distribution of goods or norms can exist.

According to Popitz, every behavioural orientation is preceded by a behavioural norm formation, and, since Durkheim, every society has also been viewed as a moralizing one. All societies recognize social habits, customs, and norms (Popitz 1980), although not all norms and morals have the status of a legal norm.[14] Additionally, according to Aubert (1973), it is necessary to discriminate between conflicts over values and conflicts over interests, and Luhmann (1980, 40–53) introduces the discrimination between normative and cognitive expectations. Therefore, it is conceivable that ideas on justice that are introduced by other nonlegal sources conflict with the 'adequate complexity of the legal system', that is, with its specific formula of justice. There will therefore be a kind of noise or interference between various ideas of fairness and normative expectations, and this would have to be found in procedural justice research, because, for a single event, legal addressees have to oscillate between different semantics and constructions of reality.

Conflicts and hence expectations can move within different systems of reference. Conflicts can be linked to various discourses: to a legal discourse and to a general social discourse within our everyday world or to other social systems such as the economic or religious system (see Teubner 1990, 134). In this way, a reciprocal diffusion of law and other social discourses is conceivable, which Teubner (1990, 134) describes as a problem of interference. Finally, this brings us to the currently much discussed issue in legal sociology and particularly in systems theory of how open or closed are social systems (in this case, the legal system).[15]

However, for the findings of procedural justice research, it is significant that the actors themselves undertake the transformation of their conflicts into a legal dispute (according to Aubert 1973, 190) in that they use the code of law in their communication about the pertinent event. When they do this, there is only one institution that can decide on this conflict; namely, the one that administers the law and continually feeds into the circulation of social communication. This aspect differentiates media theory from various substitution theories in legal philosophy[16] that also are geared to the contingence of modern societies for their explanation of the role of the procedure.[17]

Thus, the perception of fairness depends decisively on the expectations of the actors when they mobilize the legal institutions. The more that those involved hope that the judiciary will also solve or process their social conflicts, the more they will be disappointed. These disappointments are more frequent than procedural justice research would suggest, because countless mediation programs and studies confirm that, for example, crime victims particularly feel that they receive insufficient attention from the criminal justice system.[18] Their conflict with the offenders is certainly not just a normative one. On the level of the law, the actors nonetheless will perceive the decisions of the court not as unjust but as unsatisfactory.

This dissatisfaction places the legal system under pressure to form an acceptable environment for other social systems as well. The legal institutions are dependent on the use of their code. Therefore they cannot detach themselves completely from the interests and constructions of reality of their environment.[19] The same also applies to the procedures they use (Bora 1993, 61). This means that procedures can be available for certain conflicts in which negotiations must be carried out in advance, as is already the case in labour court processes and to some extent in criminal procedures,[20] in order to deal with the complexity of the conflicts within the framework of a legal procedure.[21] Therefore, the expectation orientation of the addressees of the law is decisive, and this can change historically. However, research on procedural justice will hardly be able to trace such changes. Vice versa, it holds that the more the actors are normatively oriented, the more the fairness of the procedure could be decisive. In this way, cultural differences could be explained,[22] as the law and the institutionalization of the law are always determined historically. As a result, the legal system uses its code to convey other concepts of normality to the addressees of law; through sufficient procedural control or legitimacy of the authorities, it socializes them in its customary cultural world with its specific perceptions and interpretations of life events.[23]

Ideas on legitimacy have strong explanatory power, because they are an expression of the trust in the value of the code.[24] This, as Gibson correctly supposes, will depend to a large extent on particular cultural socialization and less on the perceived fairness of single procedures. In contrast, the group value model does not focus on the central point, and this is not only because it assumes the existence of a generally valid concept of justice. Proceedings must certainly permit a structural link to other discourses, and insofar as legal procedures must always be 'environmentally acceptable'.[25] However, it is more decisive that the actors become part of the legal system and its discourse when they refer to the law.

How Procedure Turns 'Social Noise' Into Legal Order

It is only necessary for actors to have sufficient opportunity to transform their everyday descriptions of a conflict[26] into the legal discourse in as complex a manner as possible.[27] If this has occurred from the perspective of the respondents, then they perceive the procedure to be fair, and they accept the judicial reduction of complexity. Legal order from social noise has emerged through the procedure (Teubner 1990, 128; see also Luhmann 1987a, 337). Procedural justice is then nothing more than an adequate complexity of this transformation process into the legal code, and procedural justice research describes the conditions to maximize this effect. 'Standing', 'trust', 'neutrality', and 'control' are, for instance, empirically proved variables (see Lind 1994) that do not focus on allocation-oriented but only on procedural terms. Proceedings, are viewed as fair if they have imposed the least possible limitation on the complexity of the cases for either those involved or the addressees of law who are judging these proceedings. From their perspective, the addressees of law can have control only over these everyday-world[28] reality constructions; they cannot finally feel authorized and able to judge all legal interpretations.

For the structure of this transformation process, this also means that conflicts of interest or of cognitive expectations cannot be, and also need not be, decided by third persons, so that here, in contrast to normative expectations or conflicts, more open, negotiation-oriented procedures are accepted (see, e.g., Aubert 1973, 191). Although the legal system and its procedures are to a large extent normatively closed, they are cognitively open so as not to lose contact with the reality constructions of their environment (Luhmann 1987a, 337; Teubner 1989a, 104–5). From the standpoint of systems theory, procedural justice research can only make statements about the cognitive openness of legal procedures and name conditions for optimizing the procedural justice effect.

The theoretical explanation of procedural justice effects is finally to be sought less in social-psychological explanations than in the ability of the law as a communication medium to influence the constructions of reality of its actors. This, already, is the reason actors tend to perceive as right that which legal personnel tell them to be right. The legal addressees slip into this legal world and its semantic horizon. They tend to think within legal semantic boundaries because they belong to the legal system if they refer to law. The symbolic generalization of the legal code makes it additionally difficult for the law's addressees to adopt an external position. In a court case, the law strengthens this effect through its normative closure that specifically avoids reference to other nonlegal judgement criteria. These are the reasons why the law appears to be the only adequate reference system for evaluating material justice. This power of the law is the object of wide-ranging criticism (e.g., Henry and Milovanovic 1994).

The contribution of procedural justice research has been to provide convincing empirical confirmation of this effect. From the perspective of systems theory, the interesting research issue is first, how the mechanism functions through which ideas of justice emerge. The status of law in society has become much more important as a result of this research. However, this does not lead to a legitimation of the law; the issue of the evaluation of these effects is a completely different one. Secondly, the research issue cannot be to confirm a close correlation between procedural justice and material justice but, in contrast, to study how widely these perceptions of the legal addressees differ. From the standpoint of systems theory, procedural justice research can only make statements about this field of the cognitive openness of legal procedures and name conditions for its structure. Otherwise, it will fall into the trap of producing research artifacts.

Translated from the German by Jonathan Harrow at the University of Bielefeld.

Notes

1 See, for example, Bierhoff (1992), Gibson (1991), Lind et al. (1990), Lind and Tyler (1988), Thibaut and Walker (1978), Tyler (1988, 1993), Tyler and Rasinski (1991), Vidmar (1993).

2 Here, Luhmann (1984, 152) assumes a concept of contingence in the sense of things also being possible in another way; that is, the exclusion of impossibility and necessity.

3 See Habermas (1985, vol. 2, 384), Luhmann (1988, 1991), Münch (1992), Willke (1992), overview in Künzler (1989).

4 Luhmann's more recent systems theory concept of media refers to Fritz Heider's discrimination between *thing* and *medium* in the psychology of perception. For Heider, media are themselves invisible (like air and light), and things, or forms, make it possible to perceive media in a specific way. Individual legal norms are the forms that shape the medium and make it visible (Luhmann 1989, 302–8).

5 Systems theory denies the possibility of a complete understanding between alter and ego.

6 Whereby the medium of law exists in different forms as civil law, public law, or criminal law (see Willke 1992, 175).

7 These findings are based on a representative study of three thousand adults in Germany carried out as part of a research project at the University of Bielefeld (project manager: Detlev Frehsee).

8 The only purpose of this example is to illustrate the role of reference systems. At this point, it does not matter whether it is social or legal norms that are decisive for the different evaluation. Medium theory, however, suggests that legal norms play a greater role.

9 As a result of the further functional segmentation of modern societies and the attendant increasing encroachment of law, this process of legal appropriation of perceptions of justice or fairness will probably continue.

10 See, for instance, the conclusion of Lind (1994, 35), who postulates that it is motivated 'by the desire to be solidly entrenched in society and to be assured that power of state is not going to be against us'.

11 Of course, it is not the judgements of the legal personnel that are decisive here, but the perception of law by its clients.

12 In black market transactions, in contrast, the outcome of the exchange is more important than the procedure applied as, from the very beginning, these do not represent legitimate authorities of the medium of money. In addition, a comparison within the economic system is available here: namely the exchange rates of the authorized banks of issue.

13 The preceding hypothesis that legal addressees lack 'justice-free' categories to evaluate the outcomes of procedures has to be discussed in a more differentiated manner.

14 Legal norms differ from social norms only through the degree of institutionalization of the authorities that sanction them (see Popitz 1980, 32).

15 See the discussion on the theoretical problem of the structural coupling of various codes and systems through procedures (e.g., Bora 1993) and the social coherence of law (e.g. Luhmann 1987a; Teubner 1989b, 102–11).

16 According to the description in Röhl (1993, 17).

17 Compare Rawls (1971) and Wassermann (1989).

18 Sessar et al. (1986) and Boers and Sessar (1991) have empirically confirmed the important role of restitution compared to punishment.

19 From the perspective of the legal system and its institutions, these many-sided expectations then appear to be an 'overcomplexity'; that is, coordinated to the productivity of the legal system with the help of communication on fairness (Luhmann 1981, 390; 1986, 38).

20 Concerning the problematic implementation of the restitution approach in criminal process and its practice, see for example, the overview by Heinz (1993).

21 For this reason, in procedures of white-collar crime, courts bargain with the defence in almost every case (see Bussmann and Lüdemann 1995; also see the discussion in Neumann 1989, 71).

22 But the recent comparative cross-national studies show a large proportion of intercultural consistence (see Lind 1994).

23 On changing legal cultures, see also Friedmann (1985).

24 For this reason, the presence of disturbances in this circulation in individual parts of society, influences momentary norm loyalty toward and ideas on the legitimacy of legal institutions. To put it simply, when law is broadly rejected in individual groups and thus also not communicated, the circulatory system of the medium of law is partially broken, so that the relation between perceptions of legitimacy of the institutions and legal compliance is found (see Tyler 1993; Tyler and Rasinski 1991).

25 Autopoietic closure does not mean isolation (see Luhmann 1987a, 336).

26 Their social conflict, or conflict of interests, or their cognitive expectations.

27 As order from noise (see Luhmann 1987a, 337).

28 Or other systematic discourses; for example, that of the economic system.

References

Aubert, Vilhelm, ed. 1973. Interessenkonflikt und Wertkonflikt: Zwei Typen des Konflikts und der Konfliktlösung. In *Konflikt und Konfliktstrategien—Ansätze zu einer soziologischen Konflikttheorie,* edited by W. L. Bühl. München: Nymphenburger.

Bateson, Gregory. 1972. *Steps to an Ecology of Mind: Collected Essays in Anthropology, Psychiatry, Evolution, and Epistemology.* San Francisco: Chandler.

Berger, Peter L., and Thomas Luckmann, eds. 1980. *Die gesellschaftliche Konstruktion von Wirklichkeit. Eine Theorie der Wissenssoziologie.* Frankfurt am Main: Fischer Taschenbuch Verlag.

Bierhoff, Hans Werner. 1992. Prozedurale Gerechtigkeit. Das Wie und Warum der Fairneß. *Zeitschrift für Sozialpsychologie* 23: 163–78.

Blankenburg, Erhard. 1980. Mobilisierung von Recht. Über die Wahrscheinlichkeit des Gangs zum Gericht, die Chance des Erfolgs und die daraus folgenden Funktionen der Justiz. *Zeitschrift für Rechtssoziologie*: 33–64.

Boers, Klaus, and Klaus Sessar. 1991. Do People Really Want Punishment? On the Relationship of Restitution, Need for Punishment, and Fear of Crime. In *Developments in Crime and Control Research*, edited by K. Sessar and H.-J. Kerner. New York: Springer Verlag.

Bora, Alfons. 1993. Gesellschaftliche Integration durch Verfahren—Zur Funktion von Verfahrensgerechtigkeit in der Technikfolgenabschätzung und -bewertung. *Zeitschrift für Rechtssoziologie*: 55–79.

Bussmann, Kai-D. and Christian Lüdemann. 1995. *Klassenjustiz oder Verfahrensökonomie. Aushandlungsprozesse in allgemeinen und Wirtschaftsstrafverfahren*. Pfaffenweiler: Centaurus Verlag.

Derrida, Jacques. 1991. *Gesetzeskraft. Der mystische Grund der Autorität.* Frankfurt am Main: Suhrkamp.

Foucault, Michel. 1977. *Discipline and Punish: The Birth of the Prison.* New York: Pantheon.

Friedmann, Lawrence M. 1985. Transformations in American Legal Culture. *Zeitschrift für Rechtssoziologie*: 191–205.

Garland, David. 1990. *Punishment and Modern Society: A Study in Social Theory*. Oxford: Clarendon Press.

Gibson, James L. 1989. Understanding of Justice: Institutional Legitimacy, Procedural Justice, and Political Tolerance. *Law and Society Review* 23: 468–96.

———. 1991. Institutional Legitimacy, Procedural Justice, and Compliance with Supreme Court Decisions: A Question of Causality. *Law and Society Review* 25: 631–5.

Goffman, Erving. 1974. *Frame Analysis*. Cambridge: Harvard University Press.

Habermas, Jürgen. 1993. *Faktizität und Geltung*. 3d. ed. Frankfurt am Main: Suhrkamp Verlag.

———., ed. 1985. *Theorie des kommunikativen Handelns. Handlungsrationalität und gesellschaftliche Rationalisierung*. 2 vols. Frankfurt am Main: Suhrkamp.

Heinz, Wolfgang, ed. 1993. Stichwort 'Opfer und Strafverfahren'. In *Kleines Kriminologisches Wörterbuch*, edited by G. Kaiser, F. Sack, and H. Schellhoss. Heidelberg: C.F. Müller Verlag.

Henry, Stuart, and Dragan Milovanovic. 1994. The Constitution of Criminology: A Postmodern Approach to Criminology Theory. In *The Futures of Criminology*, edited by D. Nelken. London: Sage.

Honig, Michael-Sebastian, ed. 1992. *Verhäuslichte Gewalt, mit einem Nachwort zur Taschenbuchausgabe: Sexuelle Gewalt von Kindern*. Frankfurt am Main: Suhrkamp.

Hunt, Allan. 1993. Law As a Constitutive Mode of Regulation. In *Explorations in Law and Society*, edited by A. Hunt. New York: Routledge.

Künzler, Jan. 1987. Grundlagenprobleme der Theorie symbolisch generalisierter Kommunikationsmedien bei Niklas Luhmann. *Zeitschrift für Soziologie*: 317–33.

———. 1989. *Medien und Gesellschaft. Die Medienkonzepte von Talcott Parsons, Jürgen Habermas und Niklas Luhmann.* Stuttgart: Enke Verlag.

Lind, E. Allan. 1994. Procedural Justice and Culture: Evidence for Ubiquitous Process Concerns. *Zeitschrift für Rechtssoziologie*: 24–36.

Lind, E. Allan, Robert J. MacCoun, Patricia A. Ebener, William L. F. Felstiner, Deborah R. Hensler, Judith Resnik, and Tom R. Tyler. 1990. In the Eye of the Beholder: Tort Litigants' Evaluations of Their Experiences in the Civil Justice System. *Law and Society Review* 24: 953–96.

Lind, E. Allan, and Tom R. Tyler. 1988. *The Social Psychology of Procedural Justice.* New York: Plenum.

Luhmann, Niklas. 1975. *Legitimation durch Verfahren.* 2d. ed. Darmstadt: Luchterhand.

———. 1980. *Rechtssoziologie.* Opladen: Westdeutscher Verlag.

———. 1981. Gerechtigkeit in den Rechtssystemen der modernen Gesellschaft. In *Ausdifferenzierung des Rechts, Beiträge zur Rechtssoziologie*, edited by N. Luhmann. Frankfurt am Main: Suhrkamp.

———. 1984: *Soziale Systeme. Grundriß einer allgemeinen Theorie.* Frankfurt am Main: Suhrkamp.

———. 1986. *Die soziologische Beobachtung des Rechts.* Frankfurt am Main: Metzner Verlag.

———. 1987a. Closure and Openness: On Reality in the World of Law. In *Autopoietic Law: A New Approach to Law and Society,* edited by G. Teubner. Berlin: de Gruyter.

———. 1987b. Codierung und Programmierung. Bildung und Selektion im Erziehungssystem. In *Soziologische Aufklärung.* Vol. 4, edited by N. Luhmann. Opladen: Westdeutscher Verlag.

———. 1988. *Macht.* Stuttgart: Enke Verlag.

———. 1989. *Die Wirtschaft der Gesellschaft.* Frankfurt am Main: Suhrkamp.

———. 1991. Einführende Bemerkungen zu einer Theorie symbolisch generalisierter Kommunikation. In *Soziologische Aufklärung, Aufsätze zur Theorie der Gesellschaft.* Vol. 2, edited by N. Luhmann. Opladen: Westdeutscher Verlag.

———. 1993. Die Unwahrscheinlichkeit der Kommunikation. In *Soziologische Aufklärung.* Vol. 3, edited by N. Luhmann. Opladen: Westdeutscher Verlag.

Lyotard, Jean-Francois 1987. *Der Widerstreit.* München: Fink Verlag.

McIntyre, Lisa J. 1994. *Law in the Sociological Enterprise: A Reconstruction*. Boulder, Colo.: Westview.

Milovanovic, Dragan. 1986. Juridico-Linguistic Communicative Markets: Towards a Semiotic Analysis. *Contemporary Crises* 10: 281–304.

Münch, Richard. 1992. Recht als Medium der Kommunikation. *Zeitschrift für Rechtssoziologie*: 65–87.

Neidhardt, Friedhelm. 1986. Gewalt—Soziale Bedeutungen und sozialwissenschaftliche Bestimmungen des Begriffs. In *Was ist Gewalt?* edited by Bundeskriminalamt. Wiesbaden: Eigenverlag.

Neumann, Ulfried. 1989. Materiale und prozedurale Gerechtigkeit im Strafverfahren. *Zeitschrift für die Gesamte Strafrechtswissenschaft* 101: 52–74.

Parsons, Talcott. 1980. *Zur Theorie der sozialen Interaktionsmedien*. Opladen: Westdeutscher Verlag.

Popitz, Heinrich. 1980. *Die normative Konstruktion von Gesellschaft*. Tübingen: J. C. B. Mohr.

Rawls, John. 1971. *A Theory of Justice*. Cambridge: Harvard University Press.

Röhl, Klaus F. 1993. Verfahrensgerechtigkeit. Einführung in den Themenbereich und Überblick. *Zeitschrift für Rechtssoziologie*: 1–34.

Rorty, Richard. 1993. *Kontingenz, Ironie und Solidarität*. Frankfurt am Main: Suhrkamp.

Rottleuthner, Hubert. 1989. The Limits of Law: The Myth of a Regulatory Crisis. *International Journal of Sociology* 17: 273–85.

———. 1992. Grenzen rechtlicher Steuerung—Und Grenzen von Theorien darüber. *ARSP-Beiheft* 54: 123–39.

Schwartz, Martin D., and David O. Friedrichs. 1994. Postmodern Thought and Criminological Discontent: New Metaphors for Understanding Violence. *Criminology* 32: 221–46.

Sessar, Klaus, Andreas Beurskens, and Klaus Boers. 1986. Wiedergutmachung als Konfliktregelungsparadigma? *Kriminologisches Journal*: 86–104.

Spencer Brown, George. 1969. *Laws of Form*. London: Lowe and Brydon Printers.

Teubner, Gunther. 1989a. *Recht als autopoietisches System*. Franfurt am Main: Suhrkamp.

———. 1989b. Regulatory Law: Chronicle of a Death Foretold. *Social and Legal Studies* 1: 451–75.

———. 1990. Die Episteme des Rechts. Zu erkenntnistheoretischen Grundlagen des reflexiven Rechts. In *Wachsende Staatsaufgaben—sinkende Steuerungsfähigkeit des Rechts*, edited by D. Grimm. Baden-Baden: Nomos Verlag.

Thibaut, John, and Laurens Walker. 1978. A Theory of Procedure. *California Law Review* 66: 541–66.
Tyler, Tom R. 1988. What Is Procedural Justice? Criteria Used by Citizens to Assess the Fairness of Legal Procedures. *Law and Society Review* 22: 103–35.
———. 1993. Legitimizing Unpopular Public Policies: Does Procedure Matter? *Zeitschrift für Rechtssoziologie*: 47–54.
Tyler, Tom R., and Kenneth A. Rasinski. 1991. Procedural Justice, Institutional Legitimacy, and the Acceptance of Unpopular U.S. Supreme Court Decisions: A Reply to Gibson. *Law and Society Review* 25: 621–30.
Vidmar, Neil. 1993. Verfahrensgerechtigkeit und alternative Konfliktbewältigung. *Zeitschrift für Rechtssoziologie*: 35-46.
Wasserman, David. 1989. Procedural Justice and the Convicted Criminal Defendant. Paper presented at Law and Society annual meeting, June, Madison, Wisconsin.
Willke, Helmut. 1991. *Systemtheorie. Eine Einführung in die Grundprobleme der Theorie sozialer Systeme.* Stuttgart: Gustav Fischer Verlag.
———. 1992. *Ironie des Staates.* Grundlinien einer Staatstheorie polyzentrischer Gesellschaft. Frankfurt am Main: Suhrkamp.

The Author

Kai-D. Bussmann. Scientific assistant at the University of Bielefeld. Studied law and sociology at the University of Hamburg, passed the first and second examination in law, and received a doctorate in law at the University of Bremen. Has written in different criminological and sociolegal fields (mediation/restitution, court procedures of white-collar crime, family violence, systems theory). Currently project coordinator in an empirical study on family violence against children and the impact of law at the Research Centre of Prevention and Intervention in Childhood and Adolescence and lecturer on sociology of law at the University of Bielefeld.

Address: University of Bielefeld, Faculty of Law, SFB227, PO Box 100 131, 33501 Bielefeld, Germany

Abstract

Empirical research on 'procedural justice' is discussed within the theoretical perspective of systems theory. The theoretical problem is developed by looking at law as a symbolic generalized medium of communication that circulates within society. In this respect, we have to consider not only the cognitive openness of law but also its normative closure. Law as a code enables mechanisms of structural coupling with the environment of the legal system, but it constructs a specific legal reality in its environment. Although actors have expectations toward the legal system and toward legal norms, they do not have any criteria for justice within a legal world. Law as a symbolic generalized medium of communication is developed only in the legal system. If actors make judgements on law and about justice, they slip into this legal world and its terminological horizon. They tend to think within these legal semantic boundaries. For this reason, the process of judging itself and especially the fairness of a legal procedure becomes more relevant for the legal addressees than its outcome. Finally, the limits of the procedural justice research are discussed.

4 Procedural Justice As a Contested Concept: Sociological Remarks on the Group Value Model

ALFONS BORA

Much of the procedural justice research in the field of social psychology can be understood as a response to a variety of methodological individualism found, for example, in game theory or the theories of public or rational choice, which are influenced by economics. These theories are understood as attempts to establish a micro-macro link (see Alexander et al., 1987); in other words, to see collective effects as culminations of separate actions. They rest on a model positing a self-interested actor whose rationale for action is embedded in calculations of expected utility. This implies that personal utility is oriented to the intended outcome of an action and, hence, to control over that outcome. This is also the basis of the work by Thibaut and Walker (1975), in which the concept of outcome control figures prominently and procedural justice is inferred.[1] In their view the preference for procedures that are considered fair, as opposed to other procedures, results from diffuse support nurtured by the expectation of acceptable outcomes.[2] Recent procedural justice research has tried to move away from this theoretical perspective by criticizing the way it views the behaviour of individual actors. As Lind and Tyler (1988, 217, 228–30) in particular point out, the concept of a purely outcome-oriented actor is incomplete according to many empirical findings, and important modes of perception and motivational situations are ignored. They therefore distinguish between two views of procedural justice, contrasting their group value model with Thibaut and Walker's model of informed self-interest.

Translation by David Antal. Reprinted with permission, from *Social Justice Research* 8 (1995): 175–95.

According to the group value model (Lind and Tyler 1988, 230–40; Tyler 1990, 173–4), procedures are characteristics of social units. These units are called groups. Indeed, Lind and Tyler refer to society, too, as a group. Membership in such social groups is a salient aspect in the lives of individuals. Personal identities form partly in socialization processes, that is, in interaction with the norms, rules, and world views of the group in which an individual grows up. This makes aspects of social life important determinants of personal attitudes and personal behaviour. According to the group value model, these relations between social and psychological structures are conditioned by two elements, group identity and group-specific behaviour. Just as group identity provides distinguishing features that set the group off from other social arenas and thus organizes the external life of the group as it were, group-specific processes operate to structure the internal life of the group. In regulating the relations between group members, they simultaneously confer upon the members their social status. Unlike a particular decision that is perceived to be unfair, a process is a permanent institution in which the value system of the group is reflected. If, therefore, a process is deemed unfair, it tends to pose a threat to a person's standing in the group. Conversely, a process that is experienced as being fair instills a feeling of respect, even if the outcome is unfavourable. The group value model attempts to deal with the concept of a self-interested actor by starting from the idea of an actor who is oriented to social esteem and whose judgement of a process may therefore even contradict his own interest in receiving a personally favourable outcome.

The group value model can be characterized mainly by two features, conceptual subjectivism and methodological collectivism, which can also be used to point out its specific strengths and weaknesses. Subjectivism here means that the definition of procedural justice is rooted fundamentally in people's subjective assessment. That is true even of objective procedural justice, which can be described as a procedure's 'objective' conformity to the normative standards of those participating in the procedure or of persons asked to give their opinion about it. In other words, the subjectivism of the group value model stems from the theory's orientation to psychology. To that extent the model differs from rational choice approaches, which concentrate more on describing an ends-means relation and which can therefore be characterized as 'objective'. The group value model differs from them also in that it leans toward methodological collectivism, albeit only a diluted form of it.

The word 'collectivism' is intended to call attention to the fact that the group value model, unlike individualistic approaches, does not try to explain collective effects from individual actions. Instead, it accounts for a person's procedural justice judgements by pointing to socialization mechanisms and group loyalty, whereby individual effects are seen as emerging from collective facts (or what Durkheim called *faits sociaux*).

Starting from these two aspects—conceptual individualism and methodological collectivism—the following pages will outline some of the inherent limits of the group value model that become plain from a specifically sociological point of view.

Sociological Limitations of the Group Value Model

The merits of the group value model seem obvious. After all, it can help interpret phenomena that to all appearances escape rational choice models (see Lind and Tyler 1988, 228–9). First, self-interested actor models lack a foundation on which to explain the procedural justice effect—the preference for a particular procedure despite outcomes that are likely to be negative. The group value model provides a more complex and efficient approach in this regard. Whether it eventually proves to be tenable in the face of rational choice approaches is not at issue here.[3] Lind and Tyler themselves seem to argue this point cautiously. In any case, they maintain that the two approaches complement each other to a certain degree and do not claim their own concept to be universal (Lind and Tyler 1988, 240).

This conciliatory stance on the self-interested actor model need not be the final word in every respect. Perhaps the position of procedural justice research in general could be put more strongly by (*a*) abandoning inherent subjectivism for a more sociological perspective, according to which the function of procedural justice does not derive from personal judgements, and (*b*) dispensing with the distinction between methodological individualism and collectivism and, hence, with the implicit micro-macro debate as well as the rational choice models that build on it. Both proposals can be supported in greater detail if one looks closely at some of the internal difficulties with the group value model.

Latent Normative Characteristics

One of the problems with the theoretical position labelled above as conceptual subjectivism is its latent normative traits. On the one hand, the group value model must assume that the fairness of procedures can be judged reliably. On the other hand, the model's conceptual underpinnings preclude that very possibility. The model tries to wriggle out of this contradiction by using commonsense considerations. However, they prove to be normative *petitio principii*.

Take, for example, Lind and Tyler's (1988) first hypothesis: 'Frustration effects, negative reactions to apparently fair procedures, occur only when the procedure is weak; that is, when it is easy to suspect that the procedure is a sham' (207). To test this hypothesis, the scientific observer must already possess a nonsubjective standard of procedural justice. If procedural justice is to serve as an independent variable, as suggested by the hypothesis, that observer must state on 'objective' (or at the very least 'trans-subjective') grounds whether a procedure is 'strong' or 'weak'.[4] But that is scarcely possible with the theoretical means offered by the group value model, for in principle it measures procedural justice according to subjective attitudes toward discrete types of procedures.[5]

Moreover, the theoretical description does not go beyond this point. It, too, focuses on personal judgements without a criterion being formulated to handle cases in which those judgements diverge. As Lind and Tyler (1988) define it, objective procedural justice concerns the capacity to engender or enhance fairness 'by, for example, reducing some clearly unacceptable bias or prejudice' (3). In the final analysis, this points to intuition that tells one when that 'clearly unacceptable' point has been reached. What minimum percentage of positive procedural fairness judgements does a procedure need in order to qualify as fair?

Latent normativism lurks behind this approach, something that becomes evident when solutions to such obviously unsatisfactory situations are sought. In a manner of speaking, it is automatically necessary to fall back on 'fundamental' values, universal principles, and the like. The argumentation by Lind and Tyler (1988) is no exception. In replying to the obvious objection that group values are ultimately not impervious to cultural relativism, they state: 'Of course, socialized values can vary from one group to another and from one person to another, but we believe that there are also some fundamental values that affect procedural justice in all groups' (Lind and Tyler 1988, 232). And the differences between separate groups and persons at that point are based, as it were, on the ratio between universal and group-specific values: 'Judgments of procedural justice depend on the extent to which a group's procedures are congruent both with these more or less universal values and with idiosyncratic values of the group or individual in question' (Lind and Tyler 1988, 232). Therefore, a procedure's fairness cannot be measured solely according to the approval of those potentially affected, for that can vary. It must be at least complemented by external evaluation criteria.

A final observation to round out this line of reasoning is that conceptual subjectivism and normative connotations are tightly interwoven, as shown when one investigates whether Lind and Tyler's (1988) first hypothesis admits of the opposite conclusion. Do frustration effects and negative reactions to an apparently fair procedure necessarily mean that the procedure is 'weak' or 'faulty'? (Instances of this kind are cited in the section on empirical cases, below.) Are there any instruments that discriminate between 'true' and 'false' procedural justice judgements?

If procedural justice is so difficult to derive theoretically from a subjectivist model, then exploration of a nonsubjectivist approach seems justified. In light of the reasoning above, a nonsubjectivist approach would be expected to be capable of describing procedural justice as one aspect of procedures, as something supraindividual and trans-situational—in short, as a social phenomenon.

Obstacles in Collectivist Approaches

There would be some justification in asserting that the group value model seeks precisely this sociological extension by turning to methodological collectivism, as outlined above. The personal procedural justice judgement is the manifestation of the value that a group attaches to a process, and this manifestation is mediated by fair procedure. In this way procedural justice becomes an element of group morality as understood by Durkheim, who emphasized the collective origin of personal notions of morality and justice: 'Une morale est toujours l'oeuvre d'un groupe et ne peut fonctionner que si ce groupe la protège de son autorité' (Durkheim 1958, 46). But by choosing this concept, Durkheim created a dilemma for himself. The collectivist approach can no longer explain that origin of the social group; it must always posit the origin as a social given. But this assumption inevitably conflicts with what is known about social evolution. Groups and societies have formed over historical time and are constantly forming anew. This knowledge serves as the driving force underlying rational choice models, in which collective effects are considered phenomena that need explanation.

In that the group value model follows in the tradition of collectivist approaches, it lacks a way to explain the origin of group values that serve as a cause of personal judgements about justice. In this regard the group value model is no match at all for the explanatory power of individualistic theories and the questions they pose. Having acknowledged this fact, Lind and Tyler (1988) advocate accepting both models as mutually complementary. But is it advisable to leave it at that?

Perhaps not. If the field continued to be explored with both models in mind, the resulting definitional ambiguity alone would preclude observation of many cases of procedural justice, including those in which one or more participants in a procedure made purely strategic use of their possibilities. To put it differently, it has been observed that actors actually do behave 'egoistically' in certain constellations by making a personal cost-benefit calculation the basis of their decision to avail themselves of procedures and institutions.[6] In other words, what the group value model lacks on this point is a sensor for detecting the possibility that a given behaviour is not oriented to 'fairness'. Much would be gained if an 'objective' concept of procedural justice were to be developed, one that would both concentrate on the procedure itself and formally provide for the alternative of describing behaviour that was not, or not exclusively, keyed to considerations of procedural justice.

The variant of the group theory approach discussed here suffers from another defect, its sweeping generalization. The group value model makes practically no distinction between groups and societies. As pointed out above, it even refers to societies as groups. From a sociological perspective, this view seems doomed to failure. For a number of reasons, society cannot be described as a group. First, the concept of the group is drawn from interaction theory, and societies cannot be described completely in the framework of interaction theory. Much of what characterizes society cannot be explained by the face-to-face relation between persons. It comes about instead as a macro-structure, as an effect of the invisible hand operating beyond interactional relations and, all too often, even against interactional intentions (see Luhmann 1987, for the theoretical core of this idea). Second, there are too many separate groups in society for generalization to be convincing. Take fairness judgements, for example. If the group value determines the personal judgement, which group is meant? The family? Work colleagues? One's circle of friends? The government justice system? A political party? And which of these groups decides the issue if positions conflict? Whoever answers these questions by invoking inscrutable personal preferences has left the bounds of collectivist theory and no longer differs in reasoning from the methodological individualism of rational choice. Conversely, whoever answers by resorting to universalist principles, which transcend groups, must renounce conceptual subjectivism, as seen above.

These comments on the group value model can now be summarized. From a sociologist's viewpoint, the model appears to be too narrow for two reasons. Its conceptual subjectivism does not permit procedural justice to be understood as a procedure-related phenomenon explicable in terms of the function it has for the procedure. That is why a nonsubjectivist reconstruction of procedural justice would be desirable. It should also seek to avoid the drawbacks of methodological collectivism without returning to the individualism of rational choice. Recent systems theory attempts to go beyond the binary schema of the micro-macro dispute and thus transcend the aforementioned controversy surrounding methodological approaches. In the next section, I therefore try to show why it seems purposeful to add a system reference perspective to the group value approach. Let us begin with two empirical cases intended to illustrate what has been said up to this point.

Two Empirical Cases

Technology Assessment of Genetically Engineered Alterations in Plants

The first example of what can be gained by combining the group value approach with a system reference perspective is a process of technology assessment (TA) that was conducted from 1991 through 1993 by the Wissenschaftszentrum Berlin für Sozialforschung (WZB) under the auspices of the Federal Ministry for Research and Technology.[7] It dealt with the genetically engineered resistance of cultivated plants to herbicides. In this case, the tolerance for herbicides was achieved by implanting a special gene in the genome of the plants. The purpose of this engineered genetic mutation was to improve chemical weed control by enabling herbicides to kill off all weeds while leaving the transgenetic plants undamaged. The appraisal of the technology by experts was combined in this procedure with a dialogue between advocates and critics.

Approximately sixty people took part. They came from various scientific disciplines, the chemical and breeding industry, the responsible government agencies, agricultural associations, and environmental movements.

The TA was designed to be participatory. Those involved had the right to select the personnel and subject matter and to help define the related organizational tasks in an executive body (a steering committee). Whenever possible, discussion time was regulated with an eye to enabling the participants to persuade each other and thereby maximize their direct influence on the final assessment of the technology. The opening conference was devoted to selecting the technology to be studied. Although the final choice remained controversial, at least the procedure respected the desires of the participants. It is therefore likely that the idea behind participation in this TA was anchored more securely than is true of other procedures (see Bora and Döbert 1993; the procedure essentially conformed to Leventhal's rules, as explained in Bora 1993). This practice also proved to have counterproductive effects, as the course of the project showed. The concluding conference took place in the summer of 1993, after two-and-a-half years of negotiations. As the event began, the environmental groups announced that they were withdrawing from the process on the grounds that it was procedurally flawed.

This incident shows one problem of procedures like these is that of integrating dissimilar expectations of the participants. It is difficult to find a road somewhere between 'tokenism' and 'technological obstructionism'. Competing views about the responsibility of TA and about procedural principles and objectives must be combined in a way that keeps the procedure stable as a social system. Success in doing so depends partly on the patterns of interpretation (types of discourse) that are competing with each other. Empirically speaking, three concepts of procedural justice can be differentiated in the TA procedure.

For the 'scientific and technical' discourse, procedural justice was practically no issue, as shown in all the relevant records. Because information-gathering and technical solutions to specific problems were uppermost in mind, the main focus was on technical matters, where questions of justice played no role. There are therefore also good reasons to presume that control over the outcome will, by this logic, be achieved through control over the procedure. People want 'true' (or 'useful') results whether or not the procedure is 'fair'. This objective is met by means of scientific discussion in which there are methodological criteria for the acceptance of statements.

For the 'political' discourse, however, procedural justice can become an important issue under certain circumstances; namely, when it becomes necessary to demand a balance between power and informational resources. On the whole, however, the procedure is no doubt seen in terms of outcome. The decisive thing for the judgement pronounced on the procedure will be whether or not—depending on what the vested interests are—it proves useful for purposes of political mobilization or depoliticization. Such cases also figure in 'displacement theory', which holds that procedural criticism can be expected especially when procedural outcomes are dissatisfying.

Lastly, there is a 'procedure-oriented' discourse. It leaves the evaluational and informational issues an open question and centres entirely on the power of procedural rules to build structures (fairness, harmony, etc.). They create a suitable balance between cooperation and conflict in order to promote objective preparation of political decisions. The integration of the multifarious aspects of herbicide resistance issues is explicitly described as difficult. Solving this problem is one of a procedure's main inputs. This is the only type of discourse to revolve around the question of procedural justice and procedural control.

It turned out that this 'procedure-oriented' discourse was not able to balance the conflicting interests and expectations surrounding the procedure. The environmental groups especially took exception to shortcomings in procedural justice, charging that key aspects of its 'political' dimension had been neglected. As they saw it, imbalances in power, information overload, the scarcity of resources from which environmental movements suffered, and the fact that industry had begun deliberately releasing genetically altered plants made it impossible for them to continue participating for the final two days of the TA process.

Of course, it is also a political question whether and to what extent these reasons are valid.[8] In particular, it is seriously doubtful that one side in this sort of dispute can demand a moratorium from the other (without, incidentally, itself being willing to accept one—say, by temporarily halting political activities). Currently, the most likely reason that the environmental groups withdrew from the process at this late stage is that their legitimacy would have been seriously undermined in the eyes of their membership by a procedural outcome that was expected to show partial support for the technology. The environmental groups forestalled this erosion by walking out.[9]

Be that as it may, what do these incidents indicate? First, they suggest that this TA had no one kind of procedural justice to be reconstructed from the participants' subjective evaluations; the evaluations were highly controversial. Second, the occurrences cited above show that these controversial evaluations can all be described as rational attitudes if one relates them to the underlying imperative of social systems, such as science or politics. Third, they point out that 'objective' procedural justice can reasonably be thought of as a function of the procedure itself, namely, as a contribution to social integration. Before expanding on these conjectures, let us examine the second case.

Civil Hearing on the Release of Plants with Genetically Engineered Alterations

The second example also has to do with genetic engineering. Until 31 December 1993, section 18 of the Genetic Engineering Act (GenTG) mandated an oral civil hearing to be held by the Bundesgesundheitsat (federal health authority) when a genetically altered organism was released.[10] Anyone in the entire country was entitled to submit written objections, which subsequently had to be discussed with all those bringing them up. Other persons were not permitted to take part in the hearing, but were admitted without exception as guests. In this sense, the proceedings could be called semi-public. Objections had to relate to the risks and hazards of the plants in which alterations had been genetically engineered; discussion of political arguments was not allowed. These practices follow from the legal nature of the procedure, which was intended to ensure compliance with official regulations. In such cases, there is no room for debates about the political appropriateness of the law itself.[11]

Two hearings of this sort took place in early 1993 and lasted a total of ten days. The following material has been drawn from participant observation, the analysis of tape-recorded records, and background discussions with key people. One of the general characteristics of both proceedings was that the debate began with a long struggle over the agenda and charges by the objectors that the people running the gathering were biased. In both hearings, this phase lasted up to six hours or more. Another general characteristic was that the objectors persisted in trying to put the political and ethical issues, which could not legally be brought into the discussion, onto the agenda as the first point. These procedural conflicts were followed by what was usually a technical debate about the risks posed by experiments that allowed the release of plants in which alterations had been genetically engineered. Several hundred participants attended the hearings at first. Their numbers rapidly and steadily dwindled to a few dozen.

An initial analysis of the data identified six positions that differ in their evaluations of the procedure, in their reasoning, and in other ways. They can be summarized in ideal-type parlance as follows:

Position 1 The opinion of the petitioners—industrial firms, scientists, and experts—was a blend of 'scientific-technological-economical' rationality. To them, the proceedings were 'mischief', 'nonsense', 'a Punch and Judy show', and a bureaucratic obstruction to desirable developments. This attitude fixated their criticism on the formal, legal rationale of bureaucratic procedures, resulting on the whole in a rather low degree of acceptance of the proceedings.

Position 2 This attitude can be characterized as a 'scientific-technological-legal' mind set, a mix reflected mainly by scientists and lawyers from various bodies. Two aspects were seen. Scientifically, the arguments of the objectors were said to be only 'rubbish'. It was maintained that they contained 'nothing new'.[12] All the same, participants sharing this conviction asserted that due process was necessary, though they claimed that opponents would use it 'to bring the issue to a head and force the petitioners to retreat'. Because of their professional background, the people taking this stance saw the process as being highly legitimate, but they considered it desirable to have the kind of formal restrictions that ultimately were legislated.

Position 3 A type of 'legal' reference frame was recognizable in the attitude evinced by representatives of the Federal Health Office, who presided over the proceedings, and of the Federal Environment Agency and the Federal Biological Office, who also had a voice in them. These authorities were oriented strictly to procedural rules, but still called the hearing a 'gene-happening' that was 'too tedious and expensive'. They, too, therefore argued for formal restrictions.

Position 4 'Scientific-legal-political' thinking was the seed-bed for criticism of the scientific foundations of the decision for approval. Discussion of 'risk' and 'safety' and detailed scientific questions were the centre of attention. Procedural criticism, if it was raised at all, was rather moderate. To a certain extent, this was the viewpoint of the scientific experts in the ranks of the critics.

Position 5 This form of 'political' reasoning took two forms. On the one hand, the procedure was criticized in quasi-official manner as 'unfair' and 'unjust'; it was said to violate 'participatory rights because ethical, social, and political aspects may not be discussed'. On the other hand, one heard it whispered on the sly that the situation was not bad on the whole. 'After all, we have been able to mobilize a good many supporters in the region'. Among the persons of this persuasion, the legitimacy of the procedure was seen as relatively great in general, a view also manifested in calls to broaden the avenues for participation.

Position 6 In 'moral-ethical-expressive' reasoning, the dominant theme was 'disillusionment' as well as 'outrage about the farce', about 'bureaucratic tricks', and about 'legal dodges with which genuine grievances and concerns are covered up'. In the eyes of those with this attitude, the procedure clearly had little legitimacy and was able to generate little, if any, willingness to accept its outcome.[13]

This interpretation leads to the conclusion that the procedure was marked by numerous, often antagonistic attitudes toward procedural justice. It is difficult to see how the group value model could explain phenomena of this sort. These doubts arise primarily because the group value model, as shown above, applies the unit of the 'group' in a way that cannot easily apprehend such diverging attitudes. Note that this observation is not directed at empirical research, in which different attitudes are indeed observed. It bears instead on the theoretical reconstruction of those attitudes. It becomes a noticeable disadvantage that the group value model contains a notion of fairness as a 'shared concept', shared, that is, by society as a whole, thereby making it possible to derive legitimation from the individual's identification with the group.[14] But where are ideas about fairness to be taken from when obviously more than one group is involved? The theoretically engaging question at that point is how to understand a procedure's 'objective' justice under the conditions of a functionally differentiated society. The following section is an attempt to reconstruct 'objective' justice as a specific effect of integration, an outcome of procedures that take place in contexts where procedural justice is a 'contested concept'.

Theoretical Considerations of the Fairness and Structure of Procedures

The term 'contested concept' relates to an idea from political science literature (Gallie 1956; Connolly 1974). It means 'the diverse use of a partly shared concept', thereby suggesting a semantic contradiction. No one will reject the principle of procedural justice; every person will consider it worthy. Whether it exists in a specific case is debatable, however, because the shared use of the expression is based on clearly dissimilar premises. This contradiction in the use of the term 'procedural justice' cannot be resolved by distinguishing between a descriptive and a normative perspective; the contested concept typically links the two dimensions. It 'displays in our discourse over a normal range of cases a close connection between its criteria and its normative point' (Connolly 1974, 32, in reference to the word 'democracy'). This can be observed in the two cases cited above. The criteria of perspective-specific judgements on procedural justice are both normative and descriptive. As already shown, however, their respective normative rules of preference are taken from different mind sets. This relation to 'scientific', 'technical', 'economic', 'legal', or 'political' rationalities is discussed theoretically in the following passages and is called 'system reference'.

As indicated by the term 'system reference', this suggestion is theoretically embedded in recent systems theory,[15] in which procedures are seen as social systems and, hence, as communication systems. The focus of study is the function that fairness has in procedures. The hypothesis developed and explained below is that the function of procedural justice is to establish a balance between complexity and consistency in the procedure. This balance is necessary for a stable integration of diverging expectations relating to the procedure.

With systems theory providing the backdrop for these assumptions, procedural justice, like any other semantic concept, is to be viewed not as a reproduction of an 'ontological quality' (in this instance, of procedures) but as a social construct. In social constructivism as formulated in recent autopoietic systems theory, a social construct is understood as the cognitive schemata used by systems to observe themselves or other systems. To the extent that a procedure for resolving disputes functions as a social system (i.e., as a communication system), it can observe and describe itself by drawing on the schema of 'fair-unfair'. But other systems, and that may mean persons as much as groups or functional systems of society (e.g., law, the economy, and politics), can also observe a procedure and describe it with reference to the schemata specific to their respective system. Whether their observations and descriptions are fairness judgements, cost-benefit calculations, or other patterns of orientation depends solely on the rationality of the system that is observing (system reference). Modern, functionally diversified societies encompass more than one type of subsystem. Consequently, such a society has several divergent expectations of procedures for conflict resolution. In other words, modern societies are characterized by 'polycontextuality'.

These external observations become relevant for the procedure at the moment the observing systems are linked to the procedure in some way, as when they participate in it. At that point the different perspectives and rationalities are communicated in competing ideas of procedural fairness or its meaning. It is plain even from this kind of theoretical conception that the procedure can hardly be understood as an expression of the value that a group attaches to it. It seems instead to be an arena in which the views of different 'groups' meet and clash. From a theoretical perspective, a situation in which a procedure must deal with only *one* sort of procedural justice expectation is likely to be a special exception.

Typically, procedures are thus confronted with the task of integration. But for the legal system and all types of procedures derived from it, integration is a question of fairness. In explaining this point, I shall use the terms 'complexity' and 'consistency' to show how this integration is to be described as seen from inside the procedure as a social system.

For any system, the system-environment relation is a complexity differential (for more detail on this matter and the following ideas, see Luhmann 1984, 45–51). The environment is always more complex than the system. The system generates and establishes its identity, that is, the boundaries between it and its environment, through mechanisms that reduce complexity. One of the important insights of cybernetics is that complexity is reduced only if a system's own complexity is built up. This system complexity is created by restricting the possibilities of interlinkage between the elements of the system. In other words, it is structured complexity. The system must create the necessary complexity in relation to the environment in order to respond to the complexity of the environment and instill in it the willingness to accept what the system provides. A system's capacity to achieve the appropriate level of complexity is what Ashby (1956, 206) called requisite variety.[16] As shown above, for example, procedures are sometimes confronted with external expectations. Internal complexity must be built up in order to provide enough alternatives for the procedure to be able to address the external expectations. This is necessary to a certain degree in any case if the environment is to accept the outcomes of the procedure, that is, if the procedure is to be considered legitimate.

If complete requisite variety were to be achieved, there would be a need to create a systems structure that would correspond to the external expectations point for point. Internal consistency makes that impossible, however. Requisite variety would mean that the environment would, so to speak, be copied in toto within the system. It would mean, therefore, that the difference between the system and the environment would vanish. As seen from within the system, chaotic overcomplexity would be all there was to observe. That is why only a certain amount of variety is tolerable within a system. The structures must be such that they prevent too many inconsistencies. Not just any relation between the elements of the system is permitted. The theoretical term for this limitation on structural complexity is 'adequate complexity'. In describing itself, the legal system uses the concept of justice to specify its structural limitations as defined by adequate complexity (see Luhmann 1993 for a thorough treatment of this point).

Transferring this concept to the field of research on procedural justice, one can say that procedural justice is the term used in procedure-related communication to describe the standard for adequate complexity in dispute-resolution procedures as social systems. In all these cases, even when they are not intended as a direct part of the legal system, complexity is linked to issues of fairness in the same way as in law. That is because procedures of conflict resolution are designed to process or formulate normative expectations.

These highly abstract ideas are only the first step in a sociological definition of procedural justice. Let us now apply them to the observation of specific procedures. To do so, it is necessary to describe how procedures create structured complexity.

Two distinctions are used in the following passages. The first is between programmed and nonprogrammed decisions. Programmed decisions are those that apply exactly one defined programme; nonprogrammed decisions are based on more than one possible programme.[17] The second distinction is between substantive and procedural decisions. The different programmes—conditional ones of a substantive or procedural nature—constitute the structures of the social system's procedures.

The combination of programmed/unprogrammed and substantive/procedural decisions is used to formulate ideal-type descriptions of four kinds of dispute-resolution procedures featuring different grades of structural complexity. Aubert (1963) started from only two fundamental types of conflict, conflicts of interest and value conflicts. According to him, conflicts of interest result from scarcity and can, in principle, be resolved by negotiating compromises. Value conflicts are based on dissent about the normative status of an object. They are resolved through the application of legal norms.

However, restricting the law to value conflicts and deriving conflicts of interest only from scarcity does not do justice to the complexity of the phenomenon. The law does not remain confined to the treatment of value conflicts, nor does this distinction make it possible to describe mechanisms of alternative dispute resolution that sometimes originate in conflicts of interest but that often also apply legal norms. Moreover, contradictions between different interests and motives cannot always be inferred from a scarcity of resources. Nor does the distinction between value conflicts and conflicts of interest seem to account adequately for the fact that disputes can involve different time horizons. As Aubert (1963) states, conflicts of interest would be handled from the perspective of having an eye to the future; value conflicts with an eye to the past.

But this assertion is unconvincing. Value conflicts can have an explicit future dimension, as the problem of technology assessment itself shows. Sometimes the future of entire societies is said to depend on which value is given priority. The time horizon does not seem to be tied as much to the distinction between values and interests as to the one between programmed and nonprogrammed decisions. Combining these dimensions thus creates four case constellations with different types of procedures (see Table 4.1). (1) Examples of programmed procedures with programmed results are judicial and administrative proceedings with a procedural and a substantive programme (law). (2) Examples of programmed procedures with unprogrammed results can be procedures of parliamentary legislation or administrative planning decisions. They follow a procedural programme, which is likewise juristically elaborated, but they use several different viewpoints to arrive at a decision on the outcome. For that reason Luhmann calls such cases programming (i.e., norm-building) procedures. (3) The group of processes having a substantive, but no procedural, programme includes those

Table 4.1: Four Types of Procedures

Type of Decision	Substantive Decisions: Programme (Formal, binding substantive rules: application of norms)	Substantive Decisions: No Programme (No binding substantive rules: norm building)
Procedural Decisions: **Programme** (Formal, binding procedural rules)	1 substantive programme 1 procedural programme (adjudication, administrative regulation) (1)	2 or more possible substantive programmes 1 procedural programme (procedures of parliamentary legislation, administrative planning) (2)
Procedural Decisions: **No Programme** (No binding procedural rules)	1 substantive programme 2 or more possible procedural programmes (ADR, mediation, arbitration) (3)	2 or more possible substantive programmes 2 or more possible procedural programmes (policy dialogue, technology dialogue (TA), round tables etc.) (4)

forms of negotiation in which the type of result to be arrived at (e.g., a legally binding outcome) but not the specific approach is stipulated. Numerous forms of arbitration and mediation come to mind. (4) The types of procedures that are not programmed in either respect include those for norm-building, which differ from parliamentary rules of order by having no fixed procedures. Examples are roundtable discussions and dialogues pertaining to technology evaluation.

This matrix can now be applied to the empirical processes described above. From the theoretical analysis it is also possible to draw practical conclusions for designing procedures suited to a given system.

Applications of the Model

How can this analytical matrix help define the function of procedural justice in the integration of controversial normative expectations? Let us begin with type (4) procedures. The greater the number of different programmes there are within a procedure, the less structured the complexity of the entire system tends to be. With each programmatic aspect, the amount of unstructured complexity in the procedure grows, so to speak. Each of these systems may be quite flexible, since they are capable of responding to disparate demands. However, they are likely to wind up being relatively unstable because consistent decision-making becomes increasingly difficult as programmes proliferate.

Specifically, the message is that these types of procedures appear capable of dealing with an amazing variety of external demands but that they constantly run the risk of exceeding the limit of adequate complexity. They tend to become chaotic, unstable systems with a high level of structural inconsistency. Within the system, this is observed as procedural injustice. Simultaneously, however, such procedures necessarily lag behind requisite variety; they cannot really meet all external expectations.

In the case of the TA cited above, which was a type (4) procedure, it was shown that the diverging procedural justice expectations threatened from the outset to derail the proceedings, which, for their part, constantly tried to react with complexity reduction by seeking to unify the various programmatic expectations somewhat. Even before the proceedings ended, it had been forecast that the stability of the process could depend partly on the development of a unified, binding procedural programme (Bora 1993). Accordingly, the 'mistake' made by the TA could have been too much variety and too little structure.

It seems appropriate at this point to formulate the first practical consequence: Considering all that has been said above, it is not advisable to install a type (4) procedure in a highly complex environment from which numerous diverging expectations of the procedure arise. This type of procedure will always have trouble surviving under such conditions. If this diagnosis is correct, the solution would be procedural closure. Under the conditions just described, procedures ought to succeed better when the procedural programme is minimized, as with type (2) approaches.

Let us turn now to the opposite case—type (1) procedures. Each has exactly one procedural and one substantive programme. In this regard they are marked by a high degree of structural complexity.

Their only 'problem' is perhaps internal limitation, which imposes the fairness standard on them. Because their demands for consistency are relatively high, type (1) procedures cannot respond to every external event. For example, it would be an injustice if money or power (or love) was used as an argument in a legal procedure.

It seems somewhat plausible to classify the 'characteristic' case of procedural justice research into this category. Many of the relevant studies deal with procedures of comparatively great stability, such as judicial proceedings. It is immediately apparent that they do not always meet the personal expectations (e.g., moral aspects) that develop in interaction systems. Yet as social systems, these procedures remain stable for the most part because they have efficient selection mechanisms. Externally, however, they risk losing some of their acceptance and legitimation if they veer too far from personal ideas of fairness, as many studies on procedural justice have shown.

A second consequence of these considerations can therefore be formulated: If type (1) procedures lag behind external expectations, it might be appropriate to open them up.[18] In many instances it will be possible to install a type (3) procedure, something that has been documented many times in research on mediation and alternative dispute resolution.

This overview concludes with a word about 'hybrid types' of the sort encountered, for example, in the second case cited above. The trouble with the discussion in the hearing as mandated by section 18 GenTG can be described quite well if the proceedings are understood as an attempt to combine norm application and norm-building, that is, as a 'hybrid' consisting of type (1) and type (4) procedures. It can then be seen that the procedure was unable to create the necessary complexity in relation to its environment in the sphere of norm-building, here meaning especially the dispute over the intended risk concepts and visions of technology development. The legal programme reduced the complexity differential by building up structure in order to create predictable and consistent decisions. Because of the inherent limits of such structural inputs, the procedure was ill-suited to politically loaded debates about risk evaluation, with their practically unlimited store of complexity. The experiences with public participation in other environmentally relevant large projects can be interpreted the same way. If the law is to handle these types of risk communications in the judicial environment, the amount of requisite variety it requires is apt to exceed the adequate complexity that the system can tolerate.

The implications for civil hearings would thus be procedural differentiation. To differentiate procedures, one would have to test whether a distinction between norm application and norm-building could help reduce the widespread frustration and anger that these procedures seem to be provoking. In this regard, further research should examine whether it is advisable to simultaneously install different types of procedures for resolving the various legal and political questions and to combine their outcomes.

Concluding Comment

The preceding considerations have been an attempt to free the concept of procedural justice from the conceptual subjectivism and methodological collectivism in which it had become ensnared through the group value model. Concepts drawn from autopoietic systems theory make it possible to understand procedural justice as the degree of adequate complexity within a system, a dimension that serves the balance between demands for complexity and demands for consistency. It thus also promotes the integration of diverging external expectations. Conflict-resolution procedures develop different patterns of structural complexity, which can be subdivided roughly into four types. Each one facilitates a specific resolution of the problem of adequate complexity. Each therefore also results in specific problems and lends itself only to certain situations.

This concept has the advantage of being able to encompass theoretically all cases in which acceptance of the procedural outcome does not seem to be determined by considerations of fairness but, say, by utility. As suggested in the presentation of the preceding examples, cases of this kind are not rare. They stem from the rationality of social systems, as expressed, for example, in the strategic use of procedures when legal proprieties are employed politically by social movements and political parties (procedures as a power factor) or in economic life (procedures as a cost factor). This approach to understanding procedural justice is intended to eliminate the aforementioned inconsistencies in the group value model. The proposed approach is not subjectivist; it tries to avoid the quandary of having to straddle methodological individualism and collectivism. Moreover, the contributions of procedural justice research, especially that of the group value model, are preserved with the systems theory approach because their value can be localized within their respective analytical frameworks.

Notes

1 'On the whole, distribution of control appears to be the best predictor of fairness and therefore of the preference for procedures' (Thibaut and Walker 1975, 121).

2 In a study on the European Court of Justice, Gibson and Caldeira (1993) assume the opposite relation, writing that 'the data yield substantial support for the crucial hypothesis that diffuse support is important because it contributes to mass acceptance of unpopular judicial decisions' (26). See also Gibson (1991, 633).

3 Rational choice models hold that preferences for fair procedures may well not be rooted in short-term calculations of personal gain. Nonetheless, the long-term benefit that the egoistic actor can expect might explain the preference for fair procedures (Lind and Tyler 1988, 240).

4 The six procedural justice rules by Leventhal (1980) were an attempt to meet this prerequisite.

5 Lind and Tyler (1988); see the methodological suggestions in chapter 3 and the numerous empirical examples in which subjective judgement of distinct legal, political, and other procedures is used as a measure of procedural justice.

6 This is true not only of the 'repeat players', who routinely deal with conflict-resolution bodies. One can assume that every economically rational business organization—quite apart from considerations of justice—will first precisely analyse the risks involved before deciding whether to take legal action on a claim.

7 The project was directed by W. van den Daele (Berlin), A. Pühler (Bielefeld), and H. Sukopp (Berlin). The procedural organization and social science evaluation research was the responsibility of the WZB research area on 'standard-setting and the environment'. Further information on the design of the process can be found in van den Daele (1992, 1994).

8 The organizers can hardly be blamed for lack of funding. They allocated a considerable portion of the research budget to the environmental groups. Furthermore, all travel and overnight expenses were reimbursed.

9 One should also examine whether an increased frequency of such occurrences in following months suggested a nationwide trend among environmental groups to disengage themselves from grassroots participation.

10 The change in the law that required a written rather than an oral

procedure as of 1 January 1994 was due partly to the empirical problems described in the following passages (see also Bora 1994).

11 At least that is the consequence of the codification and formal rationality in positive law (see Weber 1972, 396).

12 Less drastically, it was stated that the fears of the objectors were not scientifically founded.

13 This viewpoint leans toward actionism conditioned by frustration. It could be roughly paraphrased by the slogan 'forget citizen participation, occupy the test fields'. The attempt was made to do precisely that a few weeks after the civil hearings. The action was unsuccessful and therefore probably exacerbated frustration.

14 In at least the second case described above, the group value model must refer to society at large as a 'group', for only society at large is represented by due process.

15 The following considerations rest essentially on Luhmann's theory of autopoietic systems. See Luhmann (1984, 1990) and Teubner (1988).

16 Requisite variety does not lead to the disappearance of the complexity differential between the environment and the system; it only enables the system to exist in its environment.

17 See Luhmann (1985, chapter 4, section 4). The distinction harks back to Herbert Simon. Programming in Luhmann's terminology means that there are rules for accepting a communication but not that the substantive or procedural decisions to be arrived at in due process have already been made. An important feature of all procedures is precisely the uncertainty surrounding the decision. This uncertainty is fundamental to procedural decisions as well. In those cases, it results from diverging expectations of the procedure and will be expressed as uncertainty about 'procedural justice' where the complexity of the overall system is at issue. By arriving at decisions, the procedure absorbs this procedurally related uncertainty.

18 The condition is important. Participants do not consider, say, the conventional lawsuit unfair in all cases (Lind et al. 1990).

References

Alexander, Jeffrey, Bernhard Giesen, Richard Münch, and Neil Smelser, eds. 1987. *The Micro-Macro Link*. Berkeley: University of California Press.

Ashby, W. Ross. 1956. *An Introduction to Cybernetics*. London: Chapman and Hall.

Aubert, Vilhelm. 1963. Competition and Dissensus: Two Types of Conflict and of Conflict Resolution. *Journal of Conflict Resolution* 7: 26–42.

Bora, Alfons. 1993. Gesellschaftliche Integration durch Verfahren—Zur Funktion von Verfahrensgerechtigkeit in der Technikfolgenabschätzung und -bewertung. *Zeitschrift für Rechtssoziologie* 14: 55–79.

———. 1994. Grenzen der Partizipation? Risikoentscheidungen und Öffentlichkeitsbeteiligung im Recht. *Zeitschrift für Rechtssoziologie* 15: 126–52.

Bora, Alfons, and Rainer Döbert. 1993. Konkurrierende Rationalitäten—Politischer und technisch-wissenschaftlicher Diskurs im Rahmen einer Technikfolgenabschätzung von gentechnisch erzeugter Herbizidresistenz in Kulturpflanzen. *Soziale Welt* 44: 75–97.

Connolly, William E. 1974. *The Terms of Political Discourse*. Lexington, Mass.: Heath and Company.

Daele, Wolfgang van den. 1992. The Research Program of the Research Area on 'Norm-Building and the Environment' (WZB dp FSII 92-301). Wissenschaftszentrum Berlin für Sozialforschung.

———. 1994. Technology Assessment as a Political Experiment (WZB discussion paper FSII 94-319). Wissenschaftszentrum Berlin für Sozialforschung.

Durkheim, Emile. 1958. *Professional Ethics and Civic Morals*. Translated by C. Brookfield. Glencoe, Ill.: Free Press.

Gallie, Walter B. 1956. Essentially Contested Concepts. In *Proceedings of the Aristotelian Society*, edited by the Aristotelian Society. New Series Vol. 56. Oxford: Blackwell.

Gibson, James L. 1991. Institutional Legitimacy, Procedural Justice, and Compliance with Supreme Court Decisions: A Question of Causality. *Law and Society Review* 25: 631–5.

Gibson, James L., and Gregory A. Caldeira. 1993. Compliance, Diffuse Support, and the European Court of Justice: An Analysis of the Legitimacy of a Transnational Legal Institution. Paper presented at the second Oñati workshop on procedural justice, 22 September, Oñati, Spain.

Leventhal, Gerald S. 1980. What Should Be Done With Equity Theory? In *Social Exchange: Advances in Theory and Research*, edited by K. J. Gergen, M. S. Greenberg, and H. R. Willis. New York: Plenum.

Lind E. Allan, Robert J. MacCoun, Patricia A. Ebener, William L. F. Felstiner, Deborah R. Hensler, Judith Resnik, and Tom R. Tyler. 1990. In the Eye of the Beholder: Tort Litigants' Evaluations of Their Experiences in the Civil Justice System. *Law and Society Review* 24: 953–96.

Lind, E. Allan, and Tom R. Tyler. 1988. *The Social Psychology of Procedural Justice*. London: Plenum.

Luhmann, Niklas. 1984. *Soziale Systeme. Grundriß einer allgemeinen Theorie*. Frankfurt am Main: Suhrkamp.

———. 1985. *A Sociological Theory of Law*. Edited by Martin Albrow. Translated by Elizabeth King and Martin Albrow. London: Routledge and Kegan Paul.

———. 1987. The Evolutionary Differentiation Between Society and Interaction. In *The Micro-Macro Link*, edited by J. Alexander, B. Giesen, R. Münch, and N. J. Smelser. Berkeley: University of California Press.

———. 1990. *Essays on Self-Reference*. New York: Columbia University Press.

———. 1993. *Das Recht der Gesellschaft*. Frankfurt am Main: Suhrkamp.

Teubner, Gunther, ed. 1988. *Autopoietic Law: A New Approach to Law and Society*. Berlin: de Gruyter.

Thibaut, John, and Laurens Walker. 1975. *Procedural Justice: A Psychological Analysis*. Hillsdale, N.J.: Lawrence Erlbaum.

Tyler, Tom R. 1990. *Why People Obey the Law*. New Haven: Yale University Press.

Weber, Max. 1972. *Wirtschaft und Gesellschaft*. 5th ed. Edited by Johannes Winckelmann. Tübingen: Mohr.

The Author

Alfons Bora. M.A. Born in 1957. Sociologist and lawyer. From 1983 to 1991, research fellow at the Max Planck Institute for Foreign and International Penal Law, criminology research unit, in Freiburg. Since 1991, researcher at the Wissenschaftszentrum Berlin für Sozialforschung (Science Centre Berlin, Wissenschaftszentrum Berlin), Department Normbildung und Umwelt (norm-building and environment). From 1986 to 1991, lecturer at the Institute for Sociology of the University of Freiburg/Breisgau. Since 1991, lecturer at the Free University of Berlin. Main fields of interest are sociological theory, the sociology of law, and methodology. With Karlhans Liebl, edited *Theoretische Perspektiven rechtssoziologischer und kriminologischer Forschung* (Frankfurt am Main: Campus, 1994).

Address: Wissenschaftszentrum Berlin für Sozialforschung, Reichpietschufer 50, D-10785 Berlin, Germany.

Abstract

The group value model by Lind and Tyler has had a major impact on procedural justice research. After critically examining the model, the author proposes that its underlying idea be reformulated at a more general level. The theory of autopoietic systems provides the background for an attempt to depict procedural justice as a mode for the self-description of social systems, a concept that the author relates to procedural structures that have been empirically shown to exist. Two cases from the field of genetic engineering are cited in this context.

5 The Function of Procedural Justice in Theories of Justice

AXEL TSCHENTSCHER

Introduction

Procedural theories of justice incorporate the concept of *procedural justice* as a constructive element (Kaufmann 1989). Normative theories of justice use the justice-defining function of procedural justice, which is only one of many diverse functions in the procedural justice concept. The main argument of this paper is that the applicability of the justice-defining function is very limited if no additional supportive arguments about the fairness, i.e., the quality of the procedure, are made.

This paper includes some general remarks about the terminology used (section I) and examines the role of procedural justice in theories of justice using two prominent examples of contract and discourse theories (section II). Finally, it considers deficiencies of contemporary theories of justice (section III).

Terminology

Definitions

Procedural justice is the correct application of a procedure that is likely to increase the chance of the outcome being just. In contrary, *substantive justice* is the (material) justice of the outcome itself no matter how it has been achieved. *Normative theories of justice* are theories about the kind of social arrangements that can be defended (Barry 1989, 3). These diverse concepts range from theories about the justice of single norms or institutions to theories about the world order.[1]

Procedural fairness, sometimes used synonymously with procedural justice, means correctly adhering to the formalities which define the procedure, including its interpretation (Barry 1965, 97,

100). Procedural fairness in this sense is the first element of fairness at large. The second element is background fairness, signifying the presence of all background circumstances which are required for proper application of the procedure (Barry 1990, 98). The third and most complicated element of fairness at large is the *fairness of the procedure itself*.[2]

A Tennis Game Illustration

This terminology can be illustrated with the example of a tennis game. Substantive justice is achieved if the better player wins. Procedural justice is the application of the rules of the game if that application contributes to declaring the better-playing participant the winner. Procedural fairness requires that both players abide by the rules and correctly call the points. Background fairness demands that all preconditions for a fair game be present, e.g., that each player uses his or her favourite racket. The fairness of the procedure itself requires, among other things, that the rules of the game provide for a change of sides. Without that provision, the better player might lose due to disadvantage of playing against the sun. These elements of fairness are interrelated. If, for instance, the rules were defined for the background circumstances of a perfectly symmetrical court with no wind or sunlight, a change-of-sides provision would be unnecessary for the fairness of the procedure itself. Therefore, procedural fairness requires the correct application of a fair procedure in the presence of all background circumstances. Procedural justice relies on procedural fairness because only procedures which are themselves fair and are applied fairly increase the chances of the outcome being just.

Forms of Procedural Justice

Rawls distinguishes four forms of procedural justice: perfect, imperfect, pure, and quasi-pure (Rawls 1971, 85–8, 201).

Perfect procedural justice

Perfect procedural justice is the application of a procedure that is sure to reach an adequate approximation to the just outcome.[3] The typical example is the division of a cake: the person who cuts gets the last piece. Taking equally sized pieces as the just outcome, the application of this procedure is sure to achieve an adequate approximation because self-interest will make the person do his or her best to cut equal portions. But even before the cake-slicing starts, we already know what the just outcome should and will be: equally sized pieces. Perfect procedural justice presupposes the existence of an external criterion, a principle of distributive justice, to judge the justice of the outcome (Rawls 1971, 85). Procedural justice is merely instrumental in reaching this externally justified outcome. Therefore, the function of perfect procedural justice is to actually achieve an adequate approximation to the just outcome (the realizing function).

Imperfect procedural justice

Imperfect procedural justice is the application of a procedure that is likely to reach an adequate approximation to the just outcome, but does not carry any guarantee to that effect. We can use the example of a criminal trial: the procedures applied in court are likely to lead to the conviction of the guilty—and only the guilty—defendant, but they do not guarantee that outcome. We can deduce from that definition that imperfect procedural justice has the function of increasing the chances of achieving an adequate approximation to the just outcome (the approximating function).

Pure procedural justice

Pure procedural justice is the application of a procedure that is sure to reach the just outcome because there is no independent criterion for the right result. Following Rawls, we can say that the background circumstances define the procedure.[4] Afterwards, the application of that procedure, i.e., pure procedural justice itself, defines the outcome as just. In a gambling situation, for example, the parties might choose a particular game (background circumstances) and play it adhering to its rules (application of the procedure), thereby determining a result that by definition is just, independent of the specific outcome. With pure procedural justice we have the great practical advantage of avoiding the definition of principles to meet the demands of justice (Rawls 1971, 87). It is sufficient to follow the procedure. According to its definition, pure procedural justice has the function of defining an outcome as just by defining the relevant procedures (the justice-defining function).

Quasi-pure procedural justice

Quasi-pure procedural justice is the application of a rule of choice in a situation of indeterminacy of justice, i.e., a situation where decisions in a given range are equally just (Rawls 1971, 201). Quasi-pure procedural justice has the function of defining the boundaries of discretion for the selection of one outcome within a range of equally just outcomes. The typical example is the procedure of legislation. Accordingly, Rawls uses quasi-pure procedural justice for the legislative stage of his four-stage sequence. A law that is adopted according to procedures of quasi-pure procedural justice is defined as prima facie just; i.e., just unless it can be shown that it is not in the range of equally just outcomes defined by the procedure (the discretion-defining function).

Functions of Procedural Justice

Procedural justice has a serving function inasmuch as it is seen as a means to achieve a specific outcome (Röhl 1993, 1). Regarding its serving function, procedural justice is merely instrumental, deriving justification from criteria outside of the procedure.[5] In its serving function, it is present in the forms of perfect and imperfect procedural justice: both presuppose an external criterion for the justice of the outcome. Serving, in the context of procedural justice, means either achieving or at least increasing the chances of achieving an adequate approximation to the just outcome.

The defining function of procedural justice is conceptually different from the serving function because it exclusively relies on the procedure and does not acknowledge any outside criterion as a measure for justice. Defining, in the context of procedural justice, means either defining a specific outcome as just or defining the boundaries of discretion for just outcomes.

Assigning forms of procedural justice to their respective functions will result in the scheme shown in Table 5.1.

Table 5.1: Types of Functions

Functions of Procedural Justice			
Serving Functions		*Defining Functions*	
Approximating *Function*: Imperfect PJ	Realizing *Function*: Perfect PJ	Discretion-Defining *Function*: Quasi-pure PJ	Justice-Defining *Function*: Pure PJ

Note: PJ = procedural justice.

The Functionality of Procedural Justice in Theories of Justice

Among the many different theories of justice, two will be selected to exemplify the functionality of procedural justice in their respective contexts. These two theories have a prototype status among normative procedural theories of justice: modern contractarianism is represented by Rawls's theory of justice (Rawls 1971) and discourse theory is represented by Habermas's concept in *Faktizität und Geltung* (Habermas 1992b).

Rawls's Theory of Justice

The theory

Rawls's theory of justice is well known and does not require more than a few descriptive sentences. The social arrangement that can be defended is a well-ordered society where (1) everyone accepts the same principles of justice and (2) the basic social institutions generally satisfy these principles (Rawls 1971, 4-5), making them part of the 'basic structure'.[6] The universally acceptable principles of justice are such that they could hypothetically be agreed to in an initial situation of fairness (original position).[7] To have a leading procedural principle comparable with Habermas's discourse principle, which I will describe later, we can use this formulation:

> 'Just' is a basic structure founded on principles of justice that everybody in an initial situation of fairness (original position) would agree to in the form of a social contract.

Fairness of the initial situation comprises equality, freedom, rationality, autonomy,[8] and mutual disinterestedness of the parties (Rawls 1971, 13, 14). To ensure these conditions, Rawls invents a procedure of thought, the veil of ignorance, insulating the hypothetical parties from their self-interest.[9] Behind the veil of ignorance, argues Rawls, the parties would choose two lexically ordered[10] principles of justice:

1. the principle of greatest equal liberty (equal basic rights and duties), with the list of basic liberties comprising political liberties (right to vote, eligibility for political office), liberty of conscience and thought, freedom of expression, right to property, and freedom of the person, particularly against arbitrary arrest and seizure (Rawls 1971, 61) and

2a. the principle of fair equality of opportunity; with
2b. the difference principle (social and economic inequalities resulting in benefits for the least advantaged; Rawls 1971, 14, 15, 54–117, 124).

To further support his picture of the original position, he also argues that these principles match our considered judgements[11] duly adjusted (reflective equilibrium)[12] and that they form an overlapping consensus of society.[13]

Defining the theory's principles as just

One function of procedural justice in Rawls's theory lies in finding the two principles of justice. Pure procedural justice means defining the outcome as just and thereby substituting any material assumptions about substantive justice of the outcome. In this case, the outcome is the selection of principles of justice. In Rawls's words: 'The idea of the original position is to set up a fair procedure so that any principles agreed to will be just. The aim is to use the notion of pure procedural justice as a basis of theory' (Rawls 1971, 136). The 'fair procedure' is the contractarian consideration behind the veil of ignorance: which principles would the parties choose as contractually binding if they had no knowledge about their individual position in society?

Defining the distributive outcome as just

Rawls also introduces pure procedural justice as a theoretical concept underlying the application of his second principle of justice (fair equality of opportunity; Rawls 1971, 84). Instead of focusing on the varying relative positions of individuals and how they participate in the distribution of goods, the principle of fair opportunity takes the procedural standpoint: the single process or status does not have to be 'in itself just',[14] and many complications of everyday life are discarded as irrelevant for social justice by the adoption of procedural principles (Rawls 1971, 88). As long as the principle of fair equality of opportunity is observed, every outcome is by definition just.

Defining the boundaries of discretion as just

Rawls uses quasi-pure procedural justice in the 'four-stage sequence' that he adopts to simplify the search for and application of the two principles of justice (Rawls 1971, 195-201). In this sequence, the parties of the original position first determine principles of justice (first stage) and then choose the outline of a just constitution (second stage). Afterwards, they move on to the legislative stage to explore different forms of just constitutions from a legislative perspective (third stage). Finally, in the application stage, the parties determine specific cases of civil disobedience and conscientious objection on the basis of a partial compliance theory.[15] The stages inherit the restrictions determined in prior stages while the veil of ignorance is partially lifted stage by stage. But the sequence is indeterminate in all but the first stage; only the principles of justice are sure to be chosen. With the indeterminacy of choice comes an indeterminacy of justice itself.[16] As mentioned above, indeterminacy of justice is the field for quasi-pure procedural justice: in this context, the notion of quasi-pure procedural justice acknowledges laws and policies as just if they lie within the allowed range.

Habermas's Discourse Theory

Before Rawls's approach is criticized, an example of a discourse theory of justice shall be described to broaden the picture. However, only a preliminary and limited account of Habermas's new approach can be presented here.

The theory

What Habermas calls a reconstruction of the law in his recent publication *Faktizität und Geltung* is not merely a theory of law, but encompasses a theory of justice. Indicators that Habermas's work is a theory of justice are his use of Rawls's first principle of justice to demonstrate the idea of equality and his search for a system of equal basic liberties using Rawls's concept of a disinterested participant (Habermas 1992a, 110, 151). Also, Habermas's reconstruction of the law shows that law has legitimizing power only as long as it works as a source of justice.[17] It is of special interest here that Habermas, after forming a new application of his discourse theory to the legal and social system, arrives at a concept he calls the 'procedural paradigm of the law' (*prozeduralistisches Rechtsparadigma*; Habermas 1992a, 10, 516–37). A paradigm of the law is how we look at the legal world, i.e., our 'legal world view', comprising preconceptions and intuitive background knowledge (Habermas 1992a, 468–71). Habermas contrasts his procedural paradigm with the liberal and the social paradigms[18] as well as with religious and metaphysical foundations (Habermas 1992a, 166). Under the procedural paradigm, the theory of justice in Habermas's work takes the form of a *procedural* theory of justice.

Habermas assumes that private autonomy in a more and more paternalistic society[19] requires participation in framing the principles of distribution; only with such participation is legal equality in a situation of factual inequality possible (Habermas 1992a, 516). The abstract procedure of democratic representation is no longer sufficient to provide such participation (Habermas 1992a, 516, 517). Under a procedural understanding of the law (*prozedurales Rechtsverständnis*), measures of evaluation become contingencies,[20] leaving institutionalized procedures of the democratic state and its devices of communication as the (only) generator of legitimate law.[21] The 'procedural conditions' (*Verfahrensbedingungen*) of the democratic process are to be protected best under the new paradigm (Habermas 1992a, 529, 530). Also, the procedural paradigm of the law results in procedural definitions of legal instruments, e.g., 'sovereignty'[22] or 'constitution'.[23]

Only a brief account of the line of arguments can be given here: The 'central problem' of modern democracies and the origin of Habermas's criticism is the instrumentalization of the law for political direction where the medium of 'law' cannot provide the necessary legitimization.[24] Legitimacy by legality is a paradox that cannot be solved unless specific laws, i.e., those protecting the political autonomy of citizens, are regarded as procedural generators of legitimacy (Habermas 1992a, 110, 111). Habermas connects this to the idea of self-government, where all addressees of law can at the same time see themselves as authors of law (Habermas 1992a, 153). To resolve the paradox, he transforms a discourse principle into the form of law, thereby creating the principle of democracy that itself is law-creating—a circular process for the creation of legitimate law,[25] or, in other words, a 'self-referential act to legally institutionalize political autonomy'.[26] The discourse principle says:

> All norms of action are valid that can be agreed upon in rational discourses by all persons potentially affected.

Using this principle for the medium of 'law', Habermas arrives at three basic rights of persons (greatest equal liberties, free association in membership, legal protection), finds a fourth in the necessity that (autonomous) people also act as authors of their laws (fair equal participation in the marketplace of ideas), and finally derives a fifth from those four (minimal social, technical, and ecological support; Habermas 1992a, 155–7). The procedural character becomes obvious by the fact that only the discourse principle, but no natural or moral right, is limiting the generation of new law (Habermas 1992a, 161, 162). Pragmatically formulated, legitimate law needs nothing but the mobilization of the communicative powers of a people.[27]

Defining democratic legislation as just

Generally speaking, Habermas's theory acknowledges every outcome of the law-making and law-applying processes as just if the processes are an expression of public autonomy. Basic rights are to be understood as procedural, not teleological, rights, including the discourse principle as the constitutive element. Where Rawls frames the outline of an original position for the social contract, Habermas uses the ideal situation of rational discourse as a measure for justice. Both theories, however, are similar in relying on the justice-defining function of their procedures: the outcome is just no matter what (in substance) the outcome may be.

Defining the boundaries of discretion as just

At two different points, Habermas concedes that the ideal conditions of rational discourse are not always present (if present at all) in real life situations.[28] In the first case (bargaining), the explicit purpose, to force or induce the opponent no matter how good his or her arguments are, will preclude the noncoercive consensus that is the goal of discourses (Habermas 1992a, 205). The discourse principle is supposed to work indirectly in these bargaining cases, as a discourse about procedures to regulate the bargain under a regime of fair procedural rules (Habermas 1992a, 205). In this context, Habermas uses the functionality of quasi-pure procedural justice, i.e., defining the boundaries of discretion for what kind of bargaining outcome can still be called 'just': only if a rational discourse about the procedures ensures fair equality of participation will the outcome be prima facie just (Habermas 1992a, 205, 206). In the second case (legal procedures), Habermas explicitly relies on Rawls's concept of quasi-pure procedural justice.[29] In his opinion, legal procedures incorporate the ideal conditions of communicative acts under rational discourse at least to an extent that warrants prima facie justice of the outcome, i.e., justice notwithstanding fallibility in cases of procedural failure (Habermas 1992a, 219, 220).

Criticism of the Functionality of Procedural Justice in Theories of Justice

In their attempt to avoid substantive assumptions—religious, metaphysical, or teleological considerations—about the justice of the outcome, theories of justice utilize the concept of procedural justice but do so in a very limited way: only the defining function of procedural justice contributes to their constructive line of arguments. Procedural justice in its defining function rather than its serving function means that—given the proper application of a fair procedure, i.e., fairness—any outcome is just by definition because no outside criterion is accepted.

Some problems derive from this limited use of procedural justice functionality in theories of justice: First, relying on the justice-defining function includes the assumption that no outside criterion for substantive justice is available. If this antimetaphysical assumption proved to be wrong, the defining function of procedural justice would not apply. Instead, the serving function of procedural justice would be the appropriate element to rely on in theories of justice. One does not have to promote a religious state to arrive at an alternative, i.e., an 'anti-procedural' conception of justice. It would be sufficient to assume that to some extent, justice is just a matter of intuition: we know what is just or unjust, whether or not we can find a good explanation for our judgement. Such an intuitive conception of justice would still allow for the serving function of procedural justice, i.e., we could still rely on procedures to arrive at results we intuitively approve of. But it would rule out any defining function of procedural justice: an outcome could never be just by definition, but only if the outside criterion of our intuitive assent was satisfied.

Second, relying on the justice-defining function requires that the three elements of fairness be present, the proper application of the procedure (procedural fairness), the presence of necessary circumstances of application (background justice), and the fairness of the procedure itself. Therefore, saying that a procedure defines the outcome as just does not release a theory from the obligation to prove the presence of all elements of fairness. If this second step of the argument is missing or unpersuasive, the added value of the justice-defining function becomes questionable.

Regarding the argument for the presence of all elements of fairness, procedural theories of justice often are incomplete or even unpersuasive. In the case of Rawls's theory of justice, for example, the application of his veil of ignorance procedure might be formally incorrect (no procedural fairness) because by using the maximin principle,[30] he includes a substantive assumption about the risk-avoiding nature of human decision-making that might be wrong. Rawls has to be asked this: is it really true that persons in the original position would decide in favour of a strategy that maximizes the minimum standard for individuals in a society? Why should they not, at least in some areas, be more risk-taking instead of risk-avoiding? Also, Rawls's procedure might not be fair in itself (third element of fairness) when it deprives those in the original position of their knowledge about individual capacities. If a person is not allowed to know what his or her natural gifts will be, the result of the deliberation will always be one that deprives that person of any advantages that normally come with natural gifts. Rawls's theory thereby features a socialization of natural abilities which—strong measure that it is—needs more than the argumentative support offered by him. Discourse theories, to give an example of the lack of background fairness, often fail to prove that the necessary circumstances of noncoercive and equally empowered participation[31] are present in the discourse. That might not be a problem for the hypothetical discourse, i.e., the discourse used as a model of rational thought, but it is for any form of practical discourse in parliaments or courts, politics or economics. There, the assumptions of noncoercion and equal participation might prove unrealistic and background fairness becomes an idealistic model not to be found in practice.

Conclusion

Theories of justice, insofar as they include procedural justice as a constructive element, rely on its justice-defining function. This use of procedural justice is fairly limited compared with the broad range of functions available. Little or no added value is gained by the justice-defining function if additional arguments about the three elements of fairness are missing or unpersuasive. In this second part of the argumentation, theories of justice are often deficient. This leads to an important point of criticism because, without adequate arguments for procedural fairness, the use of the justice-defining function of procedural justice in theories of justice is not much more than a formalized expression of the theorist's assumption that outside criteria of substantive justice are unavailable (the antimetaphysical assumption).

Notes

1 But see Rawls 1992, 293, 296 (describing the scope of his theory as moral conception for political, social, and economic institutions).

2 *Cf.* Bora 1993, 55, 63 (describing fairness as a principle of procedure that is achieved by observing and varying the internal structures of procedure).

3 The 'adequate approximation' is not part of Rawls's definition. *Cf.* Rawls 1971, 85 (stating that perfect procedural justice requires a procedure that is sure to reach the desired outcome). Rawls's definition, however, would not allow for cases like the cake division to be counted among the instances of perfect procedural justice: no hand can cut 'equal' pieces. The slightly different definition used here does not lead to any differences in functionality.

4 See Rawls (1971, 86), '[T]here is a correct or fair procedure such that the outcome is likewise correct or fair, whatever it is . . . the background circumstances define a fair procedure'.

5 Röhl 1993, 6 (relating the serving function to 'external' procedural justice).

6 See Rawls (1971, 9), 'A complete conception defining principles for all the virtues of the basic structure, together with their respective weights when they conflict, is more than a conception of justice; it is a social ideal. The principles of justice are but a part, although perhaps the most important part, of such a conception'.

7 See Rawls (1971, 12), explaining the propriety of the term 'justice as fairness'. Rawls uses the term 'original position' for his version of the initial situation that is the basis for contractarian models.

8 The requirement that parties act autonomously when choosing the principles of justice, that is, according to their nature as free and equal rational beings, is the element (apart from universality) that Rawls connects to Kantianism. See Rawls 1971, 251–7, 252.

9 See Rawls 1971, 136–42, 'They do not know how the various alternatives will affect their own particular case and they are obliged to evaluate principles solely on the basis of general considerations' (136–7).

10 Rawls calls the lexical order of the two principles 'priority of liberty'. See Rawls (1971, 244), 'By priority of liberty I mean the precedence of the principle of equal liberty over the second principle of justice'.

11 Rawls defines these judgements with a connection to the sense of

justice: 'Considered judgments are simply those rendered under conditions favorable to the exercise of the sense of justice, and therefore in circumstances where the more common excuses and explanations for making a mistake do not obtain. . . . And once we regard the sense of justice as a mental capacity, as involving the exercise of thought, the relevant judgments are those given under conditions favorable for deliberation and judgment in general' (1971, 47–8).

12 See Rawls (1971, 20), 'I assume that eventually we shall find a description of the initial situation that both expresses reasonable conditions and yields principles which match our considered judgments duly pruned and adjusted. This state of affairs I refer to as reflective equilibrium'.

13 See Rawls (1992, 293, 306–32), arguing why the political conception of justice is more than a *modus vivendi*.

14 This is the formulation Rawls uses to distinguish between procedurally defined justice and substantially determined justice of the outcome (Rawls 1971, 87–8).

15 Rawls locates the theory of political duty and obligation that he calls 'partial compliance theory' in the first stage (i.e., behind the veil of ignorance), whereas specific cases of citizens following rules are to be decided in the fourth stage (Rawls 1971, 199–200, 246–7, 263–91).

16 See Rawls (1971, 201), '[I]t is not always clear which of several constitutions, or economic and social arrangements, would be chosen. But when this is so, justice is to that extent likewise indeterminate'.

17 See Habermas (1992a, 180), 'But this reconstruction also shows that the law retains its power only as long as it functions as a resource of justice' (my translation).

18 See Habermas (1992a, 528), stating that the liberal and social paradigms are too concrete compared with the procedural paradigm of the law.

19 He describes as paternalistic the power of the laws over politically heteronomous subjects. See Habermas 1992a, 154.

20 See Habermas 1992a, 518, 534, stating that there is no alternative to postmetaphysical thought.

21 See Habermas 1992a, 527, 'The discourse theory of the law assumes that, on the one hand, the democratic *Rechtsstaat* is an

institutionalization of procedures and communicative prerequisites for the formation through discourse of opinions and political goals which works through legitimate law (thereby guaranteeing private autonomy), and that, on the other hand, this institutionalization facilitates (acting on political autonomy and) legitimate law-making' (my translation).

22 See Habermas 1992b. Sovereignty of a people in the perspective of discourse means political power derives from the communicative power of the citizens. Also see Habermas 1992a, 209.

23 A society is constitutional if it confronts itself using adequate forms and procedurally guided processes of assimilation, resistance, and self-correction. See Habermas 1992a, 536 (with reference to *Preuß*).

24 *Cf.* Habermas 1992a, 528.

25 See Habermas 1992a, 154, 155.

26 See Habermas 1992a, 166.

27 *Cf.* Habermas 1992a, 182.

28 See Habermas 1992a, 204, 205, regarding bargaining situations; Habermas 1992a, 220, regarding legal procedures.

29 See Habermas 1992a, 220.

30 See Rawls 1971, 152, for the maximin rule for choice under uncertainty.

31 *Cf.* Alexy 1991 (361, 362), for a table of rules and forms of rational discourses, including the rule 2.3 that no pressure against equal participation is allowed.

References

Alexy, Robert. 1991. Theorie der justischen Argumentation. Die Theorie des rationalen Diskurses als Theorie der juristischen Begründung. 2d ed., Frankfurt am Main: Suhrkamp.

Barry, Brian. 1989. *Theories of Justice. A Treatise on Social Justice.* Vol. 1. Berkeley: University of California Press.

———. 1990. Reprint. *Political Argument.* With a new introduction. Berkeley: University of California Press. Original edition, Berkeley: University of California Press, 1965.

Bora, Alfons. 1993. Gesellschaftliche Integration durch Verfahren — Zur Funktion von Verfahrensgerechtigkeit in der Technikfolgenabschätzung und -bewertung. *Zeitschrift für Rechtssoziologie* 14: 55–79.

Habermas, Jürgen. 1992a. *Faktizität und Geltung*. Frankfurt am Main: Suhrkamp.

———. 1992b. Volkssouveränität als Verfahren. In *Faktizität und Geltung*, (Frankfurt am Main: Suhrkamp). Originally published in Forum für Philosophie Bad Homburg (ed.), *Die Ideen von 1789*, (Frankfurt am Main: Suhrkamp, 1989).

Kaufmann, Arthur. 1989. *Prozedurale Theorien der Gerechtigkeit*. München: Beck.

Rawls, John. 1971. *A Theory of Justice*. Cambridge: Harvard University Press.

———. 1992. Der Gedanke eines übergreifenden Konsenses. In *Die Idee des politischen Liberalismus*, edited by Wilfried Hinsch, translated by Michael Anderheiden and Wilfried Hinsch. Frankfurt am Main: Suhrkamp.

Röhl, Klaus F. 1993. Verfahrensgerechtigkeit. Einführung in den Themenbereich und Überblick. *Zeitschrift für Rechtssoziologie* 14: 1–34.

The Author

Axel Tschentscher. LL.M., teaching and research assistant at the Bayerische Julius-Maximilians-Universität Würzburg. Studied law, journalism, and philosophy at the University of Hamburg, Cornell University, and the University of Kiel (Germany). Current focus on legal philosophy, international constitutional law, and public administrative law.

Address: Universität Würzburg, Juristische Fakultät, Institut für Rechtsphilosophie, Domerschulstraße, 97070 Würzburg, Germany.

Abstract

This paper asserts that contemporary normative theories of justice use the justice-defining function of procedural justice. The justice-defining function can be distinguished from other functions within the broader procedural justice concept. The article exemplifies the use of the justice-defining function by reference to the theories of justice of Rawls and Habermas. The main argument is that relying on the justice-defining function is persuasive only insofar as additional arguments about the three elements of fairness are presented. In this respect, theories of justice tend to be deficient.

6 Procedural Justice and Alternative Dispute Resolution

NEIL VIDMAR

Over two decades of empirical social psychology research on procedural justice have consistently demonstrated that people involved in civil legal disputes, in major and minor criminal disputes, and in conflicts arising in organizational and military settings are keenly attuned to the procedures by which the conflict is resolved (Lind and Tyler 1988; Thibaut and Walker 1975; Tyler 1990). The perceived fairness of the procedural processes contributes to overall feelings of fairness and legitimacy, independently of the resolution outcomes themselves. Indeed, sometimes procedural fairness is more important than outcome, particularly among persons who, judged from an objective standard, have lost the dispute.

For approximately those same two decades the American legal system has been experiencing a revolution in thinking regarding the procedures by which disputes, particularly civil disputes, are resolved. Scholars and practitioners of alternative dispute resolution (ADR) have urged movement away from traditional adversarial adjudication in favour of a wide array of alternative procedures, especially those that involve third-party-assisted bilateral settlement, such as mediation, judicial settlement conferences, early neutral evaluation, or summary jury trials (Menkel-Meadow 1984, 1991). Sometimes litigants adopt these procedures on a voluntary basis, but, increasingly, courts and legislatures have made them nonvoluntary. Thus, litigants find themselves assigned to settlement conferences, summary jury trials, or mandatory mediation for divorce, child custody, contract, personal injury, and a variety of other legal disputes (Menkel-Meadow 1991).

This trend in favour of ADR, and the theory behind it, provide a useful vehicle for exploring broader ideas derived from the body of social psychological research on procedural justice. Although my focus is on dispute resolution in the American legal context, I believe that many of the basic insights have implications for dispute resolution in European countries as well.

Does Settlement Provide Better Justice Than Judgement?

While we must recognize that some of the enthusiasm of judges and other court officials for ADR is based on the belief that it will help reduce their overloaded trial dockets, (Vidmar and Rice 1991) for many of the intellectual architects and practitioners of the ADR movement adjudication is actually viewed as inappropriate for resolving many legal disputes. North American adjudication has a number of characteristics which are purported to distinguish it from bilateral settlement forums: it is rule-based, adversarial, blame-fixing, coercive, public, formal, and restricted in the types of solutions that can be imposed, and disputants have no control over the final decision about how the conflict will be resolved. As a consequence of these characteristics, adjudication is said to polarize attitudes, prevent the creation of resolutions sensitive to the particular needs of disputants, cause them to feel a loss of control over the conflict, and foster frustration in both losers and winners (Menkel-Meadow 1984, 1991; Lind et al. 1990). Arbitration, another form of procedure which puts resolution power into the hands of a third party, is seen as less troublesome than adjudication since the parties may have the option of jointly choosing the arbiter; and it is less formal, and more flexible. Nevertheless, arbitration is also adversarial, tends to declare winners and losers, and removes the disputants from fashioning the final resolution to their conflict.

In contrast bilateral settlement, assisted by a mediator, is viewed by ADR proponents as a preferred, more ideal model of dispute resolution (Menkel-Meadow 1984). Proponents argue that mediation is not bound by formal rules, is conciliatory rather than adversarial, is focused on compromise rather than blame, is noncoercive, private, informal, flexible in its ability to generate solutions, and permits the disputants themselves to jointly fashion a resolution that is tailored to their unique needs and situation. As a consequence, the proponents argue that disputants have greater feelings of control and fairness, perceive the procedures and solutions to have greater legitimacy, and are more likely to comply with the terms of the conflict resolution decision than when their conflict is resolved by adjudication (Kressel and Pruitt 1989; McEwen and Maiman 1984, 1986).

Empirical data from field studies have been interpreted as supporting the view that bilateral settlements assisted by a third party are better than adjudication, or arbitration, (Kressel and Pruitt 1989a; McEwen and Maiman 1984) but in fact the studies are confounded by selection effects: different cases are selected for settlement forums than for adjudication; cases settled through these forums are different from those not settled (Vidmar 1984, 1987). What is equally important, both data and theory from procedural justice research suggest that the bilateral settlement-is-superior hypothesis is subject to severe restrictions and in many instances may simply be wrong.

Consider some findings that seem to contradict the mediation hypothesis. A study by Lind et al. (1990) compared the reactions of litigants in three state courts whose cases were resolved by trial, by court-annexed arbitration, by judicial settlement conferences, or by bilateral settlement. Contrary to the conventional wisdom that it is an aversive experience, trial was viewed as more satisfactory than bilateral settlement. Arbitration was also seen as more satisfactory than bilateral settlement. Judicial settlement conferences were seen as less satisfactory than settlements. In a different study involving cases in federal courts, Lind found arbitration to be more satisfactory than bilateral settlement (Lind 1990). In my study of a Canadian small claims court, I found no consistent relationship between litigant satisfaction and whether the case was resolved by mediation or adjudication, but I was able to document some very unhappy feelings among litigants whose cases were 'settled' by a mediator (Vidmar 1984, 1987). Laboratory experiments by Thibaut and Walker, in their seminal work on procedural justice, also found preferences for the authoritative procedures of adjudication and arbitration over mediation and negotiation (Thibaut and Walker 1975). Thibaut and Walker's basic findings have been replicated in subsequent studies involving American and European subjects (Lind and Tyler 1988).

The field studies described above are subject to selection confounds similar to studies purporting to support the advantages of bilateral settlements and thus we must interpret them cautiously. However, they do serve to raise questions about the functioning of the various forums, and about when and why people engaged in conflict might prefer procedures in which a third party authoritatively decides the resolution for them.

Coercive Elements in Bilateral Settlements

While the theory of proponents of bilateral settlement is that the parties reach a mutually acceptable solution to their conflict, studies of the actual process show that this is frequently not the case. Erlanger, Chambliss, and Melli (1987) studied 25 informally settled divorce cases and found that the process was often contentious, adversarial, nonflexible, and beyond the perceived control of one or both parties. In my small claims court study in Canada, the mediator often declared one party right and the other wrong and invoked coercive pressures to achieve a settlement (Vidmar 1985; see also Kressel and Pruitt 1989a). Starr and Yngvesson found similar winner-loser patterns in mediated outcomes in an African culture touted for its conciliatory dispute resolution processes (1975). One implication of these research findings is that, in a dispute, normative standards may clearly show one party in the right and the other in the wrong (Vidmar 1984, 1985). Another is that just because a procedure is labelled mediation, (or bilateral settlement) on the basis of its formal structure, it does not necessarily follow that the actual process will be conciliatory, based on compromise, free of reference to formal rules, or allow the parties genuine control over the final resolution.

The problem of coerciveness is exacerbated when courts require mediation, settlement conferences, or other ADR procedures. The parties not only do not enter the negotiations voluntarily, they may have little control over how the process itself is carried out and may, additionally, perceive that they do not have the freedom to reject a settlement even if legally they have the right to do so (Menkel-Meadow 1984, 1991; Vidmar and Rice 1991).

One particularly troublesome area lies in the use of mediation in cases involving domestic violence. The mediation of such disputes has become widespread in the United States and Canada in what are frequently called 'domestic issues' cases; that is, cases involving disputes over such things as divorce, child custody, and divisions of property, as well as ones where the issue is spousal violence involving the criminal law (Fischer, Vidmar, and Ellis 1993). While two of the reasons for moving these cases out of the courts are that courts have not done a very good job with them and that they create administrative problems for the courts, a third reason—the one most frequently cited—is the belief that mediation is superior to adjudication. In short, mediation has been marketed to courts and policy-makers on the grounds that it is better, fairer, and cheaper. It is said to transform and empower the parties.

Along with a number of other authors, Fischer, Ellis, and I (1993) have taken strong issue with this view when it involves issues of domestic violence—and many cases of child custody, divorce, and property division involve one party who is a victim of spousal abuse. Both in ideology and practice the tenets of mediation are usually incompatible with the reality of spousal abuse. In a lengthy paper we have analysed the unsuitability of mediation. I will summarize just a few of the ideas that we confront. Mediation sees abuse arising out of conflict but the empirical evidence indicates conflict is only the pretext for abuse; mediation focuses on future behaviour but ignoring past behaviour denies victims' experiences of violence; mediation assumes that each party participates equally in the search for a mutual agreement but in fact an abused spouse cannot participate equally; mediation avoids blame and findings of fact but the avoidance of abuse issues perpetuates that status quo of victim responsibility and abuser domination; mediation ideologists assert that the novelty of a written agreement detailing the rules of the relationship will help end violence but we show that the development of explicit rules may justify further abuse if the abuser perceives that the rules are violated. Thus, as a general rule mediation is highly unsuitable for a substantial number of cases that are classified as 'domestic issues' cases. This raises serious issues about procedural and substantive fairness when parties are pressured into mediation.

Disputants' Desire for Control

The bilateral settlement/mediation theory of ADR proponents is predicated on the assumption that disputants usually want to fashion their own resolution to the conflict. Thibaut and Walker's (1975) research led the way in showing that this assumption was not necessarily valid. Those authors conceptualized dispute resolution as involving two stages: a process stage wherein the evidence and arguments are presented, and a decision stage wherein a resolution to the dispute is reached. Their research showed that, particularly when conflict was high, disputants wanted control over the process stage but they often preferred to relinquish control over the decision stage to a neutral third party. Disputants felt that only an authoritative decision would put the conflict to an end. They did desire personal control over the process stage in order to ensure that their position was fully explained. A study by Sheppard (1985), however, showed that a procedure that allowed the third party to interfere in the process stage by asking questions or seeking clarification of evidence or arguments was judged as even more fair than standard authoritative procedures. Thus, these various data do not support the bilateral settlement/mediation theory's assumption that disputants are always desirous of controlling the total resolution process: frequently they prefer to relinquish outcome control and will, perhaps, even view infringements on aspects of the process stage positively.

The Nature of the Conflict

In a simulation experiment conducted by Houlden, Latour, Walker, and Thibaut, some prospective litigants had a claim based on equity considerations while others had a claim based on legal rights (Houlden et al. 1978). The former preferred a resolution procedure with low third-party decision control, but the latter preferred high third-party control. Many disputes involve claims of rights and the parties themselves perceive the appropriate resolution to be in win-lose terms rather than compromise. The win-lose nature of the conflict may involve explicitly stated, or tangible, issues, e.g., 'she owes me money and I want all of it' (Aubert 1963, 1967; Vidmar 1985; Vidmar and Rice 1991). Alternatively, the conflict may involve intangibles. As Lind et al. (1990, 981) observe: 'Litigants may well view their case not as a dispute about outcomes but as a clash between their own view of reality and an opposing, apparently erroneous and sometimes malicious view of reality' (Lind et al. 1990; Menkel-Meadow and Silbey 1984; O'Barr and Conley 1985, 1988; Sarat and Felstiner 1986). In such cases vindication is the goal of the disputants and their value-expressive needs may be better met by a 'judgement' rather than settlement. In addition to vindication, preferences for a third-party decision-maker tend to occur when the parties seek to set a precedent; when they have non-correspondent interests; when they have unequal power; when the relationship is not ongoing; and when bilateral settlement attempts have failed (Lind and Tyler 1988).

Expectations About Legal Procedures

Sarat and Felstiner (1986) observed private attorney-client interactions in divorce lawyers' offices. One of the most striking findings of their research was the discrepancy between the client's initial expectations that legal processes operate in the formal, impartial way that they are taught in school or portrayed in mass media and the lawyer's counselling that their expectations did not comport with legal reality: legal decision-making is often highly discretionary, subject to the interpretations of individual judges, and a formal trial is costly in time and money. Clients wanted a forum and an authority figure to whom they could explain their side of the dispute. Much dissatisfaction was expressed by clients when their expectations and the 'reality' of the legal world came face to face. The findings of Lind et al. (1990) and Lind (1990) that trial and arbitration were perceived as more fair than settlement may reflect similar expectations of litigants. Most litigants probably expected that their conflict would be subject to the ritual of a formal hearing and those whose cases were resolved in a formal hearing had those expectations met while those whose cases were resolved by settlement did not.

Additionally, it should be noted that the jury trial holds a special place in the legal socialization of American citizens, who are taught from childhood that under the U.S. Constitution they have a right to have important civil and criminal matters tried before a group of lay persons in a jury trial. Consequently, this type of resolution forum is held in high esteem (Hans 1993; Hans and Vidmar 1986; Vidmar and Rice 1991). For example. MacCoun and Tyler (1988) conducted a survey that showed a sample of American citizens had a strong preference for jury trial over trial by judge alone. They also found that twelve-person juries operating under decision rules requiring unanimity—the traditional form of jury trial—were viewed as procedurally more fair than six-person juries or juries making decisions under majority rule—at least when the consequences of a guilty verdict were serious. Thus, for Americans jury trial may provide a unique component to expectations of what constitutes procedural justice.

In short, the formality and ritual of adjudication, accompanied by a decision rendered by a judge or jury, may make it preferable to bilateral settlement in a variety of contexts and conditions.

Cross-Cultural and Dispositional Preferences

It has been theorized that disputants from some Asian cultures prefer mediation over adjudication or arbitration; and social psychological research tends to bear this out (Benjamin 1975; Hamilton and Sanders 1992; Leung and Lind 1986). However, other research suggests that, even in these cultures, when the parties do not have strong social ties and when a perceived injury is severe, they will opt for adjudication (Upham 1976).

Little research has been undertaken on individual differences in preferences for form of resolution forum, but Schuller and I (Vidmar and Schuller 1987) have documented dispositional tendencies in preferences for types of conflict resolution. Even when the type of conflict was the same, some people demonstrated a predictable preference for a conciliatory forum while others preferred one that was openly adversarial.

The above findings and theorizing should not be interpreted as grounds to reject bilateral settlements of legal disputes generally. Many disputants appear very satisfied with mediation and other types of bilateral settlement (Kressel and Pruitt 1989a). Furthermore, the Lind et al. (1990) study, in particular, may constitute an unfair test of bilateral settlement. Typically, only the lawyers attend judicial settlement conferences, and many privately negotiated legal settlements are arranged by the lawyers and then conveyed to their clients for approval. If the clients had been allowed to participate more actively in the negotiation process, had had a chance to meet their opponent in a controlled setting, and had been able to personally voice their side of the dispute, the judgements of procedural fairness may have been substantially higher. Thus, the differences in perceived fairness and satisfaction may have been due to lack of opportunity to participate in settlements rather than to characteristics of bilateral settlement per se.

Nevertheless, the various studies that I have cited raise serious questions about a predominant ADR ideology favouring bilateral settlement. They also show the clear nexus between issues raised in theoretical work on procedural justice and applied social policies. And they raise questions for which we do not, at present, have clear answers.

Some Research Questions About Procedural Justice and Dispute Resolution

The Dynamics of Judgements About Fair Procedures

Procedural justice is not consistently related to any one type of resolution forum or any one type of dispute, as some of the studies referenced above illustrate (Lind and Tyler 1988; Tyler 1990). A common denominator in judgements of procedural fairness appears to be the extent to which the procedure fosters a perception that the dispute is treated with dignity, neutrality, and importance. One component of dignity is the opportunity for disputants to 'give voice' to their side of the story. While some theorists have argued that the desire to have process control is to increase the chances of an accurate or favourable outcome, a central contribution of the research summarized in Lind and Tyler's (1988) book is to demonstrate that process control has value-expressive functions that go beyond instrumental motives. While some of the value-expression may relate to the particular dispute itself, emerging research strongly suggests that it also helps to affirm the disputants' role in the broader groups and social system of which they are members (Lind and Tyler 1988; Tyler 1990). We have much more to learn about the antecedent socialization and about the case-specific factors that give rise to judgements of procedural justice in specific contexts.

Adversarial Versus Inquisitorial Procedures

We also need to learn more about the comparative effects of formal legal procedures and how these interact with culturally derived expectations. In one study, Lind et al. (1978; see also Thibaut and Walker 1975; Lind and Tyler 1988) found that, similar to American students, French and German students preferred adversarial over inquisitional legal procedures despite the fact that the French and German students came from legal cultures that utilize the inquisitorial model. These findings have often been interpreted as indicating that an adversarial system is superior to an inquisitorial system in producing perceptions of procedural justice and in many ways the findings are consistent with other findings about the dynamics of procedural justice (Thibaut and Walker 1975; Tyler 1990). However, the Lind et al. study portrayed the inquisitorial system as one in which the disputants had no control over the process stage of dispute resolution, when in fact the actual operation of the inquisitorial system does allow for a substantial degree of litigant participation (though not to the degree allowed in an adversarial system). The Sheppard study (1985), discussed earlier leads me to predict that a replication of the Lind et al. study with a more accurate portrayal of an inquisitorial system might produce results showing the inquisitorial system to produce a greater level of procedural justice than in the original study. Of course, this is a hypothesis that only empirical research can verify.

I have also made reference to Americans' attachment to the jury system and how it plays an important role in their perceptions of procedural justice and the legitimacy of legal decisions. Germans, of course, do not utilize a jury system, but in Austria juries are used for important criminal issues. A comparative study of German and Austrian perceptions of legal decisions made with or without the aid of juries might help us to test some important theoretical hypotheses about the effect of legal culture on perceptions of procedural justice. Perhaps such a study should also compare a sample of Americans with samples of persons from one of the countries that derives its legal traditions from British common law but which no longer employs the jury system.

Finally, in the comparative legal procedure context, mention should be made regarding the relative accuracy of fact-finding between inquisitorial and adversarial systems. Leventhal (1976) has theorized that accuracy is one of the additional dimensions by which people judge procedural fairness. In their seminal work on this subject, Thibaut and Walker (1975) conducted some experiments indicating that adversarial procedures tend to produce more relevant facts and create more open-minded fact-finding among judges than do inquisitorial systems. In contrast, my students and I conducted experiments showing that adversarial procedures are more likely to promote biased witness testimony—and therefore more biased facts—than inquisitorial procedures (Sheppard and Vidmar 1980; Vidmar and Laird 1983). Comparisons between the two types of systems obviously involve multiple dimensions of accuracy and behaviour. The essential point, however, is that a better knowledge of the effects of legal procedure would help us understand procedural reactions and allow us to think about hybrid systems that might be even better than the existing ones.

Utilization of Resolution Procedures

We know that many people with grievances avoid making claims (Felstiner, Abel, and Sarat 1981; Kritzer, Bogart, and Vidmar 1991). We also know that even after claims are made, they are frequently abandoned. The potential role of procedural justice in understanding this phenomenon is demonstrated in recent work by Fischer, Campbell, and Rappaport (1994). Fischer et al. have been studying battered women who have sought court help by obtaining temporary restraining orders against their abusive mates. The willingness of the women to proceed to the next step, obtaining a permanent restraining order, appears to be related to the degree to which they believed that they obtained procedural justice in the judicial hearing granting the temporary order. To what extent might similar findings be documented in gender or race discrimination cases, or even in more traditional personal injury suits? The issue of how perceptions of procedural justice may influence the use of dispute resolution procedures in legal and nonlegal contexts has received less attention in procedural justice research than it deserves despite its obvious important implications for achieving the overall goals of social policies.

As one example, consider a dispute resolution procedure developed by the Toyota automobile corporation. The parent Toyota company was plagued by lawsuits filed by its franchise dealerships in disputes over the allocation of important sales credits to the dealerships (Ellis et al. 1994). In conjunction with the Private Adjudication Centre of Duke Law School, the company developed what is called the reversal arbitration board (RAB), which consists of neutral, independent arbitrators who hear the disputes and allocate the sales credits. The program has helped eliminate costly litigation between the parties and is generally perceived by all parties to be a success. My colleagues and I, who studied the programme, concluded that one of the reasons for its success—and the willingness of dealership owners to use it—lies in the fact that the arbitrators are independent of the Toyota Corporation, even though Toyota pays their fees and the dispute can be roughly characterized as an intracorporate dispute. Another reason is that the arbitrators develop guidelines through their rulings; we call it a 'common law of sales allocation policy'. This is a striking instance of 'law' being developed and formalized through ADR and is in contrast to most ADR procedures that attempt to avoid formal rules. A third factor is the 'asymmetric binding' nature of the RAB procedure: Toyota has agreed to be bound by the arbitrators' decisions, but the dealers have recourse to pursue the case in court if they are not satisfied with the outcome. We believe this asymmetric binding provision promotes perceptions of fairness in a situation in which one side (Toyota) has a great deal of power in relationship to the dealership. I believe that elements of the Toyota RAB procedure can serve as a model for other types of disputes between corporations and their franchisees. Another possible application may be in the design of 'inhouse' programmes for resolving complaints about race, gender, or disability discrimination.

Compliance and Legitimacy

Finally, there is the question of how procedural justice is related to compliance with the decisions of resolution forums: e.g., paying the money owed; ceasing to harass an ex-spouse. Building on his own research plus ideas derived from political science, economics, and sociology, Tyler (1990) has produced a convincing argument that people comply with law out of more than just fear of punishment or other self-interested motives. Much of compliance can be explained on the grounds that people have incorporated the values of law into their own value systems and accord law legitimacy. Fair procedures and treatment are essential to the development of legitimacy. While most of Tyler's book is directed at general compliance rather than responses to a specific settlement or judgement of a dispute resolution forum, the principles should still hold: to the extent that the procedures are seen as fair they will be accorded legitimacy and, *caeteris paribus*, incline the disputants to comply with the terms of the resolution. The debate on mediation versus adjudication is irrelevant from this perspective since procedural justice may, or may not, be provided by either forum.

Concluding Comment

I have focused on legal dispute resolution to the exclusion of important procedural justice research in organizations and with respect to political behaviour (Lind and Tyler 1988) in order to make the subject manageable in this article. At the same time I have also drawn heavily on the North American legal context in developing my ideas with full cognizance that some readers of the article may consider it too culturally bound to North America, and I may agree with them. The challenge that I make is for them to offer alternative hypotheses that are amenable to empirical verification. Through such exchanges we will learn a great deal more about an important phenomenon.

References

Aubert, Vilhelm. 1963. Competition and Dissensus: Tow Types of Conflict and of Conflict Resolution. *Journal of Conflict Resolution* 7: 26–32.

———. 1967. Courts and Conflict Resolution. *Journal of Conflict Resolution* 11: 40–51.

Benjamin, Roger W. 1975. Images of Conflict Resolution and Social Control: American and Japanese Attitudes Toward the Adversary System. *Journal of Conflict Resolution* 19: 123–37.

Ellis, René, Geetha Ravindra, Neil Vidmar, and Thomas Davis. 1994. The Reversal Arbitration Board: An ADR Model for Resolving Intra-Corporate Disputes. *Journal of Dispute Resolution* 1994: 93–110.

Erlanger, Howard S., Elizabeth Chambliss, and Marygold Melli. 1987. Participation and Flexibility in Informal Process: Cautions From the Divorce Context. *Law and Society Review* 21: 585–604.

Felstiner, William L. F., Richard A. Abel, and Austin Sarat. 1981. The Emergence and Transformation of Disputes: Naming, Blaming, and Claiming . . . *Law and Society Review* 15: 631–54.

Fischer, Karla, Rebecca M. Campbell, and Julian Rappaport. 1994. The Effect of Resource Availability on Battered Women's Decision to Follow Through with Court Orders of Protection.

Fischer, Karla, Neil Vidmar, and René Ellis. 1993. The Culture of Battering and the Role of Mediation in Domestic Violence Cases. *Southern Methodist University Law Review* 46: 2117–74.

Hamilton, V. Lee, and Joseph Sanders. 1992. *Everyday Justice: Responsibility and the Individual in Japan and the United States*. New Haven: Yale University Press.

Hans, Valerie, 1993. Attitudes Toward the Civil Jury: A Crisis of Confidence? In *Verdict: Assessing the Civil Jury System*, edited by Robert E. Litan. Washington, D.C.: Brookings Institution.

Hans, Valerie, and Neil Vidmar. 1986. *Judging the Jury*. New York: Plenum.

Houlden, Paulina, Stephen LaTour, Laurens Walker, and John Thibaut. 1978. Preferences for Modes of Dispute Resolution As a Function of Process and Decision Control. *Journal of Experimental Social Psychology* 14: 13–30.

Kressel, Kenneth, and Dean G. Pruitt. 1989a. Conclusion: A Research Perspective on the Mediation of Social Conflict. In *Mediation Research*, edited by K. Kressel and D. G. Pruitt. San Francisco: Jossey-Bass.

———, eds. 1989b. *Mediation Research*. San Francisco: Jossey-Bass.

Kritzer, Herbert M., William A. Bogart, and Neil Vidmar. 1991. The Aftermath of Injury: Cultural Factors in Compensation Seeking in Canada and the United States. *Law and Society Review* 25: 449–543.

Leung, Kwok, and E. Allan Lind. 1986. Procedural Justice and Culture: Effects of Culture, Gender, and Investigator Status in Procedural Preferences. *Journal of Personality and Social Psychology* 50: 1134–40.

Leventhal, Gerald S. 1976. Fairness in Social Relationships. In *Contemporary Topics in Social Psychology*, edited by J. Thibaut, J. Spense, and R. Carson. Morristown, N.J.: General Learning Press.

Lind, E. Allan. 1990. *Arbitrating High-Stakes Cases: An Evaluation of Court-Annexed Arbitration in a United States District Court*. Santa Monica: Rand Institute for Civil Justice.

Lind, E. Allan, Bonnie Erikson, Nehemia Friedland, and Michael Dickenberger. 1978. Reactions to Procedural Models for Adjudicative Conflict Resolution: A Cross-National Study. *Journal of Conflict Resolution* 22: 318–41.

Lind, E. Allan, Robert MacCoun, Patricia A. Ebener, William L. F. Felstiner,

Deborah R. Hensler, Judith Resnick, and Tom R. Tyler. 1990. In the Eye of the Beholder: Tort Litigants' Evaluations of Their Experiences in the Civil Justice System. *Law and Society Review* 24: 953–96.

Lind, E. Allan, and Tom R. Tyler. 1988. *The Social Psychology of Procedural Justice*. New York: Plenum.

MacCoun, Robert J., and Tom R. Tyler. 1988. The Basis of Citizens' Perceptions of the Criminal Jury: Procedural Fairness, Accuracy, and Efficiency. *Law and Human Behavior* 22: 333–52.

McEwen, Craig A., and Richard J. Maiman. 1984. Mediation in Small Claims Court: Achieving Compliance Through Consent. *Law and Society Review* 18: 11–50.

———. 1986. In Search of Legitimacy: Toward an Empirical Analysis. *Law and Policy* 8: 257–74.

Menkel-Meadow, Carrie. 1984. Toward Another View of Legal Negotiation: The Structure of Problem Solving. *University of California Law Review* 31: 754–842.

———. 1991. Pursuing Settlement in an Adversary Culture: A Tale of Innovation Co-Opted or 'The Law of ADR'. *Florida State University Law Review* 19: 1–46.

Menkel-Meadow, Carrie, and Susan S. Silbey. 1984. What Do Plaintiffs Want? Reexamining the Concept of Dispute. *Justice System Journal* 9: 151–78.

Miyazawa, Setsuo. 1987. Taking Kawashima Seriously: A Review of Japanese Research on Japanese Legal Consciousness and Disputing Behavior. *Law and Society Review* 21: 219–42.

O'Barr, William M., and John M. Conley. 1985. Litigant Satisfaction Versus Legal Adequacy in Small Claims Court Narratives. *Law and Society Review* 19: 661–701.

———. 1988. Lay Expectations of the Civil Justice System. *Law and Society Review* 22: 137–61.

Sarat, Austin, and William L. F. Felstiner. 1986. Law and Strategy in the Divorce Lawyer's Office. *Law and Society Review* 20: 93–134.

Sheppard, Blair H. 1985. Justice Is No Simple Matter: A Case for Elaborating Our Model of Procedural Fairness. *Journal of Personality and Social Psychology* 49: 953–62.

Sheppard, Blair H., and Neil Vidmar. 1980. Adversary Pretrial Procedures and Testimonial Evidence: Effects of Lawyer's Role and Machiavellianism. *Journal of Personality and Social Psychology* 39: 320–32.

Starr, June, and Barbara Yngvesson. 1975. Scarcity and Disputing: Zeroing in on Compromise Decisions. *American Ethnologist* 2: 553–66.

Thibaut, John, and Laurens Walker. 1975. *Procedural Justice: A Psychological Analysis*. Hillsdale, N.J.: Laurence Erlbaum.

Tyler, Tom R. 1990. *Why People Obey the Law*. New Haven: Yale University Press.

Upham, Frank K. 1976. Litigation and Moral Consciousness in Japan: An Interpretive Analysis of Four Japanese Pollution Suits. *Law and Society Review* 10: 579–620.

Vidmar, Neil. 1984. The Small Claims Court: A Reconceptualization of Disputes and an Empirical Investigation. *Law and Society Review* 18: 515–50.

———. 1985. An Assessment of Mediation in a Small Claims Court. *Journal of Social Issues* 41: 127–44.

———. 1987. Assessing the Effects of Case Characteristics and Settlement Forum on Dispute Outcomes and Compliance. *Law and Society Review* 21: 155–64.

———. 1990. The Origins and Consequences of Procedural Fairness. *Law and Society Inquiry* 15: 877–92.

Vidmar, Neil, and Nancy Laird. 1983. Adversary Social Roles: Their Effects on Witnesses' Communication of Evidence and the Assessment of Adjudicators. *Journal of Personality and Social Psychology* 44: 888–98.

Vidmar, Neil, and Jeffrey Rice. 1991. Jury-Determined Settlements and Summary Jury Trials: Observations About Alternative Dispute Resolution in an Adversary Culture. *Florida State University Law Review* 19: 89–104.

Vidmar, Neil, and Regina A. Schuller. 1987. Individual Differences and the Pursuit of Legal Rights: A Preliminary Inquiry. *Law and Human Behavior* 11: 299–317.

The Author

Neil Vidmar. Russell M. Robinson II, Professor of Law at Duke University School of Law, Durham, North Carolina. Doctorate social psychology from the University of Illinois (1967). Empirical work at the interface of law and social science includes studies of small claims courts, business practice acts, alternative dispute resolution, and the litigation process. Coauthor of *Judging the Jury* (New York: Plenum, 1984) and author of *Medical Malpractice and the American Jury: Confronting the Myths About Jury Incompetence, Deep Pockets, and Outrageous Damage Awards* (Ann Arbor: University of Michigan Press, 1995).

Address: Duke University School of Law, Box 90360, Durham, North Carolina 27708-0360, USA.

Abstract

In North America and elsewhere there is a movement away from traditional adversarial litigation in favour of alternative dispute resolution, or ADR. This chapter explores the relevance of procedural justice research for the development of policy regarding ADR. A procedural justice perspective helps to identify issues that can improve ADR procedures and encourage their use. It also points to the limitations of ADR and the serious problems that arise when the ideology of ADR is uncritically accepted by policy-makers. In some circumstances, traditional legal procedures may provide superior forms of procedural justice.

7 Features of Procedural Fairness: Communication in Decision-Making About Diversion and Victim-Offender Mediation

HEINZ MESSMER

Communication in Court

Unlike everyday-life approaches to interpersonal problems that may be solved by various rules of communicative understanding, communication in court is characterized by rigid limitations that function as language barriers. As legal procedures are less concerned with consensus and more with unequivocal, legally binding, and above all, quick decisions on right and wrong, they require particular procedural rules. In court, complex characteristics of antisocial behaviour must be simplified until they can be assigned to a legal norm that is codified as being generally binding. The rationality of law proves itself in implementing a decision-making strategy that no longer needs to be identical to the psychological and situational experiences of its clients. Clients, however, are particularly interested in the 'net effect of change of being' (Schumann 1979, 11, my translation). They possess detailed knowledge about events but less knowledge about due process. The transformation of lay events into judicial ones is hardly ever transparent. This problem is briefly reviewed in this paper in terms of incongruent cognitive perspectives.

In at least the German inquisitorial justice system, judges dominate court proceedings through legal process networks and habitually regulated interaction standards. For example, they control the course of conversation before the court by granting the right to speak. The judges' need for information is also highly selective. In particular, special interview techniques which require clients to rapidly switch tracks between coherent description and detailed explanation, between subjective attitude and objective perception (Kallmeyer 1983, 149), assure the judge's control over type and execution of communication. The one-sided flow of communication decisively influences not only the form but also the content of judicial negotiations.

Judges' decision-making is subject to the problem of self-immunization due to preconceived attitudes about facts. One-sided communication facilitates the judges' introspection. Their self-observation and individual norm orientation promote highly subjective decision-making preferences. As a consequence, decision-making depends on how far the deviant behaviour of others is comprehensible according to the judges' own normative standards. They can more easily empathize with interest and problem states that are familiar than with those that are far from their own experiences (see, for example, Wheeler, Mann, and Sarat 1988, 160). In addition, clients generally experience the disputed facts in an emotional rather than rational way. However, the legal process is dominated by procedures aimed at broadly excluding the psychological and social dimensions of facts (Conley and O'Barr 1990). This is particularly apparent in motive reconstruction (Dürkop 1977, 100). Where the investigation of motive remains superficial, judges' decision-making routines remain unchallengeable. Simplification of complex contents, exclusion of attempts at divergent explanations, as well as selective or presumptively exhausted information demands are major characteristics of judges' procedural dominance.

The clients' opportunity to influence procedures is correspondingly reduced. Their negotiating position is weak; often their status is mostly that of a mere provider of information (Grüner 1984; Muth 1984). In addition, their ability and willingness to provide complex descriptions of facts decreases to the extent that the implemention of preconceived communication plans is hindered. If the coherent structure of communication is interrupted by special questioning techniques, eloquence decreases, even among legally experienced status groups (Knuf 1982, 271). Lay persons are prevented from presenting themselves as factually competent speakers (Danet 1990). As it has been demonstrated that a powerful speaking style has a strong effect on the credibility, attractiveness, and acceptance of a speaker (Erikson et al. 1978; Atkinson and Drew 1979, 198; Leodolter 1975, 182), the consequences are serious. Verbal presentation always has a negative effect for clients when they are unable to comply successfully with the communicative standard of the court.

It is also no surprise that the social class variable has a strong impact on the outcome of procedures (Boy and Lautmann 1979). The restricted code of the lower class (Bernstein 1972) is not equal to the eloquence and presentation required before the court. The clients see themselves as not being understood. Here as well, the variable of social class correlates with cognitive incongruencies. According to various surveys, two-thirds of clients feel that they are not correctly interpreted before the courts (Eilsberger 1969; Boy and Lautmann 1979). What is not comprehensible can neither be experienced as appropriate nor accepted as just (Tyler 1990).

Diversion and Victim-Offender Mediation As an Alternative to Judicial Procedures

Within the last two decades, the development of juvenile justice intervention has become characterized by two informal treatment types: diversion and victim-offender mediation. Both are meant, with some critical reservations, to promote the social-integrative mechanism of social control. Diversion in Germany means dispensing with or avoiding the formal interventions of the penal law, mostly at some point between police registration and preferral of charges. A far-reaching renunciation of penal sanctions is intended in favour of nonintervention or educational measures. In addition, there is a growing development of restorative justice programmes that encourage the reintegration of victims into legal proceedings as individuals with justified claims, and encourage offenders to take responsibility for their deviant conduct.

The first programmes of victim-offender mediation in Germany were set up in the mid-1980s and shared the following guidelines: (*a*) the victim should be an individual, although corporate or organizational representatives would be accepted; (*b*) the facts of a crime should be agreed upon and the offender should have admitted guilt; (*c*) petty offences, which are generally not pursued in current legal practice, should not be the object of mediation; (*d*) the damage caused (particularly with respect to property) should not exceed the accused adolescent's restitutive capabilities; (*e*) the participation of victim and offender would be voluntary (at least formally); (*f*) victim and offender should resolve the issues at stake as directly and autonomously as possible; (*g*) the discussion would be intended to strengthen the offender's sense of responsibility for the behaviour in question; (*h*) the victim should explain the material and psychological consequences of the offence and use this as a basis to justify the claim for restitution; and (*i*) an amount of restitution could not be imposed, as it would require the approval of both parties involved (Messmer 1992).

Diversion and victim-offender mediation were both included into the ongoing practice of the Bielefeld Youth Authority. In line with the features of procedural justice, the principles of the individual programmes were guided by several basic assumptions: First, informal justice should give the people a voice that allows them to influence the course of their interest along the decision-making procedures; second, informal justice should encourage and provide a better mutual understanding regarding to the causes and effects of the deviant conduct; third, to include the affected persons into the informal procedures should strengthen the consensual domain of legally binding decisions; and fourth, to allow people to influence fact- and problem-related definitions should enhance their acceptance of the procedural outcome (see Messmer and Otto 1992).

The Bielefeld Programme: Data and Method

The following data are generated from the diversion programme located at the Bielefeld Youth Authority, which also implements, although to a lesser extent, victim-offender mediation. Due to a prosecutor's ruling, the goal of the procedure is to transfer cases from formal proceedings to the youth authority. An individual social worker must determine if educational measures are adequate and necessary for the case at hand. In the course of a diversion procedure, the social worker will arrange an interview with the client about the facts and consequences of the crime committed. Afterwards, in coordination with the offender, the social worker informs the prosecutor's office about his or her recommendations for the present case. In the course of victim-offender mediation the social worker must decide whether an extra-judicial reparation plan should be considered and whether it is practicable. This will involve the voluntary attendance of both the victim and offender, establishing clarity about the facts of the offence, and the offender's confession of guilt. In general, the social worker will contact victims and offenders separately before arranging the mediation session. For both procedures, diversion and victim-offender mediation, the factual results of the meeting ideally provide the basis for the prosecutor's decision to either drop the case or press charges.

The research discussed in this article addresses how diversion and victim-offender mediation become operational and effective in carrying out their intervention intent. On an institutional level, the evaluation research has focused mainly on the relation between social work and public prosecutor. On a procedural level, typical characteristics of the casework are examined. Finally, on an interactional level (the focus of what is to follow), interest focuses on the clients' chances to participate in and exert influence on both problem definitions and procedural outcomes. Conversations between social workers and clients are viewed as a bilateral instrument that provides a framework for negotiating situational definitions and subsequent proposals for a procedural decision. Influencing and controlling the course of a conversation (an interview) is an essential indicator of the negotiation power of the parties involved.

This study uses a total of forty-six audio-taped conversations between social workers and their clients at the Bielefeld Youth Authority recorded between June 1986 and May 1989. These involved thirty-six separate offences, mostly physical harm and damage to property but also shoplifting, burglary, and the like. Twenty-eight interviews were held to prepare a diversion recommendation only, and eighteen conversations served to prepare and implement nine victim-offender mediations.

All forty-six conversations were subjected to quantitative analysis, based on ideas of the American sociologist Thomas Scheff. Scheff has analysed the assessment of responsibility in negotiation procedures and has found that attributing responsibility is at least partially a product of social constructions. According to Scheff, the attribution of responsibility occurs in negotiation procedures where proposals and reactions to those proposals are continued until one such proposal attains the status of a final situational definition (Scheff 1968). Accordingly, the method of analysis used here is based on an operationalization and quantification of such conversational moves and strategies. Conversational moves, composed of verbal manoeuvres (such as assertions or queries), define both the factual evidence and the inherent normative responsibility during the course of interaction. They contain two distinct components. The first describes forms of negotiation, such as *how* speakers communicate information to each other or how they reciprocally evaluate the communicated information. This component is referred to as *type of move*. The second component describes the content of the negotiation, or the *subject* of the information that each speaker exchanges. This is referred to as the *negotiation level*.

A conversational move is defined as one single utterance unit of one speaker that correspondingly ends if (*a*) the speaker, (*b*) the negotiation level, or (*c*) the type of move will change; or (*d*) when there is an utterance break that will last more than two seconds. For example, a conversational move produced by the social worker like 'What did your parents do when they heard about it from the police?' will be attributed to the negotiation level <informal consequences for the offender> as well as to the type of move <demand for information>. (For a more detailed description of the individual components of a conversational move, see below.)

In addition, several victim-offender mediation conversations were completely transcribed. These were subjected to interpretative single-case analysis. To supplement the analysis of conversational moves, this method was chosen to study how problems regarding the attribution of responsibility are solved in individual cases.

Research Findings

Conversational Moves in Different Speaker Groups

An average of almost seven hundred conversational moves are used to define facts and situations in each of the forty-six conversations. Among individual speaker groups, 52.8 per cent of these conversational moves are made by social workers, 39.0 per cent by offenders, 4.1 per cent by victims, 3.2 per cent by relatives of offenders, and, finally, 0.9 per cent by relatives of victims. The higher percentages for both social workers and offenders compared to all other speaker groups is due to their presence in all conversations: other speaker groups were not always present.

Initially, this analysis deals with the conversational moves of social workers and offenders—the major participants in these conversations—and later it deals with the conversational moves of victims separately (relatives are not analysed in this study). Specific differences between diversion and victim-offender mediation will be discussed. The present data analysis is descriptive, based on the distribution of valid percentages in each speaker group according to negotiation levels and types of move respectively.

Analysis of Conversational Moves According to Negotiation Levels

When analysing conversational moves, seven different negotiation levels are distinguished, assuming that conversations about diversion and victim-offender mediation (in contrast to the formal intervention of the criminal justice system) will concentrate more on offender-related than on offence-related issues, and, moreover, that the offender will get a fair chance to define relevant issues in line with his or her normative and cognitive evaluations. Negotiation levels report on the topics on which information is imparted.

The distribution of conversational moves across the various negotiation levels (valid percentages in each speaker group) reveals that the conversations between social worker and offender focus on the reasons for deviant behaviour ('why' something happened). The discussion of relevant causes (motives, personal situations, situational aspects) is overproportionately represented and utilizes almost one-third of all conversational moves (social worker: 33.7 per cent; offender: 30.7 per cent). Informal conversations predominantly deal with explanations of juvenile delinquency. Conversational moves dealing with explanations of facts ('what' happened) are next in frequency (social worker: 13.7 per cent; offender: 14.8 per cent), followed by conversational moves concerning informal consequences of the offence for the offender (social worker: 14.5 per cent; offender: 13.2 per cent). The latter involve the discussion of any reparation and reconciliation reactions that offenders have already exhibited, and whether they have already been punished by parents or others or show remorse. This is followed by discussions on type of, extent of, and ways of implementing a proposed measure (social worker: 10.6 per cent; offender: 11.7 per cent). Almost the same proportion is used in discussions on formal legal procedures (social worker: 11.2 per cent; offender: 10.4 per cent). The discussion of legal constraints is a major indicator of how well the offender understands the status and transparence of diversion and mediation procedures. Communications on the consequences of the offence to the victim are comparatively scant (social worker: 4.0 per cent; offender: 3.8 per cent). In contrast to the discussion about the consequences of the offence for the offender, victim-related topics play a much smaller role. Lastly, conversational moves are used to monitor the course of the conversation itself (social worker: 2.6 per cent; offender: 2.2 per cent). Conversations that are not topically related to the offence such as greetings, goodbyes, warm-ups, and the like, represent 9.7 per cent of social worker, and 11.3 per cent of offender communication.

Conversations at the youth welfare office focus less on deviant behaviour as an isolated phenomenon than on its underlying causes. Nonetheless, evidence on facts of the offence is not neglected. Both are decisive for attributing responsibility for a deviant act. Information on offender-related consequences should indicate the extent of further intervention required. In contrast, the markedly lower processing of victim-related information is possibly an indication of a general deficit in the informal conversations.

Analysis of Conversational Moves According to Types of Move

In the following, the distribution of the conversational moves in both speaker groups (valid percentages) according to nine different types of move is explored. Types of move indicate how information is reciprocally exchanged. They express the relationship between a speaker and the contents of conversation pertaining to whether information is given, desired, or evaluated. Types of move can be divided roughly into two groups: whether they reveal something about the *type of communication* of a speaker or about the *evaluations of the information* given by other speakers.

With regard to *types of communication*, variables include demand for information, information on demand, unrequested information, and paraphrases. As anticipated, demand for information (questions, speech stimuli, and the like) and information on demand (answers, reactions) have a complementary distribution between social workers and offenders. Demands for information make up 20.0 per cent of the conversational moves among social workers and only 3.2 per cent among offenders. In contrast, offenders respond to a demand in 25.8 per cent of all their conversational moves and social workers only in 2.1 per cent. As far as initiatives are concerned, conversation control is clearly role-specific. Nonetheless, the distribution of unrequested information shows that offenders communicate their conversational moves proportionately more frequently without being requested (27.5 per cent) than social workers do (26.2 per cent). In addition, offenders more frequently communicate information spontaneously than on demand; they account for the dominant proportion of free speech. Paraphrases, widely used to secure understanding of the other's information, make up 3.8 per cent of the conversational moves among social workers and 1.7 per cent among offenders.

The control competence in conversations depends on the individual social worker. He or she essentially controls the flow of information through demands and through unrequested information. Offenders behave in a complementary manner. They most frequently give information for defining situations, to some extent on demand, but more frequently without being requested. If the social worker gives conversations their structure, it is the offender who mostly determines their content.

A second group of types of move provides information on how social workers and offenders reciprocally *evaluate* their communications. (Conversations beyond the communication channel between social worker and offender are excluded here, so that the total amount of valid percentages in each speaker group according to the types of move will not add up exactly to 100 per cent.) This group is dominated by statements expressing understanding, represented proportionately by 28.8 per cent of the conversational moves of social workers and 13.1 per cent of those of offenders. These signalize the listener's understanding and are mostly of a paraverbal nature (*hmm, aha*, and so on). Statements of nonunderstanding, in contrast, are much lower at 1.1 per cent among social workers and 1.8 per cent among offenders. If statements on understanding or nonunderstanding are viewed as an expression of a listener's cognitive state while processing information, their numerical incidence shows that conversations are predominantly marked by reciprocal understanding on both sides.

Explicit agreements on information make up 1.6 per cent of all conversational moves among social workers and 7.2 per cent of those among offenders. This implies that the situational definitions of offenders are of a more descriptive nature, while those of social workers are more relevant as a valued endpoint for the negotiated topic at stake. The social workers' task in conversations is predominantly to understand the offenders' situational definitions but not so much to agree with them. In contrast, their own situational definitions more frequently demand either a positive or negative evaluation from the offender. As a consequence, although social workers' contributions to the factual definition of situations are quantitatively lower, their contributions nonetheless possess more qualitative weight in decision-making procedures.

Conversational moves that cast doubt on or question situational definitions (but do not explicitly reject them) are represented with 2.7 per cent among social workers and with 1.6 per cent among offenders. Testing the correctness of situational definitions is accordingly more the domain of the social worker, while, on the side of the offender, it is more the appropriateness of the social worker's conclusions that is questioned. Explicit nonacceptance or rejection is expressed in 1.4 per cent of the conversational moves of social workers and in 2.8 per cent of the moves of offenders. This strengthens the impression that social workers' situational definitions are more based on properties that are relevant to decision-making. For social workers, explicit agreements and rejections are more or less balanced (1.6 per cent and 1.4 per cent respectively). For offenders, there is a clearer difference (7.2 per cent and 2.8 per cent respectively). A more acquiescent attitude toward the social workers' situational definitions is predominant.

The conversational structure thus reveals a composite picture that is essentially characterized by cooperation. Statements expressing understanding and agreement combined cover 30.4 per cent of the conversational moves among social workers and 20.3 per cent among offenders. In contrast, conversational moves suggesting problematic understanding situations (nonunderstanding, querying, rejection) run at 5.2 per cent among social workers and 6.2 per cent among offenders. An analysis of the types of move indicates the distinct role characteristics of the two groups. The social workers' role corresponds to the person who mostly asks for information, strengthens this by communicating understanding, safeguards intentions to understand, critically checks the content of proposals, and, without being asked, proposes decision-related situational definitions. The offenders' role is complementary: they are the providers of information, who express themselves when asked but even more when they consider it appropriate in order to determine the content of definitions. They clearly provide fewer moves to structure the course of conversation. Although the majority of their situational definitions are given according to what they consider relevant, they take a more reactive than proactive position in the conversation compared to the social worker. This is particularly expressed in their proposals of acceptance. According to these findings, the social worker appears to be a listener who strives toward understanding but does not refrain from criticism when interpreting the offenders' situational definitions, and who transforms these into decision-relevant proposals. In contrast, the offender predominantly communicates facts and evaluations about situational definitions and reacts to the social worker's transformation of this information into decision-relevant proposals.

Victims in the Negotiation Process

In the sample of forty-six conversations, twenty-eight targeted diversion while eighteen were aimed at preparing and implementing victim-offender mediation. Victims were present at ten of these latter eighteen conversations, directly confronting offenders. Compared to social workers and offenders, the negotiation profiles of victims showed some notable deviations.

First, victims are conspicuously constrained in negotiation processes. With only 4.1 per cent of all conversational moves, they are clearly underrepresented (even when their lower attendance at the interviews is taken into account). The distribution of conversational moves of victims according to *negotiation level* shows that, with 1.8 per cent of their conversational moves, victims exhibit less interest in monitoring and influencing the course of the actual talk. They also appear less interested in the discussion of formal legal procedures (7.5 per cent of their moves). In contrast, it is notable that they overproportionately refer to the facts of the offence with 24.1 per cent of their conversational moves. Apparently, there is a strong need for corrective situational descriptions, so that victims function as 'prosecution witnesses' in the conversations. Compared to all other speaker groups, victims are clearly less involved in not only the causes and motives of deviant behaviour (20.7 per cent) but also in offender-related consequences of an offence (7.8 per cent). However, this pattern is reversed for victim-related consequences of the offence, to which victims proportionately contribute the most information (11.8 per cent). The same applies to negotiations on a procedural decision. With 17.4 per cent of their conversational moves, victims have a very strong influence on solutions to be negotiated. As direct sufferers, victims are granted a major decision-making role regarding the type of a procedural decision and its implementation. The procedural outcomes that are made available to offenders essentially depend on victims.

The distribution of victims' conversational moves according to *type of move* does not differ greatly from the negotiation profile of the offenders. Although (with a proportion of 6.4 per cent) victims clearly control the course of the conversation through their demands for information more often than offenders, they respond to demands at about the same rate (24.3 per cent). In addition, victims behave in a similar way as offenders with regard to unrequested situational definitions, which make up 31.3 per cent of their conversational moves. Paraphrases (0.3 per cent) are without any importance. Compared to all other speaker groups, the proportion of victims conversational moves devoted to statements on understanding (12.5 per cent) and statements on nonunderstanding (0.9 per cent) is low; in contrast, it is high for statements on acceptance (agreement: 9.9 per cent; questioning: 2.2 per cent; rejection: 3.5 per cent).

Consistent with the victims' notable interest in defining the facts of an offence, the consequences they have suffered, and decision-related proposals, victims influence the attribution of responsibility mainly by defining the course and the effects of an offence in relation to the outcome of procedures. Like offenders, victims also function as providers of information as far as the types of communication are concerned. Yet, if their evaluative responses to proposals made by others are considered, they behave more like social workers. Victims are the most influential addressees for those situational definitions that are important for reaching decisions. Unlike social workers, however, the main objective of victims is not to reach understanding regarding delinquent conduct.

Negotiation Structures Compared: Diversion and Victim-Offender Mediation

Finally, it is important to analyse the conversational profiles of social workers and offenders as a function of conversational goals. The variable 'conversational goal' is introduced to compare the eighteen conversations used to prepare and implement a victim-offender mediation with the twenty-eight conversations that were used purely to obtain a decision on diversion. The following analyses will abstain from quotation of precise figures, to enhance comprehensibility. However, the analyses should outline the modifications that occur when the expectations of a victim are included in the ongoing procedure. It might be expected that different goals in decision-making [diversion: to probe the need for educational measures following delinquent behaviour; mediation: to restore damages and settle interpersonal conflict between victim and offender] will vary the pattern of communication in such a way that the predominant offender orientation in diversion is replaced by more practical requirements to reach a bilateral decision that also includes the needs of the victim. Accordingly, the distributions of the conversational moves of social workers and offenders in diversion and mediation are compared according to negotiation level as well as to type of move.

Negotiation levels

The analysis of negotiation levels reveals that the need to structure conversations in victim-offender mediation is three times the average found in diversion conversations among both social workers and offenders. The prospective and actual presence of victims appears to be accompanied by an increase in cognitive interest discrepancies and, accordingly, conflicting conversational dynamics. In contrast, in victim-offender mediation, we find a marked decrease in interest in formal criminal justice issues: there is a greater decrease of interest for social workers than for offenders. The formal perspective of criminal justice in mediation seems to fade with respect to the need for a consensually agreed-upon outcome. Discussions on the facts of the offence somewhat decrease for social workers as well as for offenders. Discussions on the motivational and problem background of the offenders notably drop, by one-third, for social workers and for offenders, indicating the minor importance of offender-related issues in victim-offender mediation. While the number of conversational moves concerning the consequence of an offence for the offender remains stable for social workers and only drops slightly for offenders, the conversational moves regarding the consequences of an offence for the victim clearly become more important. An approximately fourfold increase can also be seen in conversational moves regarding proposed solutions. It is very apparent that conversations aimed toward 'conflict resolution' or 'reparation' contain a disproportionate potential for negotiation-relevant solutions, while offence- and offender-related issues are dropped.

Types of move

The first group of types of move (types of communication), reveals a distinct profile regarding diversion conversations and victim-offender mediation. In mediation, social workers' demands for information on situational definitions slightly increase, while such demands double among offenders. Conversational moves that react to demands increase for social workers, while they drop by about one-quarter for offenders. The complementary role structure between questioning social workers and answering offenders becomes notably weaker in victim-offender mediation. Indeed, free speech (unrequested information) among offenders also drops slightly, while this type of move increases by about one-quarter for social workers. Paraphrases slightly decrease for social workers and rise only slightly for offenders. Obviously, social workers experience a stronger need to control and influence mediation conversations by demands for information and unrequested proposals than they do in conversations about diversion. Offenders also strengthen their influence on the course of the conversations as they more often demand information. Furthermore, for offenders the relationship between information on demand and unrequested proposals seen in diversion becomes reversed in mediation.

With regard to the second group of types of move (evaluations), the strong drop in statements on understanding in victim-offender mediation is conspicuous. In all, there are one-third fewer such statements in mediation conversations, for both social workers and offenders. This suggests increased conversational dynamics in confrontations in victim-offender mediation. Perhaps social workers and offenders want to exert more influence on situational definitions and are less interested in understanding them. There is a corresponding twofold increase in nonunderstanding (less among social workers than among offenders). However, explicit agreements on situational definitions only slightly decrease in victim-offender mediation for both social workers and offenders. Finally, the increase in reciprocally doubted or explicitly rejected situational definitions is also clearly marked: questionings in victim-offender mediation increase more than twofold for both social workers and offenders, while explicit rejections increase by approximately one-half (less among social workers than among offenders). Trends in the differences between conversations on diversion and on victim-offender mediation suggest a pattern. Among both social workers and offenders in victim-offender mediation, there is a decisive drop in reciprocal understanding statements, which is accompanied by a simultaneous increase in the willingness to contradict without essentially changing the consensual domain. While the willingness to cooperate between the speaker groups in victim-offender mediation is apparent, the style of discussing problems has clearly changed: confrontation has become more dynamic and conflicts of interest have strengthened.

There is much to suggest that openness of procedural outcome combined with the practical interests of participants in victim-offender mediation changes essential aspects of the negotiation profile of social workers and offenders, encouraging a more active articulation of interests by both parties. Difficulties in dealing with divergent interests increase markedly in victim-offender mediation. Dynamics of conflict are reflected in distinctly different evaluations of situational definitions. Sympathetic understanding is replaced by practical negotiation of interests. In victim-offender mediation, the evaluation of offenders' behaviour becomes overshadowed by idiosyncratic means to reach an acceptable end.

Structural Characteristics of Victim-Offender Mediation Conversations

The foregoing suggests some differences between the legal treatment of deviant behaviour and the more informal techniques used in diversion or victim-offender mediation. Such differences are revealed in conversations and involve in particular the reconstruction of the offender's motive, the offender's participation in and influence on the situational definitions, and cooperation and acceptance between the individual speaker groups. A comparison between diversion and victim-offender mediation has additionally shown that victim-offender mediation essentially differs from both formal legal interventions and diversion procedures on two major points: a stronger consideration of the victim's perspective in the procedure, and a broader scope of alternatives regarding a procedural decision. The net effect is that more contradictions arise between individual speaker groups. It can also be shown that victims exert a strong influence on the situational definitions of the offence as well as on prospective outcome alternatives, and that this can lead to increased cognitive discrepancies regarding these issues. The increased dynamics of conflict in victim-offender mediation support this.

Using comprehensive transcripts of mediation conversations, the course of negotiation procedures between social worker, victim, and offender can be interpreted in a more qualitative way. It is revealed that increasing negotiation scope is accompanied by increasing conflict intensity: the more that interpersonal conflicts in all their facets are articulated individually and worked out interactively, the greater the probability that differences between parties arise regarding the experience of conflict and the goals of compensation. A major finding of the transcript analyses indicates that negotiations in victim-offender mediation concentrate strongly on issues of responsibility regarding the offender's incriminating behaviour. Persons who are aware of having committed an injustice strive to maintain a positive self-concept by minimizing its consequences (see, for instance, Sykes and Matza 1957; Snyder, Higgins, and Stucky 1983; Scheff 1988; Schönbach 1990). This particularly applies to the maintenance of individual self-esteem. Furthermore, as it is evident that type and extent of compensation depend on how responsibilities are related to the extent of damage, it is understandable that each party additionally strives to fend off attributions of responsibility.

The interpretative evaluation of conversation transcripts has shown that interparty contradictions are to a large extent shaped by such attributional issues. The confrontation is mainly dominated by *justifications* with which the offenders attempt to reduce the level of injustice in various aspects of the offence. Justifications are rationalizations of behaviour; they do not deny the offence itself, but predominantly attempt to reduce the attendant injustice. In this research, offenders use justifications to avoid attributions of responsibility by externalizing assignments of guilt. Accusations are deflected onto the environment in which the offence and its consequences occurred. Specifically, accusations are deflected back to the victim. Conversation transcripts identified four different justification constructs.

The first justification construct refers to details of the recorded offence and endeavours to construct a *competing version of conflict*. The precipitating events of a conflict-laden confrontation are the focus here. For interpersonal conflicts, in general, the beginning (and thereby the cause) of conflict frequently cannot be determined precisely. This type of justification attempts to insert some normative disappointment before the officially recorded precipitating event; for instance, some provocative behaviour or an aggressive act caused by the opposing party. Thus, the disappointment retrospectively legitimizes the offender's aggressive act as a subsequent reaction. In this way, one's own incriminating behaviour can be upgraded normatively while the behaviour of the opposing party is simultaneously downgraded. Cause and effect of the conflict become reversed and role relations change in favour of the offender.

The second justification construct refers to individual norm expectations of the offender and results in *competing norm concepts*. In victim-offender mediation, a tension between individual norm orientations and generally accepted behavioural guidelines often enters the focus of negotiation. Offenders use the perspective of their own norm expectations to accuse the other party of normative deviance because he or she failed to perform acts that were to be anticipated from the offender's perspective. In case reports, the victim is accused of having violated customary rights or disregarded obligatory loyalties. In this way, conforming and deviant components of normative behaviour are once more reversed: measured against behavioural expectations of the accused offender, it is the victim who has violated norms.

The third justification construct refers to material or nonmaterial consequences of the offence expressed as *competing evaluations of the consequences of the act*. By minimizing the seriousness of features of the offence, offenders try to create the impression that the victims of their actions exaggerate the consequences. As a result, they frequently accuse the victims of trying to take unfair advantage of reparation and consequently see themselves as victims exposed to inflated reparation demands.

The fourth justification construct refers to the personality of the victim and leads to his or her *negative characterization*. Devaluing features of the opponent's (victim's) behaviour serves to focus the attention of third parties (such as social workers or mediators) on the opposing party in order to distract from the offender's own incriminating behaviour. Frequently, victims are accused of being motivated by avarice in making reparation demands, in order to undermine the legitimacy of their claims. Negative characterizations generally undermine the credibility of the opposing party. This justification construct schematically hardens the inversion of good and bad, of norm-compliant and norm-deviant behaviour.

Justification patterns attempt to rationalize the injustice of an offence by reversing the role components suggested by the facts of the formal accusation. Offenders may construct a system of beliefs and behavioural guidelines that provides legitimate support for this reversal process. Each justification is aimed at bridging the gap between what is and what should be, between actual behaviour and recognized behavioural norms, between normative order and deviance. Justification patterns form a basic principle of stigma neutralization and simultaneously try to justify a measure of tolerance for acceptable behavioural deviance before, during, and after an offence.

This research reveals that the clients' voluntary articulation of situational definitions is helpful for drawing a distinction between correct and false behaviour regulatives. Nonetheless, this gives rise to the problem that offenders not only think about their incriminating behaviour but also try to justify it. As long as they are given the opportunity to comment on the offence, their motives, and the attendant consequences, they frequently tend to rationalize their behaviour as well as neutralize the injustice committed. On the other hand, exposure of their individual perspectives simultaneously provides the opposing party with materials for a counter-argument:

only when injustice-related explanations are openly expressed can they be used as the subject of critical replies. As the transcript analysis demonstrates, even at a prenegotiation stage, errors in offender-specific justification patterns could be traced and defused by the social worker. Direct contact between victim and offender additionally overcomes neutralization trends present in the individual justification patterns: case reports have shown that victims' contributions are particularly effective in counterpointing those justifications that refer to the facts of the offence, the resulting consequences, and negative characterizations. Mediation, then, is a strong tool to counteract offender-specific techniques of delinquency neutralization (Messmer 1989, 1990).

The Notion of Justice in Informal Decision-Making Procedures

While several important criteria define the success of informal procedures, a frequently neglected topic is the extent of participation of the clients involved. The results of this study suggest that informal (compared to formal) procedures offer a broader scope of negotiation where relevant definitions are promoted according to the participants' perspectives. The reasons for deviant behaviour as well as subsequent consequences for offenders are more strongly emphasized, so that decision-making is shaped by problem-appropriate perspectives. In victim-offender mediation, the scope of negotiation is additionally increased through the presence of victims, who also demand the consideration of their own cognitive perspectives. Furthermore, this increases the range of reparation options. The data show that the individual consequences to victims as well as settlement options become topics. Since there is a direct link between attribution of responsibility, acceptance of responsibility, and reparation measures, the confrontation between the parties is correspondingly conflict-laden.

The freedom to define the issue at stake and to express arguments is an essential part of the negotiations in informal procedures. Instead of deciding on right or wrong from a higher point of view, the participants have a choice to accept or reject the definitions of the relevant other. That is why communication is a significant and proven means of fairness in conflict settlement procedures. 'Justice emerges from conflict: the procedures and values that define justice develop through negotiation among the conflicting parties. Much current work ignores the relationship between conflict and justice and the process by which justice is negotiated' (Deutsch 1985, 100). This notion implies that justice is a product of the mutual understandings of the participants and it is doubtful that it can be made only in one way. Its development in informal procedures is therefore neither legalistic nor individualistic, but rather a communicative process.

If communication about conflict is designed in such a way that both parties can define essential aspects according to their own points of view and, furthermore, if both parties are able to respond directly to the interpretations proposed by the other, mutual understanding is improved. On the one hand, communication affects the connection between reasoning and behaviour through the impact of rule-enforcing conditions, and every substantive account may reflect the errors of one's own argumentation. On the other hand, those whose behavioural motives become understandable or even explicable are experienced as being more similar to one's self than those whose behavioural motives remain nonunderstood and inexplicable. Similarity strengthens social attraction and simultaneously weakens the trend toward stigmatization (Heider 1958). Hence, recognizing similarities through mutual understanding may influence the victim's need to punish and the offender's neutralizations as well: the more understandable the opposing party's behaviour and the greater the insight into similarities, the lower the condemnations intended. Data from Umbreit (1992) indicate that, in the course of personal confrontation between victim and offender, the social process of mediation often becomes more important than the concrete outcome. Role-taking opportunities seem to make an important contribution to procedural fairness in that the participants involved learn to recognize what is cause and what is effect.

The data of the conversational analyses also point to the fact that case complexity is to a large extent concurrent with the justification behaviour of the offenders. While each justification portrays obstinate views and particular values, competing norm expectations are introduced into the procedure. Furthermore, justifications serve as a legitimate basis to acquit the offender of guilt. Both could create a balanced starting position. The freedom to fully express competing norm-orientations or facts is relevant to Rawls's understanding of justice as an appropriate initial status quo: 'A conception of justice cannot be deduced from self-evident premises or conditions on principles; instead, its justification is a matter of the mutual support of many considerations, of everything fitting together into one coherent view' (Rawls 1972, 21).

Emphasizing the different within the same, justifications often have to go into competition with legal definitions. By virtue of added information or deviant interpretations of facts, each justification intends to transgress the validity of normative expectations. While formal law will proceed according to its preconceived programme, justifications demand room in order to establish an original or obstinate view of the case. Each justification creates dissent against blame and contradicts the oligarchy of legal definitions. In line with Walzer's idea of complex equality, one might interpret the discussion of justifications as an expression of the distinct understandings that constitute a shared way of life: 'I want to argue . . . that the principles of justice are themselves pluralistic in form: . . . and that all these differences derive from different understandings of the social goods themselves—the inevitable product of historical and cultural pluralism' (Walzer 1982, 6).

As obsolete values of a mutually shared sense of justice are no longer sufficiently shared in complex, rapidly changing societies, the need for verbal understanding on consensus norms may be greater than ever. Deviant behaviour is not just a problem for society; society is also becoming a problem for the individual. Just and fair responses to deviant behaviour require negotiations over norm orientations as a premise for interventions that could function as a material base for legal socialization. Justice and the sense of justice can only be achieved and extended in cooperative relations, in which the fostering of social and personal development will be the dominant goal. Interactions that ensure understanding are an essential precondition for a procedurally fair application of law.

References

Atkinson, John M., and Paul Drew. 1979. *Order in Court: The Organisation of Verbal Interaction in Judicial Settings*. Atlantic Highlands: Humanities Press.

Bernstein, Basil. 1972. *Studien zur sprachlichen Sozialisation*. Düsseldorf: Schwann.

Boy, Peter, and Rüdiger Lautmann. 1979. Die forensische Kommunikationssituation—soziologische Probleme. In *Menschen vor Gericht*, edited by R. Wassermann. Neuwied: Luchterhand.

Conley, John M., and William M. O'Barr. 1990. Rules Versus Relationships in Small Claims Disputes. In *Conflict Talk: Sociolinguistic Investigations of Arguments in Conversations*, edited by A. D. Grimshaw. Cambridge: Cambridge University Press.

Danet, Brenda. 1990. Language and Law: An Overview of 15 Years of Research. In *Handbook of Language and Social Psychology*, edited by H. Giles and W. P. Robinson. Chichester: Wiley.

Deutsch, Morton. 1985. *Distributive Justice: A Social-Psychological Perspective*. New Haven: Yale University Press.

Dürkop, Marlis. 1977. *Der Angeklagte. Eine sozialpsychologische Studie zum Verhalten vor Gericht*. München: Fink.

Eilsberger, Rupert. 1969. Die Hauptverhandlung aus Sicht jugendlicher und heranwachsender Angeklagter. *Monatsschrift für Kriminologie und Strafrechtsreform* 52: 304–13.

Erickson, Bonnie, E. Allan Lind, Bruce C. Johnson, and William M. O'Barr, 1978. Speech Style and Impression Formation in a Court Setting: The Effects of 'Powerful' and 'Powerless' Speech. *Journal of Experimental Social Psychology* 14: 266-79.

Grüner, Hans. 1984. Kommunikation in Arbeitsgerichtsverhandlungen—Versuch einer Analyse. In *Rechtssoziologische Studien zur Arbeitsgerichtsbarkeit*, edited by H. Rottleuthner. Baden-Baden: Nomos.

Heider, Fritz. 1958. *The Psychology of Interpersonal Relations*. New York: Wiley.

Kallmeyer, Werner. 1983. Mündliche Kommunikation vor Gericht. In *Recht und Sprache*, edited by R. Wassermann and J. Petersen. Heidelberg: Müller.

Knuf, Joachim. 1982. *Polizeibeamte als Zeugen vor Gericht*. Wiesbaden: BKA-Forschungsreihe.

Leodolter, Ruth. 1975. *Das Sprechverhalten von Angeklagten bei Gericht*. Kronberg: Scriptor.

Messmer, Heinz. 1989. Tackling the Conflict: A Framework Analysis of Dispute Settlement. In *The State as Parent*, edited by J. Hudson and B. Galaway. Dordrecht: Kluwer.

———. 1990. Reducing the Conflict: An Analysis of Victim-Offender Mediation As an Interactive Process. In *Criminal Justice, Restitution, and Reconciliation*, edited by B. Galaway and J. Hudson. Monsey, N.Y.: Criminal Justice Press.

———. 1992. Victim-Offender Mediation in Germany. In *Making Amends: Mediation and Reparation in Criminal Justice*, edited by G. Davis. London: Routledge.

Messmer, Heinz, and Hans-Uwe Otto. 1992. Restorative Justice: Steps on the Way Toward a Good Idea. In *Restorative Justice on Trial*, edited by H. Messmer and H.-U. Otto. Dordrecht: Kluwer.

Muth, Jochen. 1984. Die Jugendgerichtsverhandlung aus der Perspektive des Angeklagten. In *Sozialwissenschaftliche Analysen jugendgerichtlicher Interaktion*, edited by J. Reichertz. Tübingen: Stauffenburg.

Rawls, John. 1972. *A Theory of Justice*. Oxford: Clarendon Press.

Scheff, Thomas, J. 1968. Negotiating Reality: Notes on Power in the Assessment of Responsibility. *Social Problems* 16: 3–17.

———. 1988. Shame and Conformity: The Deference-Emotion System. *American Sociological Review* 53: 395–406.

Schönbach, Peter. 1990. *Account Episodes: The Management or Escalation of Conflict*. Cambridge: Cambridge University Press.

Schumann, Karl, F. 1979. Aushandeln von Sachverhalten innerhalb des Strafprozesses. In *Interpretative Verfahren in den Sozial- und Textwissenschaften*, edited by H.-G. Soeffner. Stuttgart: Metzler.

Snyder, Charles, R., Raymond L. Higgins, and Rita J. Stucky. 1983. *Excuses: Masquerades in Search of Grace*. New York: Wiley.

Sykes, Gresham, M., and David Matza. 1957. Techniques of Neutralization: A Theory of Delinquency. *American Sociological Review* 22: 664–70.

Tyler, Tom, R. 1990. *Why People Obey the Law*. New Haven: Yale University Press.

Umbreit, Mark, S. 1992. Mediating Victim-Offender Conflict: From Single-Site to Multi-Site Analysis in the U.S. In *Restorative Justice on Trial*, edited by H. Messmer and H.-U. Otto. Dordrecht: Kluwer.

Walzer, Michael. 1982. *Spheres of Justice: A Defense of Pluralism and Equality*. Oxford: Martin Robertson.

Wheeler, Stanton, Kenneth Mann, and Austin Sarat. 1988. *Sitting in Judgment: The Sentencing of White-Collar Criminals*. New Haven: Yale University Press.

The Author

Heinz Messmer. Former associate in the Research Centre for Prevention and Intervention in Childhood and Adolescence at the University of Bielefeld (Germany). Organizer and convenor of the 1991 NATO Advanced Research Workshop on Restorative Justice held in Il Ciocco, Italy. Later, research associate at the University of Hildesheim. Currently working towards a communication-based conflict theory. Publications: *Restorative Justice on Trial: Pitfalls and Potentials of Victim-Offender-Mediation*, edited with Hans-Uwe Otto (Dordrecht: Kluwer, 1992), and Unrechtsaufarbeitung im Täter-Opfer-Ausgleich (Proceeding Injustice in Victim-Offender Mediation; Bonn: Forum).

Address: Universität Bielefeld, SFB 227, Postfach 10 01 31, D-33501 Bielefeld, Germany.

Abstract

This study deals with decision-making procedures in diversion and victim-offender mediation. The research is based on numerous conversations between social workers and clients that were audiotaped and analysed between June 1986 and May 1989 in the course of the Bielefeld diversion programme. It is shown that informal interventions in deviant behaviour follow different principles of verbal organization than those prevailing in courts. Analyses of the style and content of informal decision-making procedures reveal structural similarities and differences between social workers and clients in diversion and mediation interviews. The potential of communicative approaches regarding procedural justice is discussed.

8 Procedural Aspects of Distributive Justice

VOLKER H. SCHMIDT

Distributive and Procedural Justice in the Political Arena

The concept of distributive justice centres on the fairness or rightness of the ways in which valued goods and necessary burdens are distributed in society. Questions of justice arise as soon as it becomes apparent that the rules according to which this is done are not natural phenomena but the products of human action and decision-making. And what is made by human beings is also capable of being changed by human beings. This insight into the contingency of social institutions—and hence of their need for justification—is said to have set 'the stage for the emergence of theories of justice. For a theory of justice is a theory about the kinds of social arrangements that can be defended' (Barry 1989, 3). To provide the normative criteria in terms of which the legitimacy of such arrangements can be assessed is the task of political philosophy.

This task is not easily accomplished. Both among professional philosophers and within society at large considerable disagreement exists about what exactly justice is and entails. A view widely shared today is that any acceptable theory of justice must start from the premise that all people have an equal right to liberty and respect. But beyond that, not much agreement is found in the pertinent literature. Different philosophers have suggested different principles of justice, as well as different, and at times contrary, operationalizations of the same principles. They have grounded their conceptions in allegedly fundamental truths about human nature, the good life, society, and so forth, and yet have reached fundamentally different conclusions as to what follows from these 'truths' for the design of socially just institutions. They have invoked the powers of reason, intuition, and interpretation to back their propositions, but neither these propositions themselves nor the epistemological assumptions on which they rest have escaped questioning. After more than two thousand years of philosophical dispute it is hard to believe that unanimity in any of these questions will ever be attained.

The practical significance of moral dispute was of course limited so long as most issues of conflict of interest could be resolved by reference to a frame of collectively binding norms, customs, and traditions whose authority was symbolically represented and, if necessary, forcibly enacted by a small elite of religious and political leaders. But the structural conditions on which this model of vertical integration and legitimation from above is based—a feudalistic, predemocratic type of society—no longer prevail today. In modern, functionally differentiated societies, where 'no societal group can make the claim, with any expectation of acceptance, that it has, *a priori*, a higher insight or superior judgement than any other group' (Offe 1985, 262), it has to be acknowledged that moral disagreement is endemic: that there is a multitude of defensible conceptions of the right and the just, with no generally consented rank-order among them, but with each entailing different institutional arrangements and distributional outcomes. In the event of a dispute between two or more people holding different such conceptions, it is therefore unlikely that the contending parties will always reach a mutually agreed-upon decision. But they may agree to establish a decision procedure whose results, although not equally reflective of everyone's substantive values and interests, can be accepted as morally binding on all because they have been brought about in a manner recognized as fair by all.

This is, very roughly, the central idea underlying doctrines of procedural justice. Given the fact of moral pluralism, and considering that nobody possesses an absolute measure for the rightness of a decision, it is assumed to be in everyone's highest interest to retreat to neutral ground and, rather than aiming at a definite resolution of the conflicting claims, try to settle for 'the second best' (Raz 1986), which is to set up fair procedures for their nonviolent reconciliation. Procedural justice involves thus a shift from material principles of justice to formal rules of conflict adjudication and interest coordination. By abstracting from all particular concerns it appeals to what can be approved of from all points of view, or to what Rawls (1993) calls the 'overlapping consensus' between those who disagree in substance.

Now the prime object of political philosophy is the political order of a society. Political philosophy is concerned above all with the overall institutional design of a social system: with the rules that regulate the acquisition and distribution of political power, with the organization of the economy, with the role and authority of the state, with the rights and duties of the citizens; in short, with the basic constitutional ground rules for making society-wide decisions. A paradigmatic instance of procedural justice in the political realm is the majority principle.[1] It channels into the political process a maximum of heterogeneous interests, preferences, and potential decision criteria without predetermining by itself which of them shall become operative in it (and with what weight). Coupled with the periodicity of elections—and hence with the possibility to revise most actual policies—it makes principally acceptable to everyone affected the decisions taken by those presently in office: nobody's preferences are excluded unfairly, and today's 'losers' may be tomorrow's 'winners'. Accordingly, even those who have little (positive) reason to assent to the content of these decisions can be said to have good (negative) reasons to comply with them, because they have no reason to doubt their legitimacy.

Or so mainstream democratic theory maintains. On closer inspection, however, it turns out that the validity of the majority principle is far from self-evident and that its practical implementation poses numerous additional (decision-making) problems that are by no means trivial or negligible. For one thing, it is not clear to what kinds of questions it can be legitimately applied. This is partly a general problem of drawing a line between what can and what cannot become a legitimate object of political decision-making (consider only the unending debate over how much—if any—state intervention is permissible in the economy), and partly one of defining the specific political issues and areas in which majority decisions are appropriate (e.g., is abortion policy a suitable object for settlement through majority rule and, if so, does this imply that the losing minority has to accept any outcome?). Related to this, it is not always clear what shall count as a sufficient majority: by what margin must the majority win so that it can legitimately expect compliance? Another problem is that there are often controversies as to who the relevant majorities and the proper decision-making bodies are in a given policy area (e.g., is the federal government entitled to determine the location of airports or nuclear power plants if most of the affected residents object?). Doubts have also been raised concerning the quality of decisions reached according to majority rule (is it rational [fair] to confer equal weight on all preferences?). And so forth.

I cannot resolve these issues here. I only want to indicate and (re)call to attention that the practical legitimating capacity of majority rule, for all its theoretical soundness, is by no means incontrovertible. Below, I shall argue that the same holds true for many other procedures employed in other decision-making areas. Taken together this suggests that, just as there is no one ultimately 'first' principle of distributive justice, there are also no instances of perfect procedural justice; except for a few rather unimportant cases which need not concern us here.[2] Likewise, there seem to be only a few cases in which pure procedural justice (i.e., the abstraction from all outcome-related questions provided fair procedures are followed), is acceptable.[3] But such practical difficulties should not lead us to abandon the idea of procedural justice as such. If the idea is a coherent and desirable one—and there are good reasons to believe it is—then the empirical difficulties of realizing it fully need not undermine its normative force; they only cast doubt on the perfectionist ideals of those who continue to search for a definite 'single best' solution. The observation that their search is futile naturally provokes the question, Are there at least criteria by which we can distinguish more plausible procedures from less plausible ones? In the concluding section of the paper, I shall give a few indications as to what these might be.

Before that, I would like to do two things. First, I want to illustrate and underline the role of procedural aspects in matters of distributive justice. In my attempt to do so, I shall not touch on problems of political or, as it is also sometimes called, global justice any further. Instead, I wish to draw attention to a number of similar problems that arise at a lower level of societal decision-making, and for which the political scientist and philosopher Jon Elster has coined the term *local justice*. Secondly, I will examine two basic types of decision procedures that have been set up in response to some of these problems. Both of them are problematic in various ways. But their failures are instructive insofar as they point in the directions in which one might look for more appropriate alternatives.

Problems of Local Distributive Justice

Local justice concerns itself with the institutional allocation of goods and burdens. The concept refers to the fact that many problems of distributive justice are resolved in separate societal sectors and by relatively autonomous, intermediate institutions. The importance of the particular allocative decisions for those affected varies on a wide continuum, but in the aggregate their impact on citizens' life chances is probably no less significant than that of politics at the state level.[4] Examples range from life-and-death issues, such as the allocation of organs for transplantation or the selection of soldiers for military service in wartime, to relatively minor issues, such as the admission of children into nursery schools or of elderly people into old-age homes. Somewhere in between lie questions like the selection of employees for layoffs or the admission of students to universities, to add but two more out of a long list of local justice issues.[5]

In most such cases the number of potential candidates by far exceeds the supply of the goods in question.[6] One characteristic that these goods have in common is their indivisibility, another that their utility decreases rapidly with time because those who need or request them cannot wait long for their provision. Both factors contribute to a further intensification of scarcity, so that hard and sometimes rather painful ('tragic') choices must be made.[7] Given the stakes involved, issues of justice inevitably come into play; not least to render the outcomes acceptable for those who find themselves on the losing end of an allocative process. The question is, then, how can this acceptance be generated?

Like all matters of justice, local justice has a substantive and a procedural side. As regards the former, it is widely agreed that different principles (of justice) should govern the distribution of different goods in different sectors of society (Deutsch 1975). Likewise, the content of a principle should vary with the institutional context in which it is applied. For, to make it usable, it must be translated into specific decision criteria, and these in turn should be reflective of the key objectives sought by the institution under consideration, the nature of the good to be distributed, and so forth. In theory, this sounds reasonable enough. In practice, it is where the problems begin.

In the first place, the objectives of candidate selection are often remarkably vague, multi-referential and internally contradictory. Consider, for example, the admission policies at top universities in the United States. Their goal is not simply to transmit knowledge and to promote academic excellence, as one might perhaps expect. Rather, they see themselves as educators of future societal elites, as 'gatekeepers' for the most valued and important positions in society whose incumbents should combine intellectual distinction with 'character': with a sense of responsibility to the community, a certain breadth of interests, leadership abilities, interpersonal skills, energy, and determination. But how does one measure personality traits such as 'community orientation'? What are the best indicators of determination? And how much weight are such factors to be given anyway? The answer is, no one knows with certainty. In practice, a lot depends on the tacit knowledge and the values held by those in charge; and these values will of course differ from person to person. 'By the nature of the problem, there is no one right answer . . . reasonable people disagree on the objectives of selection' (Klitgaard 1985, 16). A related difficulty is that some of the institutions' goals may get in each other's way when pursued jointly, so that trade-offs must be made. How one should strike the balance between them is an open question, though. Again, a lot of scope is left for interpretation, which is a further source of indeterminacy. As an institution moves beyond goods-specific considerations, its objectives inevitably grow more complex—as well as more opaque.

Next, there is the problem of operationalization. It is clear that goals that go beyond what is normally seen as the central purpose of an institution are sometimes hard to justify; and if they are as vague as those just mentioned, they are also hard to operationalize. But even if extra-functional factors are ruled out, there still remain significant degrees of uncertainty and ambiguity. Consider again the case of university admissions. If one were to admit students solely on the basis of intellectual ability, one would still have to face the problem that the customary indicators of past achievement and future academic success are somewhat unreliable. High school grades, for instance, are said to be 'notoriously inexact . . . even within the same course', and, like test scores (with which they are frequently combined), 'poor predictors of later academic performance' (Klitgaard 1985, 11). If one adds to this the observation that they also tend to systematically put applicants from minority groups and lower-class backgrounds at a disadvantage (see Crouse and Trusheim 1988),[8] then their use becomes at least questionable. At the same time they are indispensable because better alternatives are not available.

A third problem is that what appear at first glance to be the obvious (sets of) principles for the distribution of a particular good in practice almost invariably have to be supplemented by other criteria, because even when applied with great strictness, they usually fail to generate the required degree of selectivity: there would still be more 'qualified' candidates than resources available. So in effect it may be quite impossible to dispense with extra-functional considerations. As Klitgaard put it in the context of university admissions: 'grades may do fairly well at separating "average" performance from "good", and "good" from "excellent". But when applicants . . . have mostly "excellents", then their grades will obviously not give much help [in deciding] among them' (Klitgaard 1985, 6). Therefore, to break ties, further factors must be taken into account. As a result, a sector's key principle (here: academic merit) is often used primarily as an eligibility standard that determines only whether an applicant will be considered a candidate. The final recipients are then selected according to other criteria and mechanisms.

This brings me to a fourth problem. In theory, it makes sense to distinguish between one type of criteria that reflects mainly goods- or sector-specific considerations and imperatives, and another that embodies wider ethical considerations, to be applied at later steps in the selection process. A prominent case is the distinction between medical and nonmedical factors for the allocation of scarce life-saving goods. In medical circles it is widely agreed that such goods should be given only to those who are 'suitable' for treatment; all others should be excluded from the outset to prevent the waste of valuable resources. It is also agreed that, whatever the criteria used for subsequent selection steps, determinations of suitability should 'rest only on scientific or medical judgements' (Caplan 1987, 15). However, in practice the line between medical and nonmedical factors is often hard to draw, rendering the status of many suitability (i.e., exclusion) criteria somewhat ambiguous, if not dubious. Consider the example of organ transplantation. Factors such as age, lifestyle, emotional stability, and social support (measured by marital status) can all play important roles as predictors that a patient will survive for a reasonable time with treatment, and that he or she will comply with a strict and stressful postoperative treatment regimen. At the same time, their assessment is inextricably intertwined with nonmedical considerations. It contains at least implicit judgements about the value of life (or the claims one has) beyond a certain age stage, about the reliability of certain (categories of) people, or about the 'rightness' of certain forms of behaviour that, like drug or alcohol abuse, may not only reduce the chances of successful treatment, but also may be the central cause of the organ failure that calls for intervention, thereby almost automatically raising the question of personal liability and 'deservingness'. But once such questions are posed, the realm of pure medical evaluation has been left and that of moral evaluation entered, with all the difficulties associated with moral pluralism turning up again.

In view of these (and numerous other) problems and ambiguities, which in one way or another arise in all local justice issues, the choice of appropriate allocation criteria is bound to be a controversial matter. There is always a multitude of potential factors which can be defended with good reasons from one point of view, and questioned with equally good reasons from another. That a large array of them *will* actually be brought up is likely, not least because in all local justice cases several types of actors are involved, either directly or indirectly, in the development of allocative policies. They are: (1) political authorities and regulators, (2) the 'providers' of the goods in question, (3) the 'recipients', and (4) 'public opinion'. Given their different institutional places and roles within the policy-making and allocation processes, each of them will view the decision-making problem in a different light and, accordingly, will favour different principles. Since none of them can be ignored for long—government officials may mandate certain rules or changes, recipients can threaten a scandal about present policies—their expectations must all be respected and considered to a certain extent. Whatever the merits of this exigency, it certainly does not facilitate the finding of unequivocal solutions.

But even when the 'relevant' criteria are (temporarily) agreed upon, the most difficult task in the whole process remains yet to be faced: 'the assignment of relative weights to the various factors that are to be considered' (Russell 1988, 1023). As Russell has shown in the context of systems of recipient selection for organ transplants, the choice of the pertinent medical factors may perhaps be justified by emphasizing their 'scientific status' or 'objectivity'.[9] When it comes to balancing them against one another and against nonmedical factors, this is no longer possible. Whichever method one chooses to balance them with, there is no way of eliminating subjective valuings altogether.

Russell's argument, although developed in a particular context, highlights a general problem of multifactor allocation systems and applies across distributive sectors and goods. In the last instance, any (local) justice scheme will contain an ineradicable element of normative contingency because other combinations of criteria and weights may be equally justifiable. Some doubts will always remain as to their material legitimacy, or at least to their appropriateness.

Given these difficulties in finding substantively compelling solutions, procedural aspects should assume a central role in fostering acceptance for those practical 'solutions' that are empirically adopted. Any allocative system will inevitably produce losers. For them, the burden of having to bear the costs of losing out is hard already. If, in addition to this, the impression emerges that the requisite decisions are reached in a questionable way; for example, because 'morally arbitrary' factors (like bias) or weakness of character (like corruptness) on the part of the selectors are allowed to creep in, then their results cannot be tolerated any longer. Conversely, if one is convinced that a sound, trustworthy mechanism is in effect, then one should find it easier to 'put up' even with hard decisions. That is to say, how one is treated may be just as important as what one gets—or doesn't get (see Lane 1988). Indirect support for this conjecture is found in much social psychological research which suggests that people are more likely to be concerned about the methods by which distributive decisions are made than about their material outcome (e.g., Tyler 1987). A 'sense of injustice', as Deutsch summarizes the findings, 'is more often aroused by complaints about the procedures involved in a distributive process than about the distributive values governing it' (Deutsch 1985, 35).

The fairness of decision-making procedures is therefore a key aspect of distributive justice. How it can be achieved is another open question, though. In the following section, I shall discuss the comparative merits and weaknesses of the basic types of procedures that are employed in local justice cases. I assume, but cannot substantiate in detail in this paper, that the empirical function of 'fair' procedures is often not so much to improve the quality of decisions (which in some instances may actually suffer from attempts at procedural 'adjustment'), but to prevent potential resentment resulting from suspicions of injustice; not to *do* justice, but to *establish perceptions* of justice. From the point of view of the allocating institutions, whose conduct may in many ways be dependent on a supportive (or at least: nonhostile) environment, this can be essential; from a normative perspective, it may well not be good enough.

Procedures of Local Justice

Principles of distributive justice can be implemented through various procedures. Local justice procedures always comprise a mix of considerations, and they are usually broken down into two or more decision steps, as indicated above. Some are 'tiered' systems, in which a candidate pool is progressively thinned by screening it first according to one criterion or set of criteria, then according to a second one, and so on until the number of recipients matches that of the available goods. Others are quota systems that use different criteria—or rank the same criteria differently—in several quotas of fixed size to achieve a certain aggregate composition of recipients.

Still others are point systems which give candidates points for a finite set of qualities and then select the person(s) with the highest scores. And some systems are complex combinations of various methods. For the sake of brevity, I shall not describe any of them in detail. Instead, I shall focus on a more fundamental difference between two basic types of procedures of which all the above systems are variants: discretionary selection on the one hand, and mechanical selection on the other.

Discretionary selection means that those responsible for making allocative decisions are relatively free to choose whomever they consider a suitable candidate. Insofar as formal rules or guidelines exist, they are not strictly binding, and they admit of substantial scope for interpretation in their implementation. One of the advantages of discretionary selection is that it allows for individualized, case-by-case decisions, so that sufficient account can be taken of specific circumstances and information pertaining to the case in question; another is that it allows for flexible and creative responses to unexpected changes in the environment. Both of these can be essential to finding adequate solutions.

At the same time, discretionary selection tends to be accompanied by a number of problems which make it extremely vulnerable to criticism. Among such problems are, first, the observation of a striking degree of variability (as well as inconsistency) in the application of selection criteria, resulting in a great deal of diversity in allocative schemes among (and within!) institutions that are essentially dealing with the same problem (Winslow 1982). The second problem is that suspicions of arbitrariness can arise due to the ensuing lack of discernible patterns or intelligible logic behind institutions' decision-making. As Calabresi and Bobbitt argue, any particular pattern may prompt criticism from somewhere, but the absence of a pattern is worse because it is taken as an indication of mindlessness or capriciousness. 'Deep anxiety and frustration', they maintain, 'are a necessary part of a process which makes a crucial decision against someone, but fails to explain why' (Calabresi and Bobbitt 1978, 61). The failure to devise clear policies, to spell out and explain their objectives and underlying rationales, and to make allocators accountable for their decisions, frequently leads to allegations, if not the reality, of discrimination, partiality, nepotism, and so forth.

Such surmises are reinforced and seemingly confirmed when, third, the aggregate selection outcomes, too, appear to be pointing in that direction. For example, in the United States empirical studies have provided repeated evidence of gender, age, and, especially, racial disparities in the allocation of scarce medical goods. As one recent examination of the allocation of kidneys in the American Midwest concludes: 'the most favored recipient of a transplant is similar to the physicians who make the final decision: a young, white man' (Kjellstrand 1988, 1309). Although none of the studies (see also Eggers 1988) could prove discriminatory behaviour on the part of the selectors, these and parallel findings from other areas suggest that the observed disparities are artifacts of discretionary decision-making, fostering perceptions of inequities and undermining a policy's social acceptance.

Mechanical selection, by contrast, is less controversial in this regard, because it is strictly formalized and hence far more predictable: once a scheme has been established, it is applied without exception, and recipient selection becomes a more or less automatic matter. By preventing the influence of 'ad hockery' (Sanders and Dukeminier 1968) and enforcing uniformity, mechanical decision-making procedures guarantee that all candidates' claims will be judged by the same standards, which is often regarded as a key prerequisite of procedural 'due process'. Coupled with this, they are 'a guard against . . . abuses. They hamstring the selectors, reducing their freedom of movement and providing fewer incentives and opportunities for corruption' (Klitgaard 1986, 100). Especially in contexts in which not only a power differential but also a conflict of interest obtains between the parties involved, they should thus inspire more normative confidence than discretionary systems. An oft-cited example supporting this conjecture is the use of strictly seniority-based layoff schemes in the United States, the main initiating force behind which is said to be 'a union desire to avoid the arbitrary exercise of authority by managers' (Addison, cited in Golden 1990, 23).

The same characteristics that account for many of the merits of mechanical decision-making—its procedural impartiality, consistency, predictability, and so forth—are also responsible for its most serious drawbacks. To reach a proper allocative decision, a variety of prima facie partly incompatible considerations must be taken into account for whose weighting there is no fixed rule or algorithm that can be used under any circumstances or in any particular case. Some procedural latitude is indispensable to allow decision-makers to respond flexibly to unprecedented difficulties, contextual peculiarities, or specific (personal) features of candidates that are not entirely foreseeable in the abstract, but are undoubtedly relevant to the decision. The price for uncompromising procedural justice, in the sense of strict equality of treatment, can be more than doubtful outcomes because it fails to address relevant individual differences, and hence important questions of material justice.[10] A reasoning of this sort underlay a decision by the German Federal Labour Law Court in 1983 to declare invalid a point system that had been developed by a lower court for the assessment and uniform treatment of contentious layoff cases. The scheme, which accorded different but fixed amounts of points for age, seniority, dependent children, and a severe handicap, while deducting a certain (equally fixed) number of points for an employed spouse, was abolished because it would overlook potentially relevant individual differences. For example, if an employee has a child with a speech defect that necessitates attendance at a special school, then this fact should be given due consideration in the layoff decision because it severely restricts the (geographical) mobility of the employee's family. Likewise, the mere fact of 'dual earnership' alone says little about the income actually available to a household (and hence about a candidate's need for the job in question), for the spouse's contribution to the family budget can vary significantly according to the type of job held, the hours spent in paid employment, and so forth. Again, to reach a well-considered judgement, such differences should be taken into account (*Entscheidungen des Bundesarbeitsgerichts* 1985, 163).

Analogous objections could be (and have been) raised against similar systems employed in other areas. If a rising number of institutions nevertheless seem to be resorting to such systems, then this is probably not primarily due to genuine concerns about the justice of their (previous) allocative policies. More important than that seems to be the public display of such concerns. Many local institutions that are responsible for making distributive decisions have been exposed to substantial scrutiny in recent years, and all kinds of criticism, sometimes well-founded, have been levelled against them. To the extent that their success, or indeed survival, depends on trust in their integrity, and on belief in the fairness of their selection rules, this can pose a major threat. In such a situation the adoption of standardized decision procedures is sometimes seen as an appropriate means to demonstrate responsiveness and to help restore the requisite trust (see Handler 1986 for a general discussion). For instance, in 1987 a national point system for 'equitable selection' of organ transplant recipients was introduced and made mandatory for all transplantation centres in the United States, following widely publicized charges of favouritism and corruption at some of the country's most prestigious clinics. Aimed at diminishing 'judgmental factors in case selection' which, as its designers (transplant surgeons themselves) acknowledge, 'in the past had probably operated to the disadvantage' of certain groups of patients (Starzl, Shapiro, and Teperman 1989, 3434), the scheme, in a 'Ulysses-like' (Wikler 1989) act of self-binding, practically removed the surgeons from the distribution process. There remain serious doubts as to the wisdom of this move from a medical or a normative viewpoint (see Schmidt 1994b), but it effectively undermined any future claims of bribery or disparate treatment, thereby protecting the organ transplant community from having its conduct questioned. Given the delicacy of the issue, this was obviously considered essential.

Conclusion

Distributive and procedural justice are multiply interrelated. In one sense this is trivial because any principle of justice must be implemented by some procedure. In another sense it is quite important because procedural questions have a significant impact on the acceptability of distributive decisions. Procedural improprieties can render difficult outcomes even more harmful, as their unveiling brings 'to mind the possibility that a more favorable outcome might have [ensued] if only more favorable practices had been followed' (Folger 1987, 150). Conversely, the likelihood of unfavourable outcomes being accepted increases when the procedures that bring them about are (perceived as) fair; all the more so when there is disagreement or uncertainty about the material standards that are to guide the requisite decisions. So far, this appears evident enough.

Now the notion of fair procedures has two aspects, one formal, the other substantive. The formal aspect refers mainly to the consistency and correctness with which a method is applied to a given problem, and to its neutrality or impartiality. The substantive aspect in part concerns the agenda for decision-making itself: the range of the issues that can be raised within a framework of institutionalized rules, and the types and roles of the actors that are given a say in the process. In addition, it concerns the degrees to which decision-makers are induced to reflect on, and possibly revise, their policies (or decisions) in the light of new information and insights. Both of these aspects are of undeniable import. However, as the preceding discussion of local justice regulations has shown, they also tend to contradict each other, so that trade-offs must be made. As a consequence, the choice of adequate procedures can be no less difficult (and contentious) than that of adequate substantive principles.

To this observation one might of course respond that the procedural alternatives discussed in this paper are pure or 'ideal' types that are hardly found in the real world, and that to the extent that they are, their respective weaknesses could be easily redressed by establishing a more balanced mixture of procedural elements. Both unregulated discretion and rigid rules are really not defensible (because they are implausible), so all that needs to be done is to apply whatever rules there are with greater latitude, while at the same time subjecting the freedom of selectors to reasonable constraints. In principle, this is probably beyond dispute. Yet in practice, it becomes immediately apparent that negative conclusions of this sort are far too vague to yield any determinate answers. For the problem is normally not a lack of insight into the necessity of balancing the pertinent concerns, but to reach agreement on where exactly the line should be drawn.

But perhaps the search for 'determinate' answers is ill-advised anyway. Perhaps the problems of justice confronted in the real world are so heterogeneous and complex that they admit only of very abstract guidelines and principles whose translation into concrete moral precepts and decision rules must then be left to the various local 'practitioners' of justice. Let me conclude, in this sense, by formulating six rather general acceptability criteria which I think any adequate 'justice' procedure must meet. Their background and underlying rationales are twofold. First, they draw upon and systematize, at a higher level of abstraction, the rules and evaluative standards commonly cited in the literature on procedural justice.[11] The aim here is to render them applicable to the widest possible number of decision-making areas and cases, while at the same time retaining their critical force. Second, they address some of the key problems and side effects resulting from attempts at implementing them in particular contexts, as discussed and illustrated in the previous section, especially in connection with mechanical procedures. The aim here is to indicate some alternative responses to those problems which led to setting up such mechanisms in the first place, i.e., to make them dispensable. In other words, the goal is to control discretion rather than to abolish it entirely.

Comprehensiveness By this I mean that the rules of decision-making must be such as to ensure (or at least permit) that all (normative and instrumental) considerations relevant to a problem do in fact appear on the agenda and figure with some weight in the process. At the same time, irrelevant factors must be excluded from consideration.

Information sensitivity Related to, but not identical with, the above point, procedures must be designed in such a way as to elicit a maximum of information pertaining to the decision-making problem.

Voice Mechanisms must be established that give those directly or indirectly affected by a decision an opportunity to be heard at some point in the process, that enable them to put on the table their views of the problem, their conceptions of justice and fairness, or their interests, with a realistic chance of influencing the outcome. To be acceptable, decisions must be resonant, at least to some extent, 'with the values of clients and publics' (Lane 1988, 177).

Transparency In order to prevent misconduct and to circumvent 'motivated irrationality'[12] (Pears 1984) or the opportunistic adjustment of standards of justice to (perceived or alleged) contextual imperatives (see Schmidt 1992), the rules of decision-making must be rendered sufficiently public.

Accountability Decision-makers must be made accountable for their decisions. In particular, they must be induced (perhaps even required) to give reasons for their decisions or their preferred decision-making rules.

Reversibility There must be provisions that allow for the reversal or correction of decisions or, if that is not possible, for modifications of the decision-making rules that generated them. More specifically, there must be independent institutional bodies that, on appeal or at random, subject the decisions to (authoritative) reviews.

It should be clear that the above criteria represent only minimal conditions which in most actual cases will have to be supplemented by further criteria, depending among others on the societal sector and level of decision-making. Moreover, they must be translated into different procedural and institutional devices, which, again, will have to be adapted to the various 'spheres of justice' and to the particular problems in question. But if all of them are given due consideration, it should be possible to overcome at least the most serious of the problems discussed in this paper.

Notes

1 The following draws on Offe 1985.

2 An oft-cited example is that of a situation in which a cake is to be shared equally among a group of people. The obvious way to achieve this goal is to have one person divide the cake and let all others choose before the person who divided it takes the remaining pieces (see Nelson 1980).

3 The distinction between perfect and pure procedural justice was introduced by Rawls. Perfect procedural justice obtains when there are (1) independent (and agreed upon) material standards for just outcomes and (2) procedures whose application is sure to bring about these outcomes. As Rawls himself notes, in matters of practical interest, perfect procedural justice 'is rare, if not impossible' (1971, 85). Pure procedural justice, by contrast, means that there is no independent criterion for substantively just outcomes. Instead, there is only agreement about the features of fair procedures. Once these are followed, any outcome has to be accepted as just and binding. In other words, the justice of outcomes derives fully from the justice of procedures.

4 It is therefore surprising that they have so far received very little systematic attention in the literature on justice. One important exemption is Walzer's book *Spheres of Justice* (1983).

5 For a fuller list, see Elster 1990, which also introduces the concept of local justice itself. A comprehensive discussion of that concept is now to be found in Elster 1992. See also Schmidt 1992 for a sociological interpretation and Schmidt 1994a for reflections on the concept's potential merits for political theory.

6 The term 'good', as it is used here, refers to both positive and negative goods. Thus, in the case of military service, the good consists in the exemption from the duty to serve.

7 For the notion of tragic choices, see Calabresi and Bobbit 1978. One might object that many of these difficulties could be avoided by resorting to market mechanisms. This would not be a very realistic suggestion, though. There is a great deal of research that shows that full marketization of such goods would arouse strong feelings of unfairness and ethical inappropriateness. This applies

even to the United States, where market allocation is probably more widely accepted than anywhere else.

8 Mainly because their living conditions are much less conducive to the unfolding of a given academic potential than are those of their white middle-class peers (and competitors).

9 Although he also emphasizes the 'very changeable and, as yet, uncertain nature of many of the major determinants of organ allocation' (Russell 1988, 1024).

10 Which requires that treatment as equals, rather than equal treatment, be secured. For the distinction between equal treatment and treatment as equals, see Dworkin 1981.

11 The most important of which are those already mentioned, e.g., impartiality, neutrality, consistency, and correctness. For a recent overview, see Bayles 1990.

12 By this I mean various forms of cognitive rationalization which relieve decision-makers of some of the (moral or other) conflicts encountered in particularly contentious or painful situations. For examples, see Schmidt 1992.

References

Barry, Brian. 1989. *Theories of Justice*. London: Harvester Wheatsheaf.

Bayles, Michael D. 1990. *Procedural Justice: Allocating to Individuals*. Dordrecht: Kluwer.

Calabresi, Guido, and Philip Bobbitt. 1978. *Tragic Choices*. New York: Norton.

Caplan, Arthur L. 1987. Equity in the Selection of Recipients for Cardiac Transplants. *Circulation* 75: 10–19.

Crouse, James, and Dale Trusheim. 1988. *The Case Against the SAT*. Chicago: University of Chicago Press.

Deutsch, Morton. 1975. Equity, Equality, and Need: What Determines Which Value Will Be Used As the Basis of Distributive Justice? *Journal of Social Issues* 31: 137–49.

———. 1985. *Distributive Justice: A Social Psychological Perspective*. New Haven: Yale University Press.

Dworkin, Ronald. 1981. What is Equality? Part 1: Equality of Welfare. *Philosophy and Public Affairs* 10: 187–246.

Eggers, Paul W. 1988. Effect of Transplantation on the Medicare End-Stage Renal Disease Program. *New England Journal of Medicine* 318: 223–9.

Elster, Jon. 1990. Local Justice. *Archives Européennes de Sociologie* 31: 117–40.

———. 1992. *Local Justice: How Institutions Allocate Scarce Goods and Necessary Burdens*. New York: Russell Sage Foundation.

Entscheidungen des Bundesarbeitsgerichts 1985. Vol. 42. Berlin: de Gruyter.

Folger, Robert. 1987. Distributive and Procedural Justice in the Workplace. *Social Justice Research* 1: 143–59.

Golden, Miriam. 1990. A Comparative Inquiry Into Systems for the Allocation of Job Loss.

Handler, Joel F. 1986. *The Conditions of Discretion*. New York: Russell Sage Foundation.

Kjellstrand, Carl. 1988. Sex and Race Inequality in Renal Transplantation. *Archives of Internal Medicine* 148: 1305–9.

Klitgaard, Robert. 1985. *Choosing Elites*. New York: Basic Books.

———. 1986. *Elitism and Meritocracy in Developing Countries*. Baltimore: Johns Hopkins University Press.

Lane, Robert E. 1988. Procedural Goods in a Democracy: How One Is Treated Versus What One Gets. *Social Justice Research* 2: 177–92.

Nelson, William. 1980. The Very Idea of Pure Procedural Justice. *Ethics* 90: 502–11.

Offe, Claus. 1985. Legitimation Through Majority Rule? Chap. 9 in *Disorganized Capitalism*. Cambridge: Polity Press.

Pears, David. 1984. *Motivated Irrationality*. Oxford: Oxford University Press.

Rawls, John. 1971. *A Theory of Justice*. Cambridge: Harvard University Press.

———. 1993. *Political Liberalism*. New York: Columbia University Press.

Raz, Joseph. 1986. *The Morality of Freedom*. Oxford: Clarendon Press.

Russell, Paul S. 1988. Organ Transplantation: How Can We Assure Equitable Distribution? *Transplantation Proceedings* 20: 1022–4.

Sanders, David, and Jesse Dukeminier. 1968. Medical Advance and Legal Lag: Hemodialysis and Kidney Transplantation. *UCLA Law Review* 15: 366–80.

Schmidt, Volker H. 1992. Adaptive Justice: Local Distributive Justice in Sociological Perspective. *Theory and Society* 21: 789–816.

———. 1994a. Bounded Justice. *Social Science Information* 33: 305–33.

———. 1994b. Some Equity-Efficiency Trade-Offs in the Provision of Scarce Goods: The Case of Livesaving Medical Resources. *The Journal of Political Philosophy* 2: 44–66.

Starzl, Thomas E., R. Shapiro, and L. Teperman. 1989. The Point System for Organ Distribution. *Transplantation Proceedings* 21: 3432–6.

Tyler, Tom R. 1987. Procedural Justice Research. *Social Justice Research* 1: 41–65.
Walzer, Michael. 1983. *Spheres of Justice*. New York: Basic Books.
Wikler, Daniel. 1989. Equity, Efficacy, and the Point System for Transplant Recipient Selection. *Transplantation Proceedings* 21: 3437–9.

The Author

Volker Schmidt. Research Fellow on the Faculty of the Social Sciences, University of Mannheim. Author of the books *Neue Technologien—verschenkte Gelegenheiten?* (1991, Westdeutscher Verlag, Opladen) with Ulrike Berger and Helmut Wiesenthal; *Politik der Organverteilung*, (Baden-Baden: Nomos, 1996) and *Lokale Gerechtigkeit in Deutschland* (Frankfurt am Main: Campus, forthcoming 1997) with Brigitte Hartmann. Main areas of work are the sociology of justice, political sociology and philosophy, medical sociology, and general social theory.

Address: Universität Mannheim, Fakultät für Soziologie III, Seminargebäude A5, D-68131 Mannheim, Germany.

Abstract

Two premises guide the understanding of the relation between distributive and procedural justice in the pertinent literature: first, that distributive and procedural justice are radically distinct concepts that cannot be reasonably related to one another; and second, that procedural justice is empirically and normatively prior to distributive justice. Both of these claims are relativized in this paper. It is argued that resorting to procedures in the event of disputes about substantive standards of just distribution is only seemingly a solution, because whatever procedure is chosen to resolve the conflict and reach a decision, it will inevitably shape the way substantive questions are treated and, hence, will have important implications for the quality and acceptance of the respective decisions. It is an error to believe that the procedural correctness of decisions suffices to achieve the requisite compliance. Therefore, procedures must themselves be devised in such a way that their outcomes are able to meet at least minimal standards of substantive adequacy. Against the background of this assumption, six acceptability criteria for procedures are suggested.

9 The Individual in the Shadow of Powerful Institutions: Niklas Luhmann's *Legitimation by Procedure* As Seen by Critics

STEFAN MACHURA

Introduction

Long before current discussions about procedural justice, Niklas Luhmann had closely examined procedure as a social institution and published his book *Legitimation durch Verfahren* (Legitimation by Procedure; first edition in 1969, second edition in 1975). Luhmann's descriptions are of central interest for the evaluation of the performance of the institution 'procedure'. Since 1969, Luhmann's sociological theory has developed in another direction. But he has not altered the main arguments of *Legitimation durch Verfahren*. It has been a milestone in the sociology of law and remains the subject of a continuing debate.

In *Legitimation durch Verfahren*, Luhmann's reference category is the maintenance of the political system in a society in which everything can change, but not all at once. This corresponds to a legal system which is based on the positivism of law and therefore is highly flexible. Hagen (1972, 486) emphasizes: Luhmann's theory

---

A former version of this chapter was published in German in *Zeitschrift für Rechtssoziologie* 14: 97–114. The author wishes to thank Anja Goldberg for the translation of the original Oñati version of the text, as well as Diane Lange and Roland Küper for additional discussions of that translation. Translations of quotations from German are Goldberg's and the author's.

is 'the theory of legal positivism, whose main issue is again ... its legitimation'.

Luhmann analyses the four institutionalized types of procedure: the court procedure, political elections, the law-making procedure and the administrative procedure.

In the following explanations, the basic structure of the procedures according to Luhmann will be elaborated. Later, the central elements in the focus of criticism will be discussed. Almost without exception, only criticism that inquires into the empirical contents or the empirically verifiable scope of Luhmann's theory will be taken into consideration. Luhmann's definition of legitimacy has, however, to be elucidated first.

Legitimation As the Adoption of Binding Decisions

Luhmann (1975, 28) comprehends legitimacy as a 'general willingness to accept yet undetermined decisions within certain tolerance limits'. The legitimation of political power in highly complex and variable societies has to be 'acquired by the political system itself' and cannot be left to a 'naturally imagined morality' (Luhmann 1975, 30).

> Legitimation by procedure and by equality of opportunity to obtain satisfying results supersedes ... prior foundations on natural law and exchange modes of forming a consensus. Procedures gain a kind of general acceptance, which is independent of the satisfying significance of the particular decision, and which carries with it the acquiescence of and the compliance with these types of binding decisions. (Luhmann 1975, 30–1)
>
> Legitimation is particularly not based on ... voluntary recognition, on personal beliefs for which the individual is held responsible, but, on the contrary, on a social climate which institutionalizes the acceptance of binding decisions as self-evident and which does not regard it as the consequence of an individual decision but as the result of the validity of an official decision. (Luhmann 1975, 34)

According to Luhmann (1975), legitimation by procedure is a learning process: a restructuring of expectations by an actual communication process that takes its course adhering to legal regulations. Legitimation is 'the adoption of binding decisions into the individual decision-making structure'.[1]

Procedure As a Decision-Oriented Social System With Limited Complexity

Luhmann classifies procedures as a special kind of social system. They are social systems geared to decision-making. As social systems they possess limited complexity. The main features of Luhmann's general sociological theory will first be reviewed. Its starting point is the complexity of the world and the contingency of all the world's structures. 'World' in this sense should be comprehended as the totality of possible events. 'World' is inconceivable and uncertain according to this conception; it is infinitely complex. The world gains reality only when being shaped by systems. Systems are formed by the stabilization of a difference between inner and outer. However, each system may be superseded by another, or even by none at all. So far, reality is just a selection from many possibilities; reality is contingent, according to Luhmann.

At each stage of development in society, the individual can and must receive more signals than he can process biologically. The complexity of the world thus has to be reduced to an extent to which human experience and action can orient itself. In addition, the human being has the special ability to create meaning. Social systems are nothing but intersubjectively constituted structures of meaning, which can be distinguished from an environment they do not belong to. People themselves are neither parts nor members of social systems, but as individuals playing roles they belong to the environment of social systems.

The 'conception of system-immanent complexity of procedure' serves as the 'central point' for Luhmann's grasp of procedure. 'The classic determination of procedure with truth as a purpose can be replaced with this conception' (Luhmann 1975, 52). The open start and the determination of one decision as the result of the procedure are characteristic for procedures. Procedures, as social systems of action which lead to one unique binding decision, are kept distinct from their environment. They make their own sense to participants, sense which connects the participants. The parties involved reduce complexity. In the 'procedure funnel' (Luhmann 1975, 115), participants in court commit themselves to a certain version of the event in dispute. The participants make individual partial decisions on certain accounts and moves, and thereby reduce the scope of the outcome, which is principally undetermined in the highly complex starting situation. 'It is especially this absorption of uncertainty by selective steps that marks the sense of the procedure and requires the limitation from the environment and irrelevant information, and thereupon causes a certain autonomy of the decision-making process' (Luhmann 1975, 47). The superior social system, which organizes the procedure, first provides only general legal rules concerning the mode of the procedure; these rules facilitate the initiation of it. In the course of the procedure, each participant's decision turns into a fact that becomes a premise for the further action of the other parties. Participants in court are bound to be consistent with their former accounts in order to remain credible. Each proceeding gains its own case history, which is binding for the participants. The parties involved have assigned roles in this procedure. These roles are differentiated from other roles of the participants in order to enhance the acceptance of the outcome of the procedure by the actors' surroundings. The principally undetermined outcome of the procedure serves to motivate the protagonists to assume a role in the procedure and to maintain it. The parties in court are aware that a judgement will be made and they assume their roles in order to affect the findings.

In another work, Luhmann (1985, 203) has put it concisely:[2]

> In the course of the procedure the participants . . . are thus made to specify their positions with a view to whatever result is still open, so that their concern can finally no longer appear to be that of just any third party. It takes on the profile of an opinion or interest as opposed to everyone's expectations—and in any case, no longer as truth or as general taken-for-granted morality. The participants find themselves as individuals again after the performance of their self-presentation in the procedure: individuals who articulate their opinions and interests, who have voluntarily established their positions as their own and therefore have hardly a chance of mobilizing an effective formation of expectation and action by third parties for their own case. Thereupon the case can be decided with the pretension that the decision that is directed at them represents the expectations of third parties. Procedures also have the aim of thus specifying the topics of conflict before releasing physical force, so that the rebel is isolated as an individual and depoliticized as such.

The defeated party is left alone to mentally cope with defeat (Luhmann 1975). A convict may find a 'relatively harmless safety valve' in blaming jurists generally (Luhmann 1975, 112). Or the person concerned may feel the constraint to learn to live up to the expectations of others.

Luhmann distinguishes between the formation and the representation of a decision. 'Legitimation by procedure' is not so much based on the purposive-rational aspect of decision-making as the 'vehicle' (Weiß) of the 'symbolic-expressive' presentation (Luhmann 1975, 124), of consensus in the procedural execution (Weiß 1977, 76). Luhmann (1975, 224) writes: 'the function of legitimation is not implemented by the choice of instruments suitable for an imagined purpose lying in the distant future, but, in many cases, by aspects of social behaviour, which very often remain latent, and by symbolic-expressive activities. The participants get involved in the procedure by the assignment of implicit roles and the nonparticipants by the dramatic presentation of the procedure, so that the process of reduction is comprehended by all of them by means of either active or symbolical mediation'. Weiß (1977, 77) explains that the availability

Figure 9.1: Models of Legitimation

I = isolated individual; I/. . . = individuals and groups; PS = political system

Model I (Habermas)

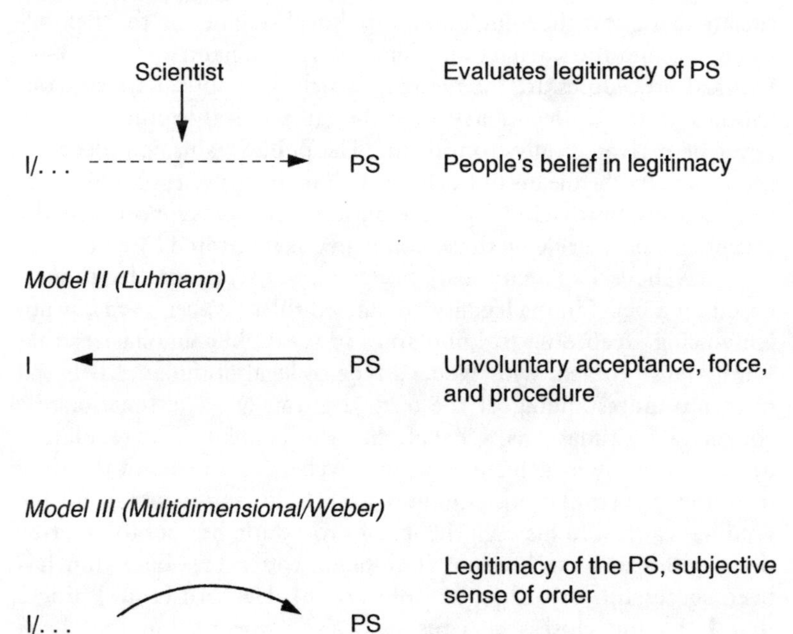

of each premise, even the most precious normative premise, as a consequence of the positivism of law is most safely politically mitigated by 'an emotional and engaged *representation* of the *existing* decision and action competences' (emphasis in the original).

Sources of Legitimation

Luhmann evaluates force and procedure as the basis of legitimacy (Luhmann 1975, 1985), which he defines without regarding its 'normative and moral aspects' (Schaper 1985, 226). (See Figure 9.1, model 2.) Force alone is not sufficient to make lasting power possible (Luhmann 1975). Its threat, however, prevents rebellion; 'physical force . . . remains an essential legitimation factor (though one in need of supplementation)' (Luhmann 1985, 202). According to Luhmann (1975), legitimation by procedure causes subordination to law in a society, which positivizes its law, (i.e., bases it on procedural decisions), and political legitimacy in a highly complex, constantly changing society. The multitude of ever-changing legal rules cannot be deduced from a conception of natural rights anymore. For all these decisions no consensus can be found with regard to each concrete case. Political legitimacy by procedure requires prerequisites in the society that allow the foundation of political stability on the 'flexibility of law and the satisfaction of interests' (Luhmann 1975, 198–9). Political procedures are the mode in which the political system contributes to its own legitimacy, even though political legitimation can never be derivated only from them. 'The public' gains confidence in the system by the means of learning (Luhmann 1975, 199). Luhmann has been disapproved of by those authors who presuppose that the acceptance of the rule by those dominated is motivated by content.[3]

Weber's explanation of his concept of rational legitimacy, based on a belief in the legality of enacted rules (Weber 1972), is not convincing, according to Luhmann (1975). Lübbe emphasizes that Luhmann's problem with Weber's type of legal dominance is based on a misunderstanding of the term 'legitimacy'. The functionalist conceives legitimacy as a belief that the content of a regulation deserves acknowledgement, not, like Weber, as a belief in the duty to follow the regulations (Lübbe 1991). Luhmann wants to fill the void he realizes. In his own theory of procedure, he tries to describe the 'legitimizing mechanism' (Luhmann 1975, 31). Luhmann has been successful, according to Röhl (1977). Heidorn (1982) judges that Luhmann closes the gaps of Weber's theory, but that he—beyond that—generalizes inadmissably. The formulation 'procedure instead of legitimation' would be more fitting for Luhmann's intentions (Heidorn 1982, 118).

Luhmann, however, stresses the factual, political deviant-isolating function of procedure. This mechanism serves the acceptance of the results of procedure against the background of a socialization process, which Luhmann describes in a pictorial style as 'social climate' and 'general acceptance' (see above). The socialization concept may, however, comprise phenomena which lead to the habitual legitimation of the results of political procedures and therefore present a functional equivalent to the mechanism outlined by Luhmann. The Federal Republic of Germany can be cited as an example: It cannot be decided yet whether the acceptance of the political system, its procedures, and decisions by its citizens is based on experience of the material capacity of the system, thus on increased prosperity,[4] or on appreciation of the central political organs and democratic constitutional decision-making. A mixture of both is likely. If the citizens gained the impression that the political procedures led to decisions which were materially inefficient or unacceptable by content or that their central political values were infringed, the aggrieved party would not always be faced with an indifferent public and the possibility might arise that decision-making in particular cases would ignite major political changes.[5] Luhmann's function of procedure as an instrument to contribute to self-legitimation and to 'operative autonomy' (1975, 173) in the political procedure and to urge citizens into a position of 'nearly unmotivated acceptance' (1975, 28) and to keep them out of the decision-making process forfeits effectiveness as soon as the citizens detect the mechanism Luhmann describes (Offe 1972, 1984). Single 'incorrect' decisions can be evaluated as exceptions by citizens; a system that founds its legitimation on its contents does not have to guarantee solutions which satisfy everybody or are just the right thing (Heidorn 1982; see Luhmann 1975, 20).

Luhmann (1975, 122–3) himself states that a basic consensus of the nonparticipants must either exist or that it 'must be feigned by the omission of uttered dissent' in order to ensure the function of legitimation. The population's belief in the system ('general confidence in the system', Luhmann 1975, 193) is therefore presupposed. Confidence is reinforced by the public nature of the process. The procedure is arranged 'like a drama which symbolizes the right and just decision' (Luhmann 1975, 124). Luhmann thus never considers 'ideological' legitimation resources to be irrelevant; the procedure must at least always be protected against them. In other places, Luhmann also mentions the significance of dimensions regarding the content of legitimation (i.e., Luhmann 1975; Heidorn 1982; more about this later on). 'Legitimation by procedure' thus provides just a partial explanation. Only as long as procedures regarding the content remain within the basic consensus of citizens do they possess the relative scope of decisions Luhmann describes; beyond this limit the belief in legality will collapse (Heidorn 1982). This is not 'unmotivated' but 'volitional acceptance' (Treiber 1975, 22) of decisions within a certain limit. Perhaps in an established pluralistic society, people are well aware that, in normal cases, there are numerous acceptable ways to solve a problem, not only one appropriate solution. The academical prominence of the positivism topic accompanies the development of such a type of society. Society is based on a common, binding set of few principles and is open to various detailed decisions in everyday life. Legal positivism is always a foundation of society but also always a threat to its very foundations, which might be shaken by legal decisions, too. This maintains a public debate on legal positivism.

With the belief of the ruled in values, the causes of legitimation in view of content and notions of natural rights still remain relevant (so also does the correctness respectively of the justice of the court proceedings and the judicial decision, which are emphasized by jurists [see Schreiber 1976; Gilles 1976]). 'The claim of the procedure to make right and just decisions by means of logical-rational argumentation and evidence and their at least tendential fulfillment are essential prerequisites for the acceptance of decisions made by national agencies' (Heidorn 1982, 93). Zimmer asks how, according to Luhmann's model of dramatic presentation, 'sanctions by elections' should be accomplished. To present them in this sense as 'the consequence of lacking effort of symbolic mediation' (1979, 259) appears to be improbable in a society with different conceptions of truth and law. Furthermore, the citizen does not need such a drama in order to accept a democratically mediated decision as a compromise in an affair 'without the claim of truth or absolute justice' (Zimmer 1979, 259).

In the context of efficiency of different types of organization, Luhmann himself describes the output of a procedure as an element promoting acceptance. The 'rationality and the capability' of a bureaucratic administration, which is largely independent of the people's consensus, can be 'a factor which supports the (political) legimitation of the entire administrative system', according to Luhmann (1975, 229).

As a functional equivalent to the mechanism described by Luhmann, procedures by socialization can obtain a kind of intrinsic value, maybe just as an instrument that is tied to particuliar decision-making situations or preferably applied in them; for example, the electoral mechanism (free, secret, equal elections) whenever representatives are to be elected (practiced already during the election of the class captain at school), and the systematic efficiency contest, whenever measurable differences are bound to turn the scale. The esteem of the type of procedure is followed by the acknowledgement of the particular procedure and its outcome. A deviation leads to difficulties with regard to psychic handling and requires the presentation of it as an exception whose necessity results from coercion or colliding values. This can also explain acceptance.

Heidorn (1982, 101) considers the 'actual content' of the rendered decisions to be the 'crucial point' of the legitimatizing effect. In the opinion of Kriele, procedures legitimatize because they increase the chances of considering all relevant aspects and of discussing priorities in a 'rationally justified', 'material-rational decision' (Kriele 1981, 37–8). Kriele's valuation standard is the 'ascertainment of truth' by procedures (1981, 190).

Habermas (1976) comprehends the legitimacy of a political order as the 'degree to which it deserves acknowledgement' which should be assessed by scientists (Heidorn 1982, 122–3). The criterion of such an assessment is whether the people's belief can withstand proof in an ideal discourse or not. Habermas thus combines the view of a critical philosopher with that of a sociologist analysing public opinion. (See Fig. 9.1, model 1, for Habermas's more philosophical approach.) He emphasizes: 'A procedure can always legitimatize only indirectly by reference to instances which are generally accepted themselves' (Habermas 1971, 244). 'Luhmann omits the fact that legality is just a derived form of legitimacy' (Habermas 1971, 243). If we take people's belief in legitimacy as a starting point, we may sometimes observe that a procedure which is seen as 'fair' enhances the legitimacy of the superior system. And we may also observe that 'legality' is sometimes seen as an embodiment of legitimacy.

In a recent book, Habermas (1993) shifts his emphasis from a critique of popular beliefs of legitimacy to a laudation of democratic procedures as guaranties of fundamental human rights. Still, he is concerned about distributive (or 'substantive') justice. Procedures are devices for that end as well as for the maintenance of human rights. Human rights are analysed in their macro-sociological dimension rather than in terms of individual concerns. Habermas (1993) answers Luhmann's system theory by stressing the chances of the citizen's political participation still given in liberal democracies. His thesis, arguing normatively and empirically, is that only real political participation of an active citizenship leads to legitimacy.

There is a lot to say in favour of this perception: 'The legitimate procedure presupposes legitimate power' (Rhonheimer 1979, 350–1). Social scientists should preserve the 'Weberian tradition' and inquire into the 'subjective' sense on which people base their acceptance of power.[6] Thus a multidimensional model of legitimation seems to be preferable. (See Fig. 1, model 3.) The acceptance of single decisions follows the legitimacy which the political system gains from the people it rules with respect to perceived contents. On which contents the ruled base their judgement can remain open. This is a question of empirical research. The term 'multidimensional model' indicates this openness and the 'double structure' of the general legitimation of the system and acceptance of its single decisions. Weber was able to gain 'depth of focus' in his analysis by examining the 'overlap of different types of legitimation', whereas Luhmann remains abstract and out of step with practice, because he only distinguishes between a greater and a lesser degree of legitimacy (Rammstedt 1976, 108–22). People may, as Weber (1972) explains, see legality as a legitimatizing factor, as long as the political order that enacts the system of law is legitimized by other factors. In normal cases, legitimacy does not depend on the content of single decisions. The peace-keeping function of procedures thus rests not only on the latent isolating effect.

Luhmann's fixation only on the self-made legitimacy of the political system is questionable because of a disregard of interactions with, for example, the economic system of society, and the segregation of the legitimacy of the political system from legitimacy that derives from other social subsystems that ensue from this estimation (Heidorn 1982, Breuer 1991). Weber showed how a growing discipline in all sectors of society produces a 'formal-operative rationality', that makes the belief in a rational legitimacy possible (Breuer 1991, 210–13).

Rational Argumentation and Learning

Confidence in the legitimizing force of rational argumentation (and in its aptitude to establish a just and correct decision) is prevalent in the juristic guild. Luhmann's 'legitimation by procedure' has therefore met the jurists' incisive criticism and often even blunt refusal.[7] The 'conventional notion of legitimation', as apostrophized by Luhmann, emphasizes the correctness, truth, and justice of the content of a decision (Luhmann 1975, 1). Luhmann does not deny the opportunities of argumentative dispute on closer examination (1975); however, he overdraws its margins and searches for other mechanisms to overcome conflicts (compare Schreiber 1976; Röhl 1987).

No matter what view is taken towards *Homo oeconomicus*'s axiom of selfishness—it seems to be a rather distorted image of the human being, in my opinion—many actions are oriented towards this maxim. Luhmann formulates that it could

> not be *rational* for the individual . . . to set back his own interest or to even put up with actual disadvantages with regard to collective advantages in view of generally acknowledged values. Even if other people benefit from these principles, it is especially rational to get one's own disadvantage compensated in the individual case and to oppose until this has taken place. The conventional concept of legitimacy therefore speculates on behaviour that is irrational from the individual point of view; it particularly cannot be combined with a theory of rational argumentation. (Luhmann 1975, 2, emphasis in the original)

The wide public, which according to Luhmann ignores a lot of procedures and obtains only selected information about other ones, accepts the procedures' outcome automatically, because it has internalized the acknowledgement of procedures and cannot acquaint itself with the arguments of the parties (Luhmann 1975; Röhl 1987).

Rottleuthner's analysis of criminal proceedings as 'distorted communication' is also an indication against unreserved confidence in the power of rational argumentation. The defendant's linguistic helplessness against the legal 'magic of language'[8] contributes to his entanglement in his role. An atmosphere of 'rigid seriousness' does not permit the defendant to dissociate himself from his role, but does obstruct meta-communication among the participants and compels the defendant to be ready to learn. The judge's noncommittal observation role disconcerts the defendant, who is constrained to self-presentation and consequently accomplishes the 'openness' of the procedure. Rottleuthner accentuates Luhmann's central elements of explanation—the 'openness' of the situation, the actors' readiness to learn, and the 'actual' entanglement in roles—in a different way, but not without force of explanation with regard to criminal proceedings (Rottleuthner 1971, 83–8).

Rottleuthner (1971) explains that Luhmann bases his accounts of the actual way procedures function on a curtailed conception of learning; i.e., learning by disappointment. This inception makes sense with regard to the explanation of the acceptance of the outcome by those aggrieved parties who could not be prompted to yield by argumentation. Learning through disappointment can also occur by means of the valid arguments of somebody else. This would again result in the traditional conception of procedure, which emphasizes the gain of insight by the involved parties. Luhmann focuses visibly on one, in fact the socially most tense, aspect of the institution of 'procedure'. The renunciation of consent in the individual case is frequently inevitable.[9] Luhmann has to admit that 'legitimation by argumentation' (Pitschas 1990, 214–16) can step beside 'legitimation by procedure', leading to an 'interplay' (Luhmann 1975, 5).

The perception of legitimacy as resulting from a process of constant restructuring of expectations, from a social learning process, is located as the weak point of Luhmann's analysis by Kielmannsegg. He asks whether this idea does not expect too much of the system and the individual (1971, 396). Is it possible to base the obligation to follow decisions only on a restructuring of expectations or must there be more? 'The individual as a kind of tabula rasa, who no longer acts according to his moral concepts, wishes and interests, but who submits unquestioningly to the prevailing state decision-making practice—this is implied in the ideal condition of Luhmann's legitimation model' (Heidorn 1982, 108). Luhmann's explanation of legitimation thus appears very unlikely. Learning only others' expectations causes no change in behaviour, creates no action according to the results of a procedure. There also has to be a change in the motivation of the actor. And here we are confronted with a gap in Luhmann's systems theory. He has no theory of action. At this point, a '*verstehende Soziologie*' in the Weberian tradition has clear advantages.

Court Proceedings

Esser emphasizes that Luhmann's elaborations about the reciprocal commitments of the parties in court proceedings originate from civil action. 'Too much activity' on the part of the judge jeopardizes 'the presentation of judicial independence', which is a condition for the 'self-entanglement of the involved parties', according to Luhmann (1975, 134). Esser judges that Luhmann described an already antiquated pattern when stressing the role of the parties, because the German judge now has a strengthened process-managing part in civil action. In contrast to Luhmann's account of the court proceedings, the preapprehension and the formation of an opinion have greater significance in court proceedings. The 'autonomy of the procedure', as accentuated by Luhmann as a controlling instrument for the interchange process between the system and the environment through system-immanent structures and processes (Luhmann 1975, 69), forfeits empirical relevance (Esser 1970). (Also opposing Luhmann's comprehension of the role of the judge, originating from a conception of a controlling and in the end deciding judge: Schaper 1985.) German jurists take the view that 'legitimation' according to Luhmann can rather be protected by means of the judge revealing his grounds for the decision and his understanding of the case—already in the course of the process (Schmidt 1973; Schaper 1985). Justice and the correctness of the judgement or the belief in them are regarded to be substantial (e.g., Zippelius 1973; Gilles 1976; Schreiber 1976; Schaper 1985). Luhmann's theory can, however, be of increased significance for the American 'adversarial process', which is governed by the principle of disposition on the part of the contending parties. But Anglo-American readers may align themselves with Zippelius (1973, 295), who points out inquiringly:

> did not the legal systems of case law virtually emerge from the judiciary, i.e., from the sense of justice of many generations of judges influenced by the prevailing legal ethics, thus from the solutions of concrete problems that have been adopted in later decisions, not at least due to their persuasive force as regards content?

Luhmann assumes that legitimation in the course of a procedure can only be 'institutionalized in connection with conditional programming of the decision-making' (1975, 133). An if-then programming serves to immunize the deciding person against criticism. Jurists have raised objections that law disclosed wide scopes of interpretation in its application on an individual case, that the legal rule had to be inquired into with regard to its normative purposes, and that the judges were responsible for the correctness of their judgements (Esser 1970; Zimmer 1979).

Procedural autonomy has also been diminished by another development described by Röhl, which involves only a fractional but nevertheless momentous part of the proceedings. The individualization of the conflict and the isolation of the involved parties are no longer functioning smoothly since the mechanism has been detected. Luhmann himself has contributed substantially to this. The individual-judicial concept of procedure could not prevent a 'politicization' by 'judiciary-oriented strategies and by a coalition formation in the surroundings of the process'. Labour courts and environmental processes can be cited as examples (Röhl 1977, 57–66). Now and then, individuals institute legal proceedings, even though the case is hopeless, in order to attract publicity, to mobilize the public, and to alter the law (Schaper 1985). This description does not apply to the bulk of the proceedings.

According to Schaper, nobody who gets involved in a procedure forfeits the prospect of social support because of this: 'It appears that the procedure not so much creates social isolation but, conversely, presupposes social isolation in order to proceed'. The legal proceeding is geared to the treatment of individual problems and hardly to the 'appropriate handling of interests with which a wide solidarity is shown' (Schaper 1985, 236).

Does court procedure in civil action really engage the parties involved in roles, as Luhmann puts it? Hegenbarth and Scholz (1979) show that parties were kept silent by the professional jurists, including their lawyers. The judge and the lawyers try to secure an undisturbed flow of juridical argumentation. In addition, many parties do not appear at civil court; they leave all activity to their lawyers. Indeed, and not only in Germany, the defendant and the plaintiff are isolated *in* the procedure (Hegenbarth and Scholz 1979). They are neither allowed to show emotion nor to use moral arguments (Hegenbarth and Scholz 1979). Thus the emotional as well as the moral conflict is not dealt with and both will often lead to further conflicts (Hegenbarth and Scholz 1979). The court procedure may decide only one station in a spiral of conflict (Hegenbarth and Scholz 1979), and lead to an acceptance of this decision in Luhmann's sense, but the next stations will be reached soon. Even in a most recent reflection on *Legitimation durch Verfahren*, Luhmann does not acknowledge this (Luhmann 1993, 332–3).

Material Ideas of Justice in Formal Procedural Principles

Procedures are not of a purely formal nature; they also have a material component with regard to content (Gilles 1976; Mandt 1991). The classic material principles of procedural justice; for instance, the acknowledgement of the parties as acting subjects of the procedure, their commitment to consistency in their procedural actions, the *audiatur et altera pars*, the judicial independence and the public nature of procedures, recur already in the social mechanisms elaborated by Luhmann, according to Zippelius. The proceedings consequently obtain their legitimacy in part from principles of procedural justice (Zippelius 1973). Interpreting these procedural principles functionally, according to their contribution to not-easily-accepted recognition by the involved parties and to an indifferent acceptance of the outcome by the public, neglects the aspect of their contribution which forms the conviction that the procedure was just. Like them, the procedural principles of political elections (equality of the weight of votes, generality of elections), which Luhmann (1975) regards from the functional angle of their contribution to the autonomy of political decisions from social integration, are themselves principles of political justice.

According to Luhmann, majority rule in the law-making process results in political power accommodating the principle of 'the constancy of added power'. This (theoretical) rule would achieve an artificial simplification of the power calculation, which would become the basis of rational action (Luhmann 1975, 176). The majority principle, however, also has a fundamental significance. As the decisive principle in the democratic constitutional state, it stands in 'close relation to the postulation of freedom and the principle of equality and does not depend on qualifications of education and property' (Mandt 1991, 339). Mandt writes 'that anybody who criticizes, defends, or suspends "only" the procedures, at the same time always criticizes, defends, or suspends certain fundamental norms, too'. Criticism of the 'elections' in communist states may serve as an example.

The Legislative Process

According to Luhmann, the wheels of the legislative process also result in the legitimation of the outcome of the procedure. Based on a case study by Grottian (1974) about an initiated amendment to the law against competitive restriction in the Federal

Republic of Germany in 1968–1972, Schmid and Treiber (1975) render the judgement that the effect of legitimation by procedure as described by Luhmann did not result. The procedure (which was conducted artfully by the head of an antitrust department of the Federal Ministry of Trade and Commerce who later became president of the anti-trust board), did not result in the acceptance of the draft bill by German industry, which had been involved in the process right from the start but made the reform fail nevertheless. The two authors conclude with the consideration: 'The objection—located on level of plausibility—that the veto power of interest groups, which are organized and capable of conflict, becomes effective in political pluralism, and that it cannot be broken by means of initiating a process of forming consent, can be raised against the thesis of the legitimizing effect of procedures (with regard to the decision-making processes of the political-administrative system)' (Treiber 1975, 177). It will be difficult for an observer of the Federal Republic of Germany to recall an example of one of the large pressure groups, capable of conflict, yielding forever to 'legitimation by procedure' either in the legislative process or later. Central concerns will be brought back to the political agenda when the opportunity arises. Now and then, resistance is even offered in the phase of the implementation of the law.

Imbalances of Power Due to the Constellation of Procedures and the Consequences

The example taken from the legislative process, the politicization of legal proceedings, as well as Rottleuthner's analysis of criminal proceedings, already point in the direction of a problem (Leibfried 1972) that was not discussed by Luhmann in *Legitimation durch Verfahren*. The constellation of interests involved in the procedure with particular competences can cause imbalances of power, which have serious consequences. Who can appear in the proceedings, and with which rights on the basis of his other resources, and which structure of power results from this, is of central significance for the legitimacy of the procedure's outcome and the decision-making process, even for legitimacy in Luhmann's restricted sense.

'From an empirically informed perspective', Pitschas (1990, 214–5) shows himself not convinced by Luhmann's accounts of 'legitimation by procedure':

> the mere display of power in procedures in order to make others accept a passed decision has always revealed its 'poorness', e.g., in the behaviour of those submitted to law, who have always maintained their position of yearning for freedom and justice opposed to assigned role behaviour and imposed encumbrances of interactions. . . . Anyway, the social reality of the citizens' claim to repel, to program, or to let state decisions be controlled or to play a part in them in some other way 'in' and 'by' procedures, remains.

Procedures lose their legitimizing effect once their function is 'detected' (Offe 1972, 133–4). This has already happened, at least partially, as can be demonstrated by the example of citizens' action groups. Attempts to integrate and pacify the action groups (Rucht 1984, recognizing in this respect the possibility of a 'legitimation by procedure') by means of participation in the procedure are no longer the reliable instruments of the authorities. Pitschas's perception of procedure (1990, 215) as a 'process of social agreement' and not of cunning 'entanglement' with the purpose of 'self-legitimation' of 'state power' describes the social ideal. Luhmann, however, sees the increased rationality in rigidly conditionally programmed administrative procedures, and not in a procedure of cooperation with the persons involved (Luhmann 1975). 'Rationalization always means: functionally specified orientation. Functionally specified orientation, however, requires the release from other functions, especially from those of obtaining consensus and legitimizing decisions' (Luhmann 1975, 218). According to Luhmann, development should tend towards the segregation of the political system into two parts, one part responsible for legitimation and one administrative part freed from this burden. Not in vain has Rammstedt gained the impression that, in the end, Luhmann bases his conception of legitimacy, which is reduced to the acceptance of the authority's decisions, 'on a generalized hierarchical structure of the administrative state' (Rammstedt 1976, 116).

Luhmann analyses elections (together with majority decisions) as procedures of the political system which just keep the citizens away from the decisions, letting them get rid of their protest in a harmless way (Luhmann 1975), and by which the political system legitimizes itself and acquires 'operative autonomy'. Kevenhörster (1978) refutes the thesis of the just symbolic-expressive significance of polling with reference to the investigations of empirical electoral research. According to its findings, electoral behaviour, which turns the election decision into an act of a general (with regard to the political system as a whole) as well as a selective (with regard to concrete political decisions) allocation of legitimacy by the voters, also has an instrumental component oriented content (Kevenhörster 1978). The protest of electors, (e.g., voting for extreme parties) may very well jeopardize a political system and restrain its 'operative autonomy'.

Conclusion

Luhmann contributes much to the explanation of procedures. The headwords are: legal framework, acceptance and segregation of roles, binding power of procedural history, possibility of dividing the instrumental making and the symbolic-expressive account of the decision, learning by disappointment also, and the possibility of the social isolation of the aggrieved party. The analysis shows some deficits. 'The performing and the legitimizing margins of procedures'—with the subject of a ramified 'ungovernableness' debate—are not discussed by Luhmann (Heidorn 1982). The human being is, in Luhmann's view, relying on and even standing in the shadow of social systems with their independent functioning, and not—surely to a limited extent—stepping out from their embrace and restructuring them. Luhmann was able to partially elucidate how procedures promote acceptance, but not the self-legitimation of the political system without reference to contents. The critics of Luhmann's approach convey insight also with regard to legitimacy, legitimation, and procedural justice.

More than a decade after the publication of *Legitimation durch Verfahren*, Luhmann wrote in a footnote (1981, 71) that he places his own definition in 'legitimation by procedure' in disposition, because it 'provoked much unnecessary controversies'. One may find other words for 'legitimation'. Many unnecessary controversies? Probably not, because Luhmann challenged his critics to much productivity, which not least sharpened awareness of aspects of distributive and procedural justice. But after all this, the debate has not reached a final point. There is another perspective possible.

Towards an Alternative Model of Procedure and New Research

Recent empirical research shows the importance of how people evaluate what happens in a procedure before a decision is made. These evaluations influence peoples' judgements about outcome fairness and procedural justice. They also influence trust in institutions and their personnel as well as their legitimacy. An overview of this mainly American literature was given by Lind and Tyler 1988; Tyler and Lind 1992. These two American authors did not refer to Luhmann's 'legitimation by procedure'. However, their group value theory can be taken as a contrasting model to Luhmann's (Machura 1994a, 1994b). According to Lind and Tyler, people learn in a procedure about their standing in the social group to which they belong and on which they are dependent. They want to be treated as promised in the group values. These values are acquired during socialization within the group. Affected persons look especially at the behaviour of people in authority positions towards them. Similar is the psychology of persons not personally affected. As long as the procedures seem fair, people are ready to accept single unjust decisions (Tyler 1990). Unfair procedures are unacceptable for them because they are likely to result repeatedly in unjust decisions (Tyler 1990).

From the perspective of the group value theory, a system that uses 'legitimation by procedure', as described by Luhmann, will lose legitimacy in the long run. A dramatic staging does not meet the requirement of honesty. People learn to expect certain standards of behaviour of authority. They also learn to expect output rationality and efficiency of procedures. But this is of minor importance compared with the former, as the group value theory puts it. Authorities have to conform to four dimensions of procedural justice (Tyler and Lind 1992; Lind 1994). People want to experience 'standing' (to feel that they are respected group members). They want to gain a feeling of 'trust' in the benevolence of the authority. They want to experience the 'neutrality' of the authority and they want to have a 'voice' to influence the decision. Of the four aspects of procedural justice, voice is of minor importance, Lind and Tyler argue. In contrast to Luhmann's, their model of man is not curtailed to the *Homo oeconomicus* model.

Reading Lind and Tyler, one is reminded of many arguments formulated by Offe, by Habermas, by the defenders of procedural rationality of processes, and by the other authors cited above. Lind and Tyler's core model of the individual in group relation may be criticized or endorsed. It provides an alternative. With their social psychological perspective and with their empirical work, Lind and Tyler encourage new research on procedure, focusing less on philosophical or juridical reasoning as the debate that at least German scholars are familiar with. Instead, Lind and Tyler focus on the evaluations of people.

The first results of procedural justice research using the Lind and Tyler approach in Germany can already be presented. According to Luhmann, losers in court tend to be upset about the jurists. This is not always true and perhaps is not even the typical reaction. In a study of juvenile prisoners, Haller found that their evaluations of their judges were quite differentiated (Haller 1987; Haller and Machura 1995). Lay assessors were seen as tendentially enhancing procedural justice (Haller and Machura 1995). Defendants in county courts evaluated their judges and their lawyers positively; public prosecutors were seen in more differentiated ways but still stood in high esteem (Machura 1994b).

In contrast to Luhmann's model, winning or losing is not always the decisive criterion for affected persons. Instead, procedural justice and distributive justice contribute a lot to satisfaction with outcomes (Haller and Machura 1995), evaluations of jurists (Machura 1994b), and trust in legal institutions (Machura 1994a).

It has to be mentioned here that Luhmann (1975) tends to restrict his analysis of court trial to civil procedures. He suspects that there may be differences with regard to the psychology of criminal procedures. The two studies cited are on criminal procedures. But for a long time, parts of the literature have extended Luhmann's argumentations to this field. More important seems to be that empirical research on legitimizing aspects of procedures has now started in Germany (and also in the Netherlands; see Wemmers 1996). It should be broadened to various types of procedures and conflicts.

Notes

1 Luhmann (1975, vii, preface to the second edition).

2 This book, *A Sociological Theory of Law* (a translation of Luhmann's book *Rechtssoziologie*) contains a chapter on legitimation which gives a brief, to a certain degree radicalized, version of *Legitimation durch Verfahren*.

3 Hennis (1976, 19): 'Niklas Luhmann . . .: a theory of legitimacy as an instruction of how to remove this problem through eager sweeping, i.e., procedure'; Kielmannsegg (1971), Zippelius (1973), Ryffel (1974), Menzel (1980), Tönnies (1987), Pitschas (1990), Lübbe (1991).

4 About this perception in the scientific German literature, see Menzel (1980). Czybulka (1989, 65–6), e.g., states: 'too biased'.

5 Heidorn (1982). Zippelius's (1973) arguments with regard to the

material outcomes. Law-making on the use of nuclear power and citizens' reaction is quoted as an instance by Zimmer (1979).

6 See Weiß (1977), Heidorn (1982), Weber (1972).

7 For juridicial criticism, see Esser (1970). Rottleuthner's criticism of Luhmann culminates in the assertion that Luhmann would not try out the 'systematically distorted interaction' in court on a 'model of undiluted communication' (Rottleuthner 1971, 81).

8 The linguistic barriers are an important subject of the research on the sociology of law; see Röhl (1977).

9 Lübbe (1991). Gilles (1976) emphasizes that, in a highly complex society, no one is able to form a conviction for every question to be decided. Luhmann approves as far as criminal law is concerned: Schreiber (1976).

References

Breuer, Stefan. 1991. *Max Webers Herrschaftssoziologie*. Frankfurt am Main: Campus.

Czybulka, Detlev. 1989. *Die Legitimation der öffentlichen Verwaltung*. Heidelberg: C. F. Müller.

Esser, Josef. 1970. *Vorverständnis und Methodenwahl in der Rechtsfindung*. Frankfurt am Main: Athenäum.

Gilles, Peter. 1976. Verfahrensfunktionen und Legitimationsprobleme richterlicher Entscheidungen im Zivilprozeß. Zur Kritik N. Luhmanns am Richtigkeitspostulat der sog. klassischen Verfahrenslehre. In *Festschrift für Gerhard Schiedermair zum 70. Geburtstag*, edited by G. Lüke and O. Jauernig. München: Beck.

Grottian, Peter. 1974. *Strukturprobleme staatlicher Planung*. Hamburg: Hoffmann und Campe.

Habermas, Jürgen. 1971. Theorie der Gesellschaft oder Sozialtechnologie? Eine Auseinandersetzung mit Niklas Luhmann. In *Theorie der Gesellschaft oder Sozialtechnologie—Was leistet die Systemforschung?* edited by J. Habermas and N. Luhmann. Frankfurt am Main: Suhrkamp.

———. 1976. Legitimationsprobleme im modernen Staat. In *Legitimationsprobleme politischer Systeme*, edited by P. Graf Kielmannsegg. Opladen: Westdeutscher Verlag.

———. 1993. *Faktizität und Geltung*. 3d ed. Frankfurt am Main: Suhrkamp.

Hagen, Johann J. 1972. Legitimation durch Verfahren. *Juristische Schulung* 11: 485–8.

Haller, Volkmar. 1987. Zum Einfluß von Urteilshöhe und empfundener distributiver und prozeduraler Gerechtigkeit auf die Urteilszufriedenheit sowie auf die Beurteilung von Richter und Gerichtsbarkeit bei jugendlichen Strafgefangenen. Diss. Faculty of Psychology, Philipps-Universität Marburg.

Haller, Volkmar, and Stefan Machura. 1995. Procedural Justice at German Courts As Seen by Defendants and Juvenile Prisoners. *Social Justice Research* 8: 197–215.

Hegenbarth, Rainer, and Regine Scholz. 1979. Konfliktlösung ohne Kommunikation: Die Organisation der Sprachlosigkeit in Zivilprozessen. *Informationsbrief für Rechtssoziologie* 15: 88–118.

Heidorn, Joachim. 1982. *Legitimität und Regierbarkeit.* Berlin: Duncker and Humblot.

Hennis, Wilhelm. 1976. Legitimität. In *Legitimationsprobleme politischer Systeme*, edited by P. Graf Kielmannsegg. Opladen: Westdeutscher Verlag.

Kevenhörster, Paul. 1978. Legitimitätsdoktrinen und Legitimierungsverfahren in westlichen Demokratien. Zu Bestimmungsfaktoren und Defiziten der Systemlegitimierung. In *Die Rechtfertigung politischer Herrschaft, Doktrinen und Verfahren in Ost und West*, edited by P. Graf Kielmannsegg and U. Matz. Freiburg (Breisgau): Alber.

Kielmannsegg, Peter Graf. 1971. Legitimität als analytische Kategorie. *Politische Vierteljahresschrift* 12: 367–401.

Kriele, Martin. 1981. *Einführung in die Staatslehre.* 2d ed. Opladen: Westdeutscher Verlag.

Leibfried, Stephan. 1972. Sozial-Technologie. *Neue Politische Literatur* 17: 119–21.

Lind, E. Allan. 1994. Procedural Justice and Culture: Evidence for Ubiquitous Process Concerns. *Zeitschrift für Rechtssoziologie* 15: 24–36.

Lind, E. Allan, and Tom R. Tyler. 1988. *The Social Psychology of Procedural Justice.* New York: Plenum.

Lübbe, Weyma. 1991. *Legitimität kraft Legalität. Sinnverstehen und Institutionenanalyse bei Max Weber und seinen Kritikern.* Tübingen: J. C. B. Mohr (Paul Siebeck).

Luhmann, Niklas. 1975. *Legitimation durch Verfahren.* 2d ed. Darmstadt: Luchterhand.

———. 1981. Selbstlegitimation des Staates. In Legitimation des modernen Staates, edited by N. Achterberg and W. Krawietz. *Archiv für Rechts- und Sozialphilosophie*, suppl. 15. Wiesbaden: Steiner.

———. 1985. *A Sociological Theory of Law.* Edited by Martin Albrow. Translated by Elizabeth King and Martin Albrow. London: Routledge and Kegan Paul.

———. 1993. *Das Recht der Gesellschaft.* Frankfurt am Main: Suhrkamp.

Machura, Stefan. 1994a. Procedural and Distributive Justice as Seen by

German Defendants. Paper presented at Law and Society annual meeting, 17 June, Phoenix, Arizona.

———. 1994b. Trust and Procedural Fairness: How Are Lawyers, Judges, and Public Prosecutors Seen by German Defendants? Paper presented at the thirteenth World Congress of Sociology, 18 July, Bielefeld, Germany.

Mandt, Hella. 1991. Legitimität. [I] Theorie und Geschichte. In *Wörterbuch Staat und Politik*, edited by D. Nohlen. Bonn: Bundeszentrale für politische Bildung.

Menzel, Hans-Joachim. 1980. *Legitimation staatlicher Herrschaft durch Partizipation Privater?* Berlin: Duncker and Humblot.

Offe, Claus. 1972. *Strukturprobleme des kapitalistischen Staates*. Frankfurt am Main: Suhrkamp.

———. 1984. Politische Legitimation durch Mehrheitsentscheidung? In *An den Grenzen der Mehrheitsdemokratie. Politik und Soziologie der Mehrheitsregel*, edited by B. Guggenberger and C. Offe. Opladen: Westdeutscher Verlag.

Pitschas, Rainer. 1990. *Verwaltungsverantwortung und Verwaltungsverfahren*. München: Beck.

Rammstedt, Otthein. 1976. Zum Legitimationsverlust von Legitimität. *In Legitimationsprobleme politischer Systeme*, edited by P. Graf Kielmannsegg. Opladen: Westdeutscher Verlag.

Rhonheimer, Martin. 1979. *Politisierung und Legitimitätsentzug. Totalitäre Kritik der parlamentarischen Demokratie in Deutschland*. Freiburg (Breisgau): Alber.

Röhl, Klaus F. 1977. *Gegenwartsströmungen der Rechtssoziologie*. Berlin: Sektion Rechtssoziologie in der Deutschen Gesellschaft für Soziologie and arbeitskreis für rechtssoziologie e. V. Informationsbrief für Rechtssoziologie, special edition 1.

———. 1987. *Rechtssoziologie*. Köln: Heymann.

Rottleuthner, Hubert. 1971. Zur Soziologie richterlichen Handelns (2). *Kritische Justiz* 4: 60–88.

Rucht, Dieter. 1984. Recht auf Widerstand? Aktualität, Legitimität und Grenzen 'zivilen Ungehorsams'. In *An den Grenzen der Mehrheitsdemokratie. Politik und Soziologie der Mehrheitsregel*, edited by B. Guggenberger and C. Offe. Opladen: Westdeutscher Verlag.

Ryffel, Hans. 1974. *Rechtssoziologie*. Neuwied: Luchterhand.

Schaper, Jürgen. 1985. *Studien zur Theorie und Soziologie des gerichtlichen Verfahrens*. Berlin: Duncker and Humblot.

Schmid, Günther, and Hubert Treiber. 1975. *Bürokratie und Politik*. München: Fink.

Schmidt, Eike. 1973. *Der Zweck des Zivilprozesses und seine Ökonomie*. Frankfurt: Athenäum.

Schreiber, Hans-Ludwig. 1976. Verfahrensrecht und Verfahrenswirklichkeit. *Zeitschrift für die gesamte Strafrechtswissenschaft* 26: 117–61.

Tönnies, Sibylle. 1987. Ist das Recht ein Biotop? *Rechtstheorie* 18: 105–19.

Treiber, Hubert. 1975. Verfahren als Herrschaftsmechanismus: Zu Niklas Luhmanns 'Legitimation durch Verfahren'. *Kriminalsoziologische Bibliographie* 8: 19–24.

Tyler, Tom R. 1990. *Why People Obey the Law*. New Haven: Yale University Press.

Tyler, Tom R., and E. Allan Lind. 1992. A Relational Model of Authority in Groups. *In Advances in Experimental Social Psychology*. Vol. 25, edited by M. Zanna. New York: Academic.

Weber, Max. 1972. *Wirtschaft und Gesellschaft*. 5th ed. Edited by Johannes Winckelmann. Tübingen: Mohr.

Weiß, Johannes. 1977. Legitimationsbegriff und Legitimationsleistung der Systemtheorie Niklas Luhmanns. *Politische Vierteljahresschrift* 18: 74–85.

Wemmers, Jo-Anne. 1996. *Victims in the Criminal Justice System*. Amsterdam: Kugler Publications.

Zimmer, Gerhard. 1979. *Funktion-Kompetenz-Legitimation. Gewaltenteilung in der Ordnung des Grundgesetzes*. Berlin: Duncker and Humblot.

Zippelius, Reinhold. 1973. Legitimation durch Verfahren? In *Festschrift für Karl Larenz zum 70. Geburtstag*, edited by G. Paulus, U. Diederichsen, and C.-W. Canaris. München: Beck.

The Author

Stefan Machura. Born in 1962. Studied sociology, political science, and social economy at Ruhr-Universität Bochum. Doctoral thesis *Die Kontrolle öffentlicher Unternehmen* (The Control of State-Owned Enterprises), 1993, Wiesbaden: DUV. Has published articles on sociological theory, state administration, state-owned enterprises, court trials, and procedural justice. Currently Wissenschaftlicher Mitarbeiter (Researcher) at the Chair for Sociology and Philosophy of Law, Ruhr-Universität Bochum.

Address: Cäcilienstrasse 21, D-59759 Arnsberg, Germany.

Abstract

Niklas Luhmann's book *Legitimation durch Verfahren* (Legitimation by Procedure) is of central interest for the evaluation of the performance of the social institution 'procedure', and contributes much to the explanation of procedures. But, as this paper discusses, Luhmann's intention to show

how the political system promotes self-legitimation without reference to contents fails. Critics of his book have conveyed further insight into legitimacy, legitimation, and procedural justice. Machura argues for a 'multidimensional model' of legitimacy and for a 'legitimacy by fair procedures'.

10 Subjective Procedural Justice and Civil Procedure

CHRISTOPH RENNIG

Introduction

Disadvantageous decisions are more likely to be accepted and observed if they are arrived at by means of a fair procedure. This finding has been confirmed repeatedly (Lind and Tyler 1988; Tyler 1990; Tyler and Lind 1992) within a tradition of social psychological research that from the outset has focused attention on the judicial system (Thibaut, Friedland, and Walker 1974; Walker, LaTour, Lind, and Thibaut 1974; Walker, Lind, and Thibaut 1974; Thibaut and Walker 1975). Nevertheless, this body of research does not supply a set of easy-to-follow directions for the organization of legal procedure. There seem to be at least three complications:

1. There is no single form of fair legal procedure. Research into the relative effect on subjective procedural justice of some aspects of legal procedure has produced inconsistent results. Casper, Tyler and, Fisher (1988), and Landis and Goodstein (1987), for example, report divergent findings as to the effect of plea bargaining on defendants' perceptions of the fairness of criminal procedure. Furthermore, there is evidence that the matter in dispute and the social, cultural, and ethnic background of the persons involved also affect perception of procedural justice (Leung and Lind 1986; Barrett-Howard and Tyler 1986; Barrett and Lamm 1989; Vidmar and Schuller 1987; Valente and Mace 1993).
2. Subjective procedural justice is not the only variable affecting the acceptance of the justice system and compliance with the system's decisions. Undoubtedly, it is an important variable in this respect, probably the most important one. But effects of other variables like absolute or relative outcome or of subjective distributive justice on the evaluation of the justice system cannot be denied (see Lind and Tyler 1988; Tyler 1990; Tyler and Lind 1992). Thus, any legal policy

aiming to safeguard the acceptability of the justice system would fortunately miss its target if it did not accompany any efforts in the field of subjective procedural justice with an attempt to eliminate or at least reduce an eventual structural injustice in terms of *outcomes*.

3. Ensuring acceptance of and compliance with courts' decisions is not the only purpose of legal policy. Of course it is an important political aim, but only in conjuction with other aims. To give just two examples: It is of equal importance, at least in most states where the rule of law prevails, that equal access to justice be given to all citizens—regardless of a potential influence of equal access to justice on subjective procedural justice. And probably everywhere, legal policy is subject to limited financial and personnel resources. This enumeration is not at all exhaustive, but it may suffice as a basis for explaining the general orientation of German legal policy in the field of civil procedure in recent years.

One main end of this policy was and is the reduction of the case-load of the civil courts. The easing of this burden is seen as a means to enhance the acceptability of the civil justice system and its decisions, because it is expected to enable the courts to handle cases more thoroughly and more speedily. Furthermore, reduction of case-load is seen as a means to slow down the increase in the budgetary expenditures of the civil justice system. The promotion of pretrial settlement and of alternative dispute resolution will remain important approaches, too. From the point of view of legal policy, these kinds of procedures appear to serve two purposes: namely, to reduce the civil courts' case-load, and, in certain types of disputes, to produce an outcome superior in terms of acceptability and pacification. Since some conceivable means of easing case-load, such as raising court fees while abolishing legal aid, are incompatible with the ideal of equal access to justice, alternative dispute resolution has been and is seen as one of the most promising ways to keep cases away from civil courts.

Several recent legislative acts have been aimed at enhancing the attractiveness of alternative dispute resolution. Other administrative or legislative efforts to reduce the case-load of the civil courts or to accelerate legal proceedings concentrated on organizational reforms inside the courts and on changes in civil procedure. The latter shall be discussed in this article with special regard to empirical findings on determinants of subjective procedural justice.

These recent changes in civil procedure have partly taken into account relevant results of research in the fields of sociology of law, comparative law, business administration, and economics. Part of this research was carried out within the research programme of the Federal Ministry of Justices 'Analysis of the Structure of the Judicial System'. But research on subjective procedural justice has neither been used in developing legal political strategies nor been carried out within the aforementioned research programme so far.

This article is intended to give an idea of how civil proceedings in Germany operate by providing empirical data on the German civil justice system and by explaining the general structure of German civil procedure as well as recent changes in civil procedure. In addition, it will accompany this outline with empirical findings about the factors that determine subjective procedural justice and develop hypotheses on the subjective procedural justice of civil proceedings under German civil procedure. The final section will address the question of how to safeguard acceptance of the civil justice system and subjective procedural justice under conditions of high case-load.

Data on German Civil Jurisdiction

The Germans seem to like civil proceedings. In 1989, the number of judges per one hundred thousand inhabitants was twenty-eight in the old Federal Republic of Germany,[1] twenty in Austria and Belgium, ten in France, and six in the Netherlands (Blankenburg 1992).[2] Statistics on the number of civil proceedings per one hundred thousand inhabitants shows a similar picture: in 1989, there were 10,800 proceedings per one hundred thousand persons in Austria; 9,400 in the old Federal Republic of Germany; 4,700 in Belgium; and 1,600 in France and the Netherlands (Blankenburg 1992).

Data on per capita average annual premiums for legal-costs insurance coverage are also worth mentioning. In 1989, such expenditures in the old Federal Republic of Germany were the highest in Western Europe (see Table 10.1).

Together with the data cited above, these figures indicate a relatively high readiness of the German population to use legal services. On the other hand, they may also indicate limited faith on the part of some people in their fellow citizens' ability to resolve disputes amicably and in the courts' administration of justice.

But 1989, to which the above data refer, was not the year in which the case-load of the civil courts in the old Federal Republic of Germany reached its peak. A look at the changes in the number of

Table 10.1: Average Per Capita Annual Premiums for Legal-Costs Insurance Coverage

Nation	Average Annual Expense (in ECUs)
Germany	23,959
Austria	18,136
Switzerland	9,964
Belgium	9,035
Netherlands	5,088
Spain	3,035
France	1,560
Great Britain	1,041
Italy	0,398
Greece	0,160

Source: Jagodzinski, Raiser, and Riehl (1991, 287).
Note: ECU = European Currency Units.

new civil suits per year since 1978[3] in the old Länder shows that this number went up from 1.13 million in 1978 to 1.68 million in 1986, then fell to 1.59 million in 1989 and later evened out at about 1.55 million in 1990 and 1991. More recent increases in the number of civil suits shall not be discussed here because the legislative acts that are addressed later in this article were based on the situation in the 1980s.

An important indicator of how the civil justice system is coping with its case-load is the change in the backlog of cases from one year's end to the next year's end. That shows whether the civil justice system is making headway in settling its arrears. In the old Federal Republic, the number of cases carried forward into the new year increased from 477,000 in 1978 to 717,000 in 1986, then fell to 667,000 in 1989, and finally reached 671,000 in 1990 and in 1991.

This means that from 1978 to 1986, the number of civil suits went up by about 30 per cent of the 1978 amount. During the same time span, the backlog increased by about 50 per cent. From 1986 to 1991, the number of civil actions went down by about 10 per cent of the 1986 amount, while the backlog only decreased by about 7 per cent. From 1989 to 1990, there was even a decrease in new civil suits and an increase in the backlog.

These data indicate that the German civil justice system in the early 1980s was already operating at its limits. On the other hand, it can be seen that during the 1980s, as their case-load became heavier, the civil courts disposed of, or had to dispose of, a growing number of suits. The disposals by civil courts of first instance increased from 914,000 in 1978 to 1.31 million in 1987 and then went down to 1.199 million in 1991. During the same time span, the number of judges in service at the civil courts of first instance did not increase to the same extent, as is shown in Table 10.2:

Table 10.2: Number of Judges at Civil Courts of First Instance Per End of Respective Year (old Länder only)

Year	Number of Judges
1978	3,251
1987	3,707
1991	3,865

Two assumptions may be derived from this data:

As the German civil justice system is operating at full capacity, its case-load affects the factual thoroughness of case handling by the civil courts. If over a certain period a more or less constant number of judges disposed of an increasing number of cases, then the time spent on individual cases must have decreased. If time spent indicates thoroughness, then it can be concluded that a growing case-load leads to a loss of thoroughness.

But even if the system is under pressure, a certain minimum of time is undoubtedly spent on a single case. If the increase in the backlog exceeds the increase in new suits and the decrease in the backlog lags behind the decrease in new actions, then the courts must surely be handling their cases with a certain standard of thoroughness, if time taken for the disposal is the criterion. What determines this standard is not clear.

The picture of the conditions in the German civil justice system would be incomplete without data on alternative dispute resolution, because the case flood troubling the courts is not the only characteristic of the system as a whole. Institutions of alternative dispute resolution have constantly been extended since the early 1970s (Morasch 1984).

Contrary to widespread prejudices, lawyers play an important role in pretrial settlement. In 1986–87, 70 per cent of the civil cases in which one of the parties was counselled by a lawyer were settled extrajudicially. This rate fell to 30 per cent in cases where both parties were represented by a lawyer (Wasilewski 1990, 36).

A recent study by Stock et al. (1995) provides information on the supply of and the demand for alternative dispute resolution in four German cities (Lübeck, Nuremberg, Rostock, and Leipzig) in 1991 and 1992. The data listed in the study afford an insight into the relation between cases handled by institutions of alternative dispute resolution and those handled by the civil courts of first instance. The estimate[4] of this relation includes a correction for case transfer between institutions of alternative dispute resolution. With one exception, these institutions were handling many more cases than the civil courts of first instance, regardless of whether debt-settlement orders are included or excluded, as is shown in Table 10.3:

Table 10.3: Ratios of Cases Handled by Institutions of ADR to Civil Suits and to Civil Suits Plus Summary Proceedings for Debt-Settlement Order in Four German Cities (1991)

	ADR Cases to:	
City	Civil Suits	Civil Suits + Summary Proceedings
Lübeck	6:1	2:1
Nuremberg[a]	10:1	1:1.25
Leipzig	10:1	8:1
Rostock	23:1	4:1

Note: ADR = alternative dispute resolution.
[a]Due to the city's economic structure, the Nuremberg court has a very high rate of summary proceedings for debt-settlement orders. Such proceedings have to be opened at the court whose district comprises the location of the creditor, and Nuremberg is the headquarters of the consumer finance company of a mail-order-house that claims to be the continent's largest.

These findings, especially those obtained in Lübeck and Nuremberg, primarily reflect pretrial activities of lawyers. A comparison of cities in the western part of Germany (Lübeck, Nuremberg) with cities in the new Länder (Rostock, Leipzig) indicates a greater demand for alternative dispute resolution in the eastern regions. This difference may have been caused by the fact that, in 1991 and 1992, the civil justice system in the new Länder still was being built up, and cases could not be handled speedily. Furthermore, alternative means of settling local disputes and small-claims cases were promoted very strongly in the former German Democratic Republic. This tradition may still have influenced the way in which legal adversaries handled conflicts.

Alternative dispute resolution seems to be used less frequently in Germany than in some other European countries. In the old Federal Republic, about 2 per cent of all traffic accidents were followed by a civil suit, while at the same time in the Netherlands this was the case for 0.2 per cent of all traffic accidents (Simsa 1992). At first glance, the difference between 98 per cent and 99.8 per cent for extrajudicial settlements may not appear salient. But transferring the Dutch rate to Germany would mean nothing less than reducing the number of civil suits following traffic accidents by 90 per cent.

German Law of Civil Procedure

Fundamental Regulations

The following outline of German civil procedure refers to civil suits that are tried and decided by a judgement. Other existing forms of procedure or disposal are not examined. Nor is there any detailed explanation of stages or types of trial that seem to bear little relation to empirical findings on subjective procedural justice.

According to sections 23 and 71 of the Judicature Act (Gerichtsverfassungsgesetz [GVG]), two kinds of courts have original civil jurisdiction: the *Amtsgerichte* (local courts) and the *Landgerichte* (regional courts). The civil jurisdiction of the *Amtsgericht* includes matters not exceeding a value in dispute of ten thousand Deutschmarks (DM), and, regardless of the amount in dispute, most landlord and tenant cases and a few other kinds of cases. The *Landgericht* has first-instance jurisdiction in most matters exceeding a value in dispute of ten thousand DM and, regardless of the amount in dispute, in all claims of liability in respect to a government official, and in some exceptional kinds of case. The fundamental procedural regulations are the same for the *Amtsgericht* as for the *Landgericht*, with two important exceptions:

Amtsgericht decisions are always taken by one judge. The *Landgericht* principally decides through a civil chamber of three judges. But the chamber may, if certain conditions are met, transfer responsibility for trying and disposing of a case to one of its members. This transfer to a judge sitting alone is provided for in section 348 of the Code of Civil Procedure (Zivilprozeßordnung [ZPO]).[5] The percentage of cases tried and decided by a judge sitting alone varies dramatically among the *Landgerichte* of the old Federal Republic, from near zero to above eighty. This variation cannot be explained by variations in characteristics of cases or of litigants involved. Compliance with local traditions, and not with statutory regulations, seems to be an influential factor (Rottleuthner, Böhm, and Gasterstädt 1992, 35–112).

In the *Landgericht*, both parties must be represented by a lawyer (section 78 ZPO). Only through their lawyers can the litigants make valid declarations. If the lawyer does not appear at the trial, the party he or she represents is deemed absent (with possible negative procedural consequences), even if the party actually is present. In the *Amtsgericht*, representation by lawyers is not required by law, but is of course possible. The proportion of actions brought to the *Amtsgerichte* with at least the plaintiff represented by a lawyer has been continuously increasing and amounted to 86 per cent in 1991. In the same year, in 46 per cent of the *Amtsgericht* cases both parties engaged a lawyer. This proportion has been increasing, too. The ratio of *Amtsgericht* cases with neither side being represented by a lawyer fell to 11 per cent.

In general, legal action is taken by sending a statement of claim to the court. The court sends the statement of claim to the defendant, who has to present a statement of defence if he wants to prevent himself from being adjudged at once. The petition laid down in the statement of claim and any partial acknowledgement by the defendant limit the range of possible judgements. Furthermore, the court must not look for evidence on its own initiative. Thus, the parties have the power to define the matter in dispute—both in respect to the proceedings as a whole and in respect to single stages of the proceedings. On the other hand, having once received the statement of claim, the court can exercise strong influence on further proceedings. The court decides which of the litigants' allegations are legally relevant at all with respect to a justification or a dismissal of the action, and, on these grounds, what are the issues of fact. Furthermore, the court shall in every phase of the proceedings, from the pretrial stage to the end of trial, attempt to induce the litigants to compromise on the matter in dispute.[6] The taking of evidence during the trial is conducted by the judge or by the presiding judge of the civil chamber, as appropriate.

The parties have a constitutional right to comment on the facts on which the court's decisions are grounded, one consequence of which is that the court may not base decisions on evidence upon which the litigants have had no opportunity to comment.[7] But if a party is represented by a lawyer, then, as far as civil procedure is concerned, this constitutional right is still observed if the court only hears the lawyer. Additionally, section 137 (4) of the ZPO provides that a litigant on petition has to be heard by the court.[8] The difference between the two modes is that the hearing pursuant to Article 103 (1) of the Basic Law is a statutory requirement, while the hearing under section 137 (4) of the ZPO only has to take place upon the party's petition. Litigants and their lawyers receive an official copy of the written judgement that as a rule contains a statement of facts and reasons for the decision. Exceptions concerning the content of the written judgement are discussed below.

Most judgements of the courts of first instance can be appealed against on questions of fact *and* law (*Berufung*). In the proceedings on appeals of this kind, the litigants may allege new facts and introduce new evidence. Some of the judgements of the courts of second instance, i.e., the judgements terminating the *Berufung* proceedings, can be appealed on questions of law *only* (Revision). The option to appeal a judgement mainly depends on the gravamen imposed on the litigant wishing to appeal. The appeal on questions of fact *and* law (*Berufung*) is admissible if the value of the subject of the complaint exceeds fifteen hundred DM.[9] Appeals of an *Amtsgericht*'s decision are filed with the *Landgericht* that in this case also is a court of appeal. Appeals of a *Landgericht*'s decision of first instance are filed with the *Oberlandesgericht* (higher regional court). An appeal on questions of law only ('Revision') is admissible only against judgements passed in second instance by an *Oberlandesgericht*. The nonadmission of appeals, be it on questions of fact and law or on questions of law only, has another consequence: if there is no provision whatsoever for appealing a particular judgement, the court may refrain from giving a statement of facts in the written judgement.[10]

Recent Amendments of Laws Ruling Civil Proceedings

Only some of the past decade's amendments to laws ruling civil proceedings can be assumed to bear relation to subjective procedural justice. The guiding line of the legislation of particular interest here seems to have been, first of all, reduction; i.e., reduction of the number of judges needed for disposing of a certain number of proceedings of first instance, reduction of the amount of—or at least of the increase in—appellate proceedings, reduction of the time needed for the taking of evidence. Whether these efforts might have reduced subjective procedural justice, too, will be considered later in the chapter.

The critical values of a lawsuit or of the subject of the complaint defining the competences of the *Amtsgericht* and the *Landgericht* with respect to original civil jurisdiction and controlling for the options to appeal against judgements of first instance, were raised continuously.[11] In the 1990s, these rises clearly exceeded inflation.

The value separating the *Amtsgericht/Landgericht* competences was raised from three thousand DM to five thousand DM in 1982, to six thousand DM in 1990, and to ten thousand DM in 1993.[12] This increase of the threshold moved cases from the *Landgericht* to the *Amtsgericht* and thus had three main consequences:

1. The total number of judges needed to dispose of a certain number of civil proceedings of first instance was reduced, because the *Amtsgericht* decisions are always taken by one judge, while the *Landgerichte* regularly decide by a civil chamber of three judges (some chambers more often than others).
2. For a certain proportion of cases the number of judges trying the individual case was reduced from three to one. This is true for cases where the value of the subject of the complaint falls between the old and the new critical value.
3. The number of judgements that can be appealed for questions of *law only* was reduced as well, as this kind of appeal is only admissible if the decision to be appealed was taken by an *Oberlandesgericht*. This condition is only met if the original decision was taken by a *Landgericht*, not by an *Amtsgericht*.

The value of the subject of the complaint separating cases where an appeal on questions of *fact and law* is admissible from cases where it is inadmissible was raised from five hundred DM to seven hundred DM in 1982, to twelve hundred DM in 1990, and to fifteen hundred DM in 1993.[13] This kept cases out of the *Landgerichte* as courts of second instance.

The options to appeal have been reduced further by amendments included in the law that came into force on 1 March 1993. Before that date, the *Landgerichte* tried all nonpecuniary claims, and in nonpecuniary claims appeals on questions of facts and law were generally admissible. Beginning 1 March 1993, all nonpecuniary claims where the value of the subject of the complaint does not exceed ten thousand DM have been tried by the *Amtsgerichte*. Appeals of *Amtsgerichts*' decisions of those cases are only admissible if the value of the subject of the complaint exceeds fifteen hundred DM.

All the aforementioned amendments increased the proportion judgements of first instance that can not be appealed. In 1990, appeals were inadmissible for 30 per cent of the cases disposed of by the *Amtsgerichte* and for 23 per cent of all civil cases disposed of by courts of first instance (*Amtsgerichte* and *Landgerichte*). If the regulations that took effect in 1 April 1991 are projected on the statistical data of the whole year of 1991, then proportions of 44 per cent (cases disposed of by the *Amtsgerichte*) and 34 per cent (cases disposed of by civil courts of first instance) result. The effects of the amendment that came into force 1 March 1993 can only be estimated at the moment. Meanwhile, appeal is inadmissible in about 45 per cent of the cases disposed of by the *Amtsgerichte* and in about 39 per cent of all civil cases disposed of by courts of first instance. Another consequence should be recalled. If an appeal is inadmissible, giving a statement of fact in the written judgement is at the discretion of the court (ZPO, section 313a [1] [1]; see note 12).

Another change of civil procedure might have been initiated when section 495a of the ZPO took effect on 1 April 1991.[14] This section provides that, if the value of the matter in dispute does not exceed a certain amount, the arrangement of the proceedings is at the discretion of the judge at the *Amtsgericht* (so-called simplified procedure). This means, for example, that the taking of evidence is not limited by a catalogue of admissible evidence and that the litigants need not be heard themselves if they are represented by lawyers, not even upon petition. First, the limit of the value of the matter in dispute for a case that could be tried in simplified procedure was one thousand DM. In 1993, the critical value was raised to twelve hundred DM. In 1991, about 40 per cent of the civil cases disposed of by the *Amtsgerichte* and about 14 per cent of all civil cases disposed of by courts of first instance theoretically could have been tried under section 495a of the ZPO. The respective proportions for 1993 can be estimated at about 40 per cent (*Amtsgericht* cases) and 34 per cent (all civil cases of first instance).

The law that came into force 1 March 1993 extended the possibilites of a civil chamber to transfer a lawsuit for decision to a judge sitting alone. The wording of section 348 of the ZPO 'The civil chamber *may* transfer the lawsuit for decision to one of its members as a judge sitting alone . . .' was replaced by 'The civil chamber *shall as a rule* transfer the lawsuit for decision to one of its members as a judge sitting alone . . .'.[15] This might increase the number of cases transferred to a judge sitting alone and enable the civil chambers to dispose of more cases within a certain period.

Findings on Subjective Procedural Justice and the Context of German Civil Procedure

Empirical and experimental research has shown that quite a few variables affect subjective procedural justice. Nonetheless, little is known about litigants' or other citizens' evaluations of German civil procedure, and even less is known about either the characteristics of German civil procedure that affect—or at least probably affect—these evaluations or the causes of their influence. Most of the research on subjective procedural justice has addressed questions of criminal procedure or managerial relations and has been carried out outside Germany. None of the respective studies using German subjects have referred to civil procedure. The gaps in empirical knowledge about the perceived fairness of German civil procedure cannot be filled by interpolations from research results at hand. Such conclusions would be incorrect, because the matters in dispute as well as social and cultural factors probably affect the perceived fairness of (court) proceedings (Leung and Lind 1986; Barrett-Howard and Tyler 1986; Barrett and Lamm 1989; Vidmar and Schuller 1987; Valente and Mace 1993). The studies done so far do not fit with German civil procedure as to either matter at issue or subjects' cultural background.

The next step that can be made is to derive questions needing further examination and substantiated hypotheses from the research at hand. In the following section, the characteristics of German civil procedure are looked at from the perspective given by the results of empirical research on procedural justice. As hypotheses and not interpretations are aimed at, this section is neither intended to exhaustively report all the results that have been gathered so far nor to smooth inconsistencies in the results and interpretations of different studies.

Three prominent variables—prominent both with respect to research tradition and number of studies examining them—are *decision control*, *process control*, and *voice*. The latter are sometimes used as synonyms (Lind and Tyler 1988, 8; Tyler and Lind 1992, 144).

Some studies found positive correlations between subjective procedural justice and the increase in *decision control* (Tyler 1988; Houlden et al. 1978; Tyler, Rasinski, and Spodick 1985). While plea bargaining as a possible form of defendants' decision control significantly enhanced perceived fairness of criminal procedure in the study of Landis and Goodstein (1987), Casper, Tyler, and Fisher (1988) found no effect of mode of disposition on subjective procedural justice. And as to civil procedure, some findings show that procedures with high decision control of the third party are sometimes preferred to mediation or forms of alternative dispute resolution, where the parties have high decision control (Sheppard 1985, Vidmar 1993).

It can be concluded that decision control at least under certain conditions affects the perceived fairness of the procedure. Thus, observing section 279 of the ZPO might have a positive effect on subjective procedural justice of German civil proceedings. The aforementioned section encourages the court to try to induce the litigants to compromise in every stage of the proceeding.[16] A 'true' compromise is a solution of conflict voluntarily chosen by both parties, i.e., a decision controlled by them, not by the court. The procedure leading to that kind of disposal gives the opponents decision and process control and thus should receive high ratings of procedural fairness. But the reality of compromising at the trial may be different. The parties sometimes may feel pressed to compromise by the court, because the judges feel overloaded, not qualified to decide on the difficult case, etc. If the litigants feel pressed, perceived decision control and, as a consequence, subjective procedural justice, should be rather low. Thus, observation of section 279 of the ZPO can have quite different effects on the perceived fairness of the procedure, depending on the behaviour of the individual judge.

Enhancing *process control* (i.e., especially the opportunity to present evidence and thus to influence the choice of facts the decision is based on) and *voice* (i.e., the capacity to have one's opinion heard) repeatedly have been shown to heighten procedural fairness (Walker, LaTour, Lind, and Thibaut 1974; LaTour 1978; Sheppard 1985). This is first of all true for procedures with high decision control of a third party, like court proceedings (Houlden et al. 1978; Tyler 1988; Lind and Tyler 1988, 109).

For managerial relations, it has been demonstrated that 'voice' can result in a 'frustration effect'. Subjective procedural justice can be decreased, if 'voice' leads to the impression that the statements given are not considered duly by the decision-maker. This is the case, for example, if on the side of the litigants the perception is fostered that the decision-maker judged the claim as completely justified but nevertheless granted only an inferior outcome (Folger 1977; Cohen 1985). Bierhoff (1992) reports respective findings of a series of studies carried out with German subjects.

The importance of due consideration of litigants' statements favours the rational-instrumental or social-exchange interpretation of the voice effect. Giving a party voice increases subjective procedural justice only if voice is perceived as a means for decision control. But there is also evidence for the concurring value-expressive interpretation that assumes that having the opportunity to express one's view is rewarding in and of itself, even if it does not result in decision control (Tyler et al. 1985). Further support for the value-expressive-model comes from the study of Haller (1987; see also Haller and Machura 1995) that was carried out with juvenile delinquents jailed in Germany. The perceived fairness of the proceedings increased when defendants felt the court had given them opportunity to present their own view of their case. The assumption that these subjects felt (post hoc) they had enhanced decision control is not very plausible, because perceived opportunity to present one's own view and length of sentence were correlated positively (and significantly). For the subjects, opportunity to present their view of the case might have meant opportunity to explain themselves and where they stood.[17]

The facultative or compulsory representation by lawyers also may affect voice and, subsequently, subjective procedural justice. A lawyer sometimes does not make all the comments on the case, on the evidence, and on the trial, that the litigant wishes to be made. In those cases the litigant may feel he or she had little or no voice. Casper et al. (1988) found that in criminal cases the length of time defendants could talk with their lawyers about the case significantly affected the perceived fairness of the procedure. This effect may have been caused by the defendants' impression that they had voice *in relation to their lawyer*; it may also have been caused by a more concise presentation of the defendants' views through well-prepared lawyers, i.e., perceived voice *in relation to the court*.

The relational model of authority proposed by Tyler and Lind (1992) includes effects of due consideration of litigants' views on trust in the court, of fact-based decision-making on perceived neutrality of the court, and of both trust and perceived neutrality on subjective procedural justice. Some authors have argued that a certain process control of the third party might foster complete and undistorted sampling of facts (Sheppard 1985). From this point of view the active role that German civil judges play in the taking of evidence may be perceived as safeguarding fact-based decision-making. Litigants' impressions as to due consideration of their views by the court are probably affected by at least two variables: (1) perceived communication of these views to the court and (2) comments given by the court on these views. As far as the first variable is concerned, the behaviour of the lawyers may be crucial, as pointed out before. Feedback on how the court has taken the parties' statements into consideration is given by the written judgement including the statement of facts and the reasons for the decision. A complete written judgement is given in 'normal' civil procedure. But as has been shown above, this 'normal' procedure need not be observed in a growing proportion of cases. If the value of the subject of the complaint does not exceed fifteen hundred DM, a statement of facts in the written judgement is not required (ZPO, section 311a [1] [1]). This may result in a lack of feedback on how the court considered the litigants' views.

Moreover, if the value of the matter in dispute does not exceed twelve hundred DM, the judge can make use of the simplified procedure (ZPO, section 495a), i.e., arrange the proceedings at his discretion. Litigants represented by lawyers then need not be heard at all, not even on request. The aforementioned cases may be, but do not *have to be*, tried in simplified procedure. Data concerning the actual frequency of proceedings taken under section 495a of the ZPO are not available yet. And it is yet unknown what simplified procedure means in practice. It sometimes might mean some kind of a roundtable talk where the parties have satisfactory voice, but it also may mean a procedure fostering perceptions of incomplete fact sampling and of lack of due consideration of litigants' views.

Presence or absence of an *option to appeal* also affects ratings of procedural justice, especially those of German subjects. Sheppard (1985) showed option to appeal to be generally relevant. Barrett and Lamm (1989) found a significant effect of option to appeal in a study with German students, contrary to the results of Barrett-Howard and Tyler's (1986) identically designed study with American students. On a poll taken in Berlin in 1988, 83 per cent of the respondents stated that they preferred judiciaries with several instances to those with only one instance, even if trying a case at several instances took a few years ('Vertrauen', 1988).

As options to appeal probably enhance perceived fairness of procedure, it can be assumed that the recent amendments to the ZPO that continuously reduced the proportion of civil cases that can be appealed have lowered the perceived fairness of civil procedure and the acceptance of the civil justice system.

Limiting the options to appeal will have yet another consequence. Courts of appeal do not only have the function to review the individual adjudgement that is appealed against. By doing so they also give guidelines for the jurisdiction of the lower courts. Options to appeal to a certain degree compel the lower courts to comply with these guidelines. Thus, limiting options to appeal will foster divergencies between lower courts as to the adjudgements of comparable cases. Moreover, it might even increase the case-load of the lower courts. In any dispute, divergency between decisions of different courts gives the lawyers of both litigants a greater chance to find a precedent of any other local court supporting their party's view. As a consequence, readiness to settle the dispute extrajudicially might decrease. Moreover, divergency in the adjudgement of comparable cases reduces the *consistency of decisions* of the civil jurisdiction as a whole. And some studies have shown that consistency over cases or persons affects subjective procedural justice (Barrett-Howard and Tyler 1986; Barrett and Lamm 1989; Haller and Machura 1995).

From a theoretical perspective it should be pointed out that consistency over cases, as far as it is conceived as judging comparable cases equally, is also a matter of distributive justice, as it means following the rules of equity.

Consistency may be relevant to subjective procedural justice in yet another respect—*consistency of a judge's behaviour* at the trial. Some findings indicate that the dignity of the procedure and the respect with which the parties feel treated by the judge or other authorities are correlated significantly with perceived procedural fairness (Tyler 1988; Casper et al. 1988; Lind and Tyler 1988, 221–242; Tyler and Lind 1992, 153; Haller and Machura 1995). If the judge behaves inconsistently and, for example, does not treat both parties equally, at least one of the litigants will perceive the proceedings as lacking dignity and the judge as unrespectful. It is not clear whether strict statutory regulations foster consistency of judges' behaviour at the trial. Judges' behaviour should be, but in fact sometimes is not, guided by statutory regulations.

One example of firm behavioural styles overriding statutory regulations is the most discretionary application of section 348 of the

ZPO by German civil panels mentioned above (Rottleuthner et al. 1992, 35–112).

If strict statutory regulations would lead to greater consistency of a judge's behaviour, then giving the judges more discretionary powers, as with the simplified procedure pursuant to section 495a of the ZPO, should increase the probability both of the proceedings being perceived as undignified and of the judge being seen as biased and unrespectful. These assumptions can be only speculative; empirical research as to the effects of the simplified procedure is necessary.

Thoroughness of case handling is another variable affecting subjective procedural justice. Haller and Machura (1995) report ratings of the judge's sense of duty and feelings that the court had sufficient information on the case to be significantly correlated with judgements of the fairness of criminal procedure. Both sense of duty and completeness of information sampling can be considered as indicators of thoroughness of case handling.

It might further be assumed that proceedings are perceived as more thorough if the cases are tried by a chamber instead of a single judge. The study done by Rottleuthner et al. (1992) comparing single-judge with chamber disposals does not directly address this issue, but allows for a crude operationalization of acceptance and perceived thoroughness of the disposals. Rottleuthner et al. examined decisions of civil chambers of several *Landgerichte* with decisions that members of the respective chamber had taken as judges sitting alone to whom the chamber had delegated the case according to section 348 of the ZPO. The authors report proportions of appeals, which might indicate acceptance, and proportions of successful appeals, which might indicate thoroughness. On these measures, no significant differences between chamber and single-judge decisions could be observed if case characteristics were controlled for (Rottleuthner et al. 146–62). As this study does not allow for a rigorous test of the hypothesized relation between number of judges deciding and perceived thoroughness, it is still possible that consumers of German civil jurisdiction perceive three professional judges together to act more thoroughly than one. But consideration of the aforementioned data shows that this assumption may be wrong.

The perceived thoroughness of the civil justice system as a whole probably depends on the options given to appeal of adjudgements. A case having been tried by several instances may appear to be handled more thoroughly than a case tried only by one instance. In the poll taken in Berlin that has already been mentioned above, 83 per cent of the respondents stated they preferred several instances and eventual lengthy trials to one instance ('Vertraven', 1988).

One factor surely affecting the thoroughness of case handling is the case-load of the civil courts. It has already been pointed out that, as the case-load exceeds a critical amount, the time the courts (can) spend on trying individual cases is reduced. Once the critical point is passed, growing case-load can be assumed to lower subjective procedural justice.

Therefore, the main purpose of the recent amendments to the ZPO (reduction of the case-load) should not necessarily come into conflict with attempts to enhance the perceived procedural justice of the civil justice system. But some of the means used to reach that end will presumably cause fairness of civil procedure to decrease. Most crucial is the limitation of options to appeal. Making appeals inadmissible undoubtedly eases the burden of the courts of appeal, but at the same time probably brings more legal disputes to the lower courts. Moreover, taking away options to appeal probably reduces subjective procedural justice in three ways: first, directly, because options to appeal enhance perceived procedural fairness; second and third, indirectly, because reduction of options to appeal probably fosters inconsistencies and may lower perceived thoroughness of the civil justice system as a whole, and because consistency and thoroughness affect subjective procedural justice. The cases that cannot be appealed are not at all a *quantité négligeable*. They can be estimated to make up about 39 per cent of all cases disposed of by civil courts of first instance in 1993.

The simplified procedure (ZPO, section 495a) may have negative effects on subjective procedural justice, too. It might affect voice given to the litigants and perceptions of neutrality of the court, of the dignity of the procedure, and of the accuracy of fact sampling. But these assumptions are much weaker than those concerning the limitations of options to appeal, as little is known about how simplified procedure is carried out in practice. This form of procedure is worth closer empirical examination.

Conceivable Strategies of Legal Politics

As pointed out in the introduction, legal politics must try to bring the following aims into accordance: (1) enhancement (or at least safeguarding) of subjective procedural justice of the civil justice system, (2) reduction of the case-load of the civil courts, (3) providing (or safeguarding) equal access to justice. A fourth topic is related to all purposes mentioned above: support of alternative dispute resolution.

The relationship between subjective procedural justice and case-load can be assumed to be curvilinear. As subjective procedural justice of the civil jurisdiction increases, civil courts should become more attractive as forums of dispute resolution. The two variables should be correlated positively; case-load should go up as perceived fairness is enhanced. But from a certain critical point, any further increase of case-load may result in a lack of thoroughness of case handling which seems to affect subjective procedural justice negatively. From this point, case-load and subjective procedural justice presumably are correlated negatively; subjective procedural justice decreases as case-load grows even further. The assumed curvilinear relationship is presented in Fig. 10.1. It should be pointed out that the case-load of the civil courts is of course affected by many variables other than subjective procedural justice, e.g., economic factors.

The relation between case-load and subjective procedural justice is not assumed to be a perfect one. Therefore it is conceivable that a legal political measure affects only perceived fairness and not the case-load. In this case, the whole curve would move up or down along the ordinate, as the dotted curves in Fig. 10.1 demonstrate. It is also possible that legislatory efforts, such as reducing options to appeal, affect both subjective procedural justice of the system as a whole and case-load. In this case, the curve is moved vertically (change of the general level of subjective procedural justice) and the actual position of the civil justice system on this (new) curve is also moved horizontally (change in case-load). As exemplified by letters 'A' and 'B' in the figure, it might be possible that a decrease of the general level of procedural justice still leads to an increase in the actual level of perceived procedural fairness, a sufficient decrease of the case-load being granted for. The latter process seems to have been hoped for when the recent amendments to the ZPO were passed.

As to the left half of the curve (Fig. 10.1), it is mainly equal access to justice that links subjective procedural justice with case-load. It is assumed that the case-load increases because the courts become a more and more attractive forum for settling everyone's disputes. Vidmar (1993) pointed out that many of the characteristics of procedure that lead to low procedural fairness ratings (like lack of respectful treatment of parties, lack of dignity of procedure,

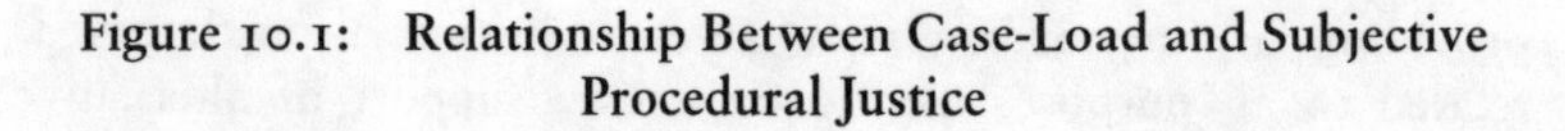

Figure 10.1: Relationship Between Case-Load and Subjective Procedural Justice

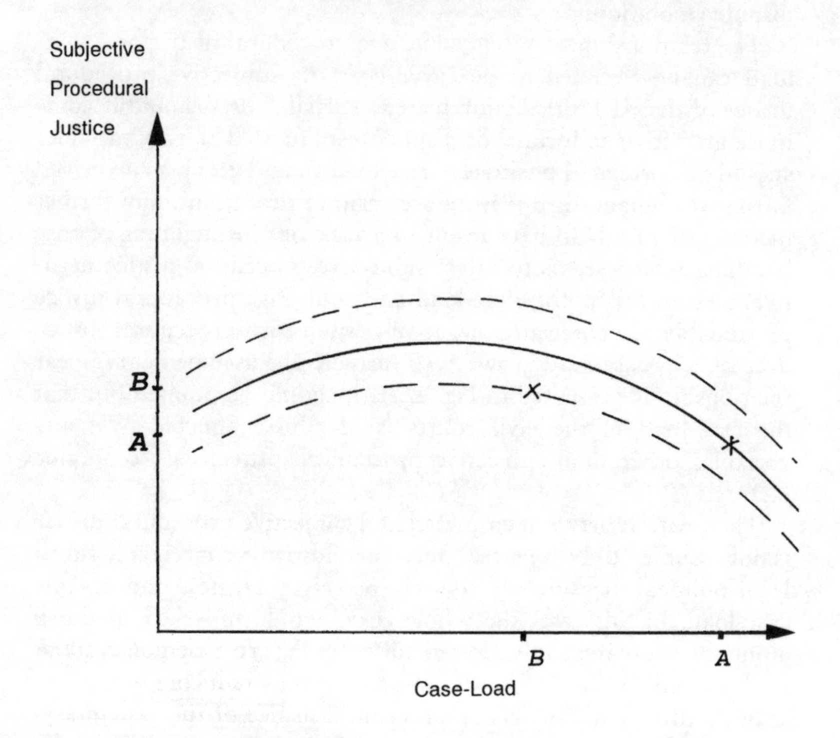

lack of neutrality, etc.) prevent people from trying their case before a court and thus result in unequal access to justice. As to the right half of the curve, it is difficult to hypothesize how equal access to justice could be related to decreasing subjective procedural justice and increasing case-load. The lowering of perceived fairness was assumed to be caused by a decrease of thoroughness of case handling. That decrease may, but need not neccessarily, affect equal access to justice. The two variables might be unrelated beyond the critical point of case-load.

Equal access to justice may be restricted even while case-load is going up. A greater number of civil suits does not necessarily mean that everyone brings his action with equal probability and chance.

The increase in new suits may still lag behind the increase in disputes considered by the parties to be worth to be tried by a court. Here, the attractiveness and perceived fairness of alternative dispute resolution become crucial. As long as resolving disputes by alternative means is perceived as being attractive and as fair as having the case tried by a civil court, procedures of alternative dispute resolution can replace court procedures, and vice versa. But some research findings question the equivalence of the two respective procedural systems (Sheppard 1985, Vidmar 1993). If alternative dispute resolution is seen as some kind of second-class settlement, then being compelled to make use of it instead of trying one's case will be perceived as refusal of equal access to justice. And, it seems, people sometimes are compelled to bring their case to institutions that offer alternative dispute resolution, because they cannot expect the court to come to an adjudgement within a tolerable period. The data presented by Stock et al. (1995), mentioned above, support this assumption. In the two cities in the eastern part of Germany where, at the time when the study was done, the civil courts were even more overloaded than in the western part, demand for and use of alternative dispute resolution was much higher than in the western cities (see Table 10.3). Thus, it seems that disputants make greater use of alternative dispute resolution as the case-load exceeds the critical point. As long as alternative dispute resolution is rated as fair and accepted as well as normal civil procedure, it will prevent the right half of the curve in Fig. 10.1 from going down as shown in the figure: Disputes that cannot be handled thoroughly by the courts any more are given to institutions offering alternative means of resolution. Being directed to these insitutions does not affect the fairness of the procedure, as these institutions are a part of a system of conflict resolution seen as equivalent to the courts. Subjective procedural justice remains near its peak even as case-load grows (and only as long as institutions of alternative dispute resolution have the capacities demanded for).

But this sounds like a fairy tale. It has to be taken into account that institutions of alternative dispute resolution are often not equivalent to courts in terms of perceived fairness of procedure, acceptance of the institution, and compliance with decisions. Therefore, alternative dispute resolution cannot give full relief to a justice system already positioned in the right half of the curve.

These considerations could, of course, be differentiated further. But for now, they may suffice for purposes of orientation. We can assume that the German civil justice system still is positioned somewhere in the right half of the curve. And as we cannot hope for alternative dispute resolution to bend the right half of the curve represented in Fig. 10.1 upwards, the subjective procedural justice of the system can be enhanced or at least safeguarded only in two ways: by reducing the case-load or by enhancing the case-handling capacity of the system. The latter was done with organizational reforms within the judiciaries and, above all, with the aforementioned measures reducing the number of judges trying and deciding an individual case. Both the shifting of a great proportion of civil cases from the *Landgerichte*, where as a rule chambers decide, to the *Amtsgerichte*, where only one judge decides, and the easing of transferring lawsuits for decision from the *Landgericht*'s chamber to a judge sitting alone enabled a constant number of judges to try more cases and thus enhanced the capacity of the civil justice system.

The method mentioned first—reducing the case-load—has to be adopted too, for organizational reforms of the judiciaries and reforms of procedural law can increase the case-handling capacity of the system only for a certain time span. If the factors affecting the number of new civil suits are not approached, the system will be operating at its limits again sooner or later. The reduction of the number of new civil suits brought to the German courts is a question not only of civil procedure but also of civil law. Better acceptance of the civil law and its regulations by the population may prevent some civil suits. Furthermore, modes of alternative dispute resolution should be developed in the direction of neutral, thorough, and as dignified as possible procedures. Last but not least, the culture of dispute resolution in Germany is in question. Easy-to-follow directions are not at hand.

Notes

1 The term 'old Federal Republic' is used to denote the area that the Federal Republic of Germany comprised until 2 October 1990, (i.e., the former West Germany). 'Old Länder' is a synonym. The term 'new Länder' is used to denote the area of the former German Democratic Republic, which since 3 October 1990 has been part of the Federal Republic of Germany.

2 These figures include all judges in each state, not only civil judges. Thus, the high ratio of judges in the Federal Republic of Germany also reflects the high degree of differentiation of the German justice system into several branches of jurisdiction, each of which has sev-

eral (normally three) tiers. The five main branches, also mentioned in the Basic Law (Grundgesetz [GG]), are the ordinary judicature, which exercises civil and criminal jurisdiction; the labour judicature, which is a special form of civil judicature; the administrative judicature; the jurisdiction of the social courts, which is a special form of administrative jurisdiction; and the fiscal jurisdiction, which is another special form of adminstrative jurisdiction (cf. Grundgesetz, Article 95 [1]). In addition, there are the constitutional courts of the Federal Republic itself and of most of the states within the Federal Republic (Länder), and some other special branches of the judiciary.

3 The estimate was made by the author, using data reported by Stock et al. (1995).

4 The estimate was made by the author, using data reported by Stock et al. (1995).

5 Before 28 February 1993, section 348 of the ZPO was worded as follows (my translation):

> §348. (Judge of the civil chamber sitting alone)
> (1) The civil chamber may transfer the lawsuit for decision to one of its members as a judge sitting alone, unless:
> 1. the matter involves special difficulties from the factual or legal point of view; or
> 2. the case has fundamental legal significance.
> (2) The chamber may decide on the transfer to the judge sitting alone without an oral hearing. The decision may not be contested.
> (3) The case may not be transferred to a judge sitting alone if hearings were already held on the main issue before the civil chamber on the day set for the hearings, unless in the meantime a provisional, partial or interlocutory judgement was issued.
> (4) The judge sitting alone may, after hearing the parties, return the case to the civil chamber if it appears that, as the consequence of a substantial change in the state of the proceedings, the decision is of fundamental importance. A retransfer to the judge sitting alone is barred.

6 This is laid down in section 279 of the ZPO:

> §279. (Amicable settlement; attempt at conciliation')
> (1) The court shall bear in mind in every stage of the proceedings an amicable settlement of the case or of individual points of

controversy. It can refer the parties for an attempt at amicable settlement to a commissioned judge or a requested judge.

(2) The personal appearance of the parties may be ordered for an attempt at amicable settlement. If such appearance is ordered, § 141 (2) is applicable mutatis mutandis.

7 See Article 103 (1) of the Basic Law (Grundgesetz [GG]): 'In court, the legal right to be heard in the process is granted for everyone'.

8 See ZPO, section 137 (4): 'In proceedings with lawyer representation, not just the lawyer but also the party shall be allowed to speak if he so petitions'.

9 See ZPO, section 511a (1): 'An appeal is inadmissible if the value of the subject of the complaint does not exceed one thousand five hundred Deutschmarks'.

10 See ZPO, section 313a (1) (1): 'The statement of facts is not required if it is certain that an appeal may not be lodged against the judgement'.

11 These critical values are laid down in section 23 of the Judicature Act (GVG), as far as the original jurisdiction by the *Amtsgericht* and by the *Landgericht* is concerned, and in section 511a of the Code of Civil Procedure (ZPO; see note 9), as far as the option to appeal on questions of fact and law is concerned. The legislative acts meant to ensure the functioning of the civil justice system just raised the sums of money in the respective regulations.

12 The respective versions of GVG, section 23, took effect 1 January 1983, 1 April 1991, and 1 March 1993.

13 The respective versions of ZPO, section 511a, took effect 1 January 1983, 1 April 1991, and 1 March 1993.

14 Section 495 a of the ZPO reads as follows:

§495a. (Procedure at the court's discretion, content of the judgement)

(1) The court may rule the procedure at its discretion if the value of the object of the litigation does not exceed one thousand two hundred Deutschmarks. Upon petition an oral hearing is held.

(2) The court decides on the lawsuit by a judgement where a statement of facts is not required. The judgement need not contain the grounds of the decision if the essential terms have been placed on the record.

15 See note 5 for the old version of ZPO section 348. The new version of section 348 (1) in effect since 1 March 1993, is:

> The civil chamber shall as a rule transfer the lawsuit for decision to one of its members as a judge sitting alone if:
> 1. the matter does not involve special difficulties from the factual or legal point of view, and
> 2. the case has no fundamental legal significance.

The rest of ZPO section 348 remained unchanged.

16 See note 6.

17 From Haller's findings it can also be concluded that the severity of outcome the court expects affects the giving of voice to the parties.

References

Barrett, Edith J., and Helmut Lamm. 1989. The Role of Procedural Justice in the Allocation of Limited Resources: A West German Perspective. *Social Justice Research* 3: 21–30.

Barrett-Howard, Edith J., and Tom R. Tyler. 1986. Procedural Justice As a Criterion in Allocation Decisions. *Journal of Personality and Social Psychology* 50: 296–304.

Bierhoff, Hans Werner. 1992. Prozedurale Gerechtigkeit: Das Wie und Warum der Fairneß. *Zeitschrift für Sozialpsychologie* 23: 163–78.

Blankenburg, Erhard. 1992. Droht die Überforderung der Rechtspflege? *Zeitschrift für Rechtspolitik* 25: 96–102.

Casper, Jonathan D., Tom R. Tyler, and Bonnie Fisher. 1988. Procedural Justice in Felony Cases. *Law and Society Review* 22: 483–507.

Cohen, Robert L. 1985. Procedural Justice and Participation. *Human Relations* 38: 643–63.

Folger, Richard. 1977. Distributive and Procedural Justice: Combined Impact of 'Voice' and Improvement on Experienced Inequity. *Journal of Personality and Social Psychology* 35: 108–19.

Haller, Volkmar. 1987. Zum Einfluß der Urteilshöhe und empfundener distributiver und prozeduraler Gerechtigkeit auf die Urteilszufriedenheit sowie auf die Beurteilung von Richter und Gerichtsbarkeit bei jugendlichen Strafgefangenen. Diss., Faculty of Psychology, Philipps-Universität Marburg.

Haller, Volkmar, and Stefan Machura. 1995. Procedural Justice at German Courts as Seen by Defendants and Juvenile Prisoners. *Social Justice Research* 8: 197–215.

Houlden, Pauline, Stephen LaTour, Laurens Walker, and John Thibaut. 1978. Preferences for Modes of Dispute Resolution As a Function of Process and Decision Control. *Journal of Experimental Social Psychology* 14: 13–30.

Jagodzinski, Wolfgang, Thomas Raiser, and Jürgen Riehl. 1991. Auswirkung der Rechtsschutzversicherung auf die Rechtspflege. *Zeitschrift für Rechtssoziologie* 12: 287–301.

Landis, Jean M., and Lynne Goodstein. 1987. When Is Justice Fair? An Integrated Approach to the Outcome Versus Procedure Debate. *American Bar Foundation Research Journal* 4: 675–707.

LaTour, Stephen 1978. Determinants of Participant and Observer Satisfaction with Adversary and Inquisitorial Modes of Adjudication. *Journal of Personality and Social Psychology* 36: 1531–45.

Leung, Kwok, and E. Allan Lind. 1986. Procedural Justice and Culture: Effects of Culture, Gender, and Investigator Status on Procedural Preferences. *Journal of Personality and Social Psychology* 50: 1134–40.

Lind, E. Allan, and Tom R. Tyler. 1988. *The Social Psychology of Procedural Justice*. New York: Plenum.

Morasch, Helmut, ed. 1984. *Schieds- und Schlichtungsstellen in der Bundesrepublik Deutschland*. Köln: Bundesanzeiger.

Rottleuthner, Hubert, Ellen Böhm, and Daniel Gasterstädt. 1992. *Rechtstatsächliche Untersuchung zum Einsatz des Einzelrichters*. Köln: Bundesanzeiger.

Sheppard, Blair H. 1985. Justice Is No Simple Matter: Case for Elaborating Our Model of Procedural Fairness. *Journal of Personality and Social Psychology* 49: 953–62.

Simsa, Christiane. 1992. *Praxis und Zukunft der außergerichtlichen Regulierung von Verkehrsunfällen*. Speyer: Forschungsinstitut für öffentliche Verwaltung bei der Hochschule für Verwaltungswissenschaften Speyer. Köln: Bundesanzeiger.

Stock, Johannes, Petra-Ida Thünte, Heimfrid Wolff, and Erhard Blankenburg. 1995. *Schnittstellen von außer- und innergerichtlicher Konfliktbearbeitung im Zivilrecht*. Köln: Bundesanzeiger.

Thibaut, John, Neremiah Friedland, and Laurens Walker. 1974. Compliance with Rules: Some Social Determinants. *Journal of Personality and Social Psychology* 30: 792–801.

Thibaut, John, and Laurens Walker. 1975. *Procedural Justice: A Psychological Analysis*. Hillsdale, N.J.: Lawrence Erlbaum.

Tyler, Tom R. 1988. What Is Procedural Justice? Criteria Used by Citizens to Assess the Fairness of Legal Procedures. *Law and Society Review* 22: 103–35.

———. 1990. *Why People Obey the Law*. New Haven: Yale University Press.

Tyler, Tom R., and E. Allan Lind. 1992. A Relational Model of Authority in Groups. In *Advances in Experimental Social Psychology.* Vol. 25, edited by M. Zanna. New York: Academic.

Tyler, Tom R., Kenneth A. Rasinski, and Nancy Spodick. 1985. The Influence of Voice on Satisfaction With Leaders: Exploring the Meaning of Process Control. *Journal of Personality and Social Psychology* 48: 72–81.

Valente, Ernest, and Robyn R. Mace. 1993. A Comparision of the Experiences of Afro-American Disputants and White Disputants in Related-Party Misdemeanor Criminal Court Cases. Paper presented at Law and Society annual meeting, 29 May, Chicago.

Vertrauen in die Justiz. Ergebnisse einer Umfrage in Berlin. 1988. *Deutsche Richterzeitun* 22: 392.

Vidmar, Neil. 1993. Verfahrensgerechtigkeit und alternative Konfliktbewältigung. *Zeitschrift für Rechtssoziologie* 14: 35–46.

Vidmar, Neil, and Robert A. Schuller. 1987. Individual Differences and the Pursuit of Legal Rights: A Preliminary Inquiry. *Law and Human Behavior* 11: 299–317.

Walker, Laurens, Stephen LaTour, E. Allan Lind, and John Thibaut. 1974. Reactions of Participants and Observers to Modes of Adjudication. *Journal of Applied Social Psychology* 4: 295–310.

Walker, Laurens, E. Allan Lind, and John Thibaut. 1974. The Relation Between Procedural and Distributive Justice. *Virginia Law Review* 65: 1401–20.

Wasilewski, Rainer. 1990. *Streitverhütung durch Rechtsanwälte.* Köln: Bundesanzeiger/Deutscher Anwaltsverlag.

The Author

Christoph Rennig. Born in 1954. Received diploma in psychology in 1981 and doctorate in law in 1985 at Philipps-Universität Marburg. From 1985 to 1991, research assistant at Philipps-Universität Marburg, Faculty of Law. From 1991 to 1995, public prosecutor, from 1992 to 1995 assigned to the Federal Ministry of Justice, Department of Empirical Legal Research. Currently, a judge at the Amtsgericht Frankfurt am Main. Fields of research are judicial decision-making, eyewitness identification, procedural justice, criminal law, and procedure. Published his dissertation, *Die Entscheidungsfindung durch Schöffen und Berufsrichter in rechtlicher und psychologischer Sicht* (Decision-Making by Lay Assessors and Judges in Legal and Psychological Perspectives) in 1993 (Marburg: Elwert).

Address: Beethovenstrasse 4, D-65812, Bad Soden, Germany.

Abstract

German civil procedure has not yet been the subject of empirical research in procedural justice. This article is intended to develop hypotheses on the subjective procedural justice of German civil procedure by providing empirical data on the German civil justice system and by contrasting the general structure of German civil procedure as well as its recent changes to empirical findings about the factors that determine subjective procedural justice in general. It is assumed that the high case-load troubling German civil courts may affect procedural justice by reducing the thoroughness of case handling. Recent legislative efforts to cope with the case-load have reduced the options to appeal and the proportion of cases where giving reasons for an adjudgement is compulsory. This is supposed to lower subjective procedural justice. Organizational reforms and a shift of cases from civil chambers to single judges are presumed to safeguard thoroughness of case handling without endangering subjective procedural justice. Modes of alternative dispute resolution are discussed with respect to subjective procedural justice and the limited resources of the civil justice system.

Index